THE TURKISH MEDIA

THE TURKISH MAFIA
A History Of The Heroin Godfathers

Frank Bovenkerk & Yücel Yeşilgöz

*Translated from the Dutch
by Rosalind Buck*

Milo Books Ltd

Published by Milo Books in 2007

This publication has been made possible with financial support from the
Foundation for the Production and Translation of Dutch Literature.

ISBN 978 1 903854 73 0

Typeset by e-type

Printed and bound in Great Britain by Cox and Wyman, Reading

About the Authors

Frank Bovenkerk is professor of criminology at the Willem Pompe Institute for Criminal Law and Criminology at the University of Utrecht in the Netherlands. An expert on organised crime, he worked for the Dutch Parliamentary fact-finding Van Traa Commission on police investigation methods. He has published several books, including the best-selling story of a cocaine cartel queen, *La Bella Bettien,* which was made into a movie.

Yücel Yesilgöz is a criminologist who published his dissertation on Turkish immigrants in Dutch criminal courts in the Netherlands in 1995: *Allah, Satan and The Law.* He is part of the Willem Pompe research project on crime and criminal law in multicultural society.

Contents

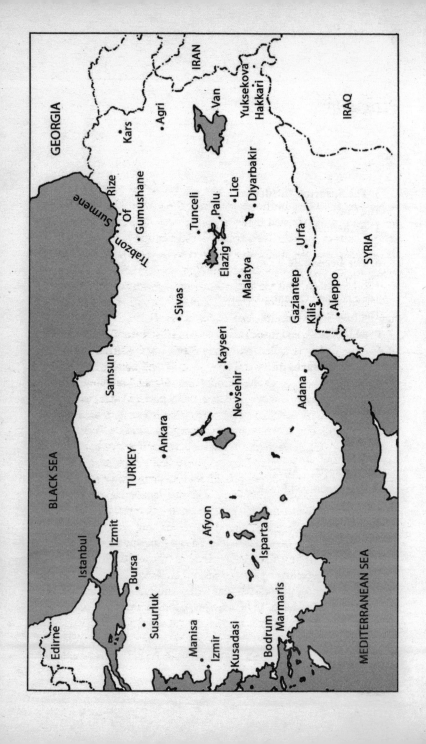

Prologue

In November 1996, a traffic accident near the town of Susurluk exposed the close ties that existed between the underworld and so-called police special units in Turkey. The revelation shocked the entire nation. From that moment on, the mafia was daily news – up to and including the discovery almost ten years later of the 'Constitution with the Red Jacket' in an Ankara sauna. This top secret document showed that the higher military had its own conception of ruling Turkey, a 'democracy' that has seen four military coups since the end of World War II.

These incidents, and many more, are considered proof of the existence of what in Turkey is called the 'Deep State' – a mysterious alliance of chauvinistic elements of the military, security and intelligence services, the judiciary and even organised crime. Once hidden from view, this state no longer seems deep – it even emerges every now and then, and without shame. In the ten years preceding Susurluk, there had already been rampant speculation as to the role mafia organisations in Turkey played in the armed conflict between the state and the Kurdish independence movement PKK. In Western Europe, police and the judicial authorities were confronted with the spin-offs. Heroin has long been smuggled from Turkey. Today, human trafficking and the laundering of criminally obtained money are also rife. The Turkish and Kurdish communities in England, France, Germany, the Netherlands and other countries in Western Europe are plagued by extortion and violent crime.

The public outside Turkey knows little of this, as the discussion in the Turkish media and other publications is conducted in a language they don't speak. Police, the judicial authorities and the intelligence services in Western Europe have, until now, kept their knowledge and insight largely to themselves. There is now good reason to devote attention to this shady world: it is throwing Turkey itself into upheaval and, moreover, entire sections of the emigrant communities in Western Europe appear to be involved. This book is therefore intended as an attempt to describe the equally fascinating and sinister history of organised crime in and outside Turkey in a language other than Turkish.

Although it has always been our intention to produce an impartial criminological analysis, we have continually been forced to also consider the political implications of the problem. In their analyses, a lot of Turkish authors stick to the essentially nationalistic view that is politically correct in Turkey and which, in honour of the first president of the Republic and great reformer, Kemal Pasha, is referred to as Kemalism. Other authors follow the Marxist view, often in such a dogmatic manner that they actually place themselves outside objective political science. It is also hard to see a lot of the analyses from the Kurdish left-wing perspective as anything other than propaganda. Such limitations are, in principle, incompatible with serious study. In our view, they can only flourish on the basis of the view of the sociologist Max Weber, which boils down to the fact that objectivity is unfeasible, but that the scientist is obliged to aspire to as high a degree of objectivity as possible. That does not mean to say that authors on this subject are not permitted to hold a political opinion, but that it is not relevant here.

Frank Bovenkerk & Yücel Yeşilgöz

Introduction

On 5 March 1992, a horrified policeman found the charred remains of three men on the banks of Lake Brielle, in the Netherlands. They had evidently been murdered elsewhere, hacked into pieces and dumped there, then drenched in petrol and set alight to prevent identification. Enquiries led to a Turkish café in Rotterdam, the Şato-bar, and a forensic reconstruction of events suggested that, the previous evening, the three men had been forced down to the cellar, where they were stood against a back wall and mown down with machine-gun salvoes. Shortly afterwards, in a residential building in Rotterdam, another trio of corpses was discovered. All three had their throats slit. In both cases, the victims and the perpetrators came from Turkey, though a young Dutchman had also participated in the second massacre. Even the hard-bitten Rotterdam police, no strangers to brutal murders in a big city, were appalled by both the scale and methods of the killings. And in the course of that year, they were to link these six murders to another five.

It had started with a gangland killing in a car park near Brussels the previous autumn, when a Surinamese drug dealer was shot dead. The motive was probably a 'rip' deal – a bogus drug-buy in which the dealer is robbed rather than paid. The subsequent murder of a Turkish Kurd took place on New Year's Eve 1991. Four days later, a Turk was found in a flat in Rotterdam, having been shot four times in the head. He had been running a *zula*, or storage place, for heroin. The suspects in the Lake Brielle murders struck again later that year in Amsterdam, bringing the total in the series up to ten or eleven.

The reconstruction of the series of murders generated the following picture. The Rotterdam heroin market was, at that time, primarily in the hands of a crime 'family'. The man killed on New Year's Eve was the son of the family patriarch. They were Kurds from the renowned heroin-smuggling centre of Lice, in Southeast Turkey, the area in the province of Diyarbakir where the underworld is assumed to have been then run by

Baba (Godfather) Behçet Cantürk. That added a political dimension to the case: Cantürk was a strongly left-wing, Kurdish *baba* who donated a proportion of his income to the Kurdish freedom struggle and, in doing so, directly or indirectly supported the armed Kurdish PKK movement. An informer told the police that the family procured large shipments of heroin in Iran, which they brought into the Netherlands by truck via Germany and Belgium. On arrival in Rotterdam, the shipments were divided into portions of ten kilos and sold to smaller dealers, such as the Moroccans. The Turkish authorities corroborated this story. When it came to Kurdish crime groups, the Turkish police cooperated well and the Dutch police were allowed to interrogate several suspects in Turkey.

The family had several Turkish and Kurdish relations working for it in Rotterdam and managed to keep the organisation closed. Initially, they went unnoticed, as the leaders were smart enough to replace their person-nel from time to time and the police therefore had no time to get to know new suspects. Revenue from the trade was not spent in the Netherlands, so no one had noticed that they had become rich; they were all registered as unemployed and received benefit from the Social Services.

The only family this group tolerated in addition to its own was that of a cousin by marriage, who also came from the town of Lice. It had now come to the attention of the local boss of the family in Rotterdam that this cousin was planning to start his own business and was using the family transport to do so. The New Year's Eve murder was the definitive signal that the cousin was planning to break the hegemony of the family. He had enlisted the services of a special Turkish hit squad of three men with a reputation as unscrupulous assassins. The father of the family in Lice decided to send his other sons, Kadri and Akif, to Rotterdam to find out what was going on. They established who had put out the contract on their brother and returned to Turkey. The idea was evidently to challenge the family and acquire a place in the Rotterdam market. In response to that challenge, instructions were issued from Turkey for the murders that were to end at Lake Brielle.

In the police and judicial scene in the Netherlands and its neighbour-ing countries, this bloodbath drastically changed opinions on the danger of organised crime. The event was unprecedented in the Netherlands and prompted a huge police investigation into murder, grievous bodily harm, smuggling, participation in a criminal organisation and unlawful depriva-tion of liberty. Yet at the end of the investigation, the police team involved was disbanded and the detectives, as usual, immediately threw themselves into their next case.

One man, however, did not want the significance of such an extraordinary case to be overlooked. Henk Jansen, head of the organised crime department in Rotterdam-Rijnmond, wondered whether academic criminologists might be capable of reconstructing and recording the events. Jansen had good reason for asking this, as the case had not actually been closed satisfactorily. Although his efforts had led to long prison sentences for a number of minor members of the Turkish-Kurdish criminal organisation in Rotterdam, the men who really wielded the power and who had commissioned the murders remained out of reach in Southeast Turkey. It would be good, he thought, to have a picture of the entire scope of the case, as an affair of international dimensions. After all, to understand anything about the drug trade in Western Europe you have to realise that the important decisions in this market are taken elsewhere.

The detectives involved had interpreted the Lake Brielle case as relatively primitive. In their opinion, it had been stupid to attract the attention of the Dutch authorities with so much violence. Moreover, the heroin market in the Netherlands is fairly accessible, so from the point of view of competition those murders had not been necessary. The retaliations pointed to more than just the instrumental violence that is part and parcel of all organised crime. In this case, honour, reputation and revenge were at stake and the Dutch had had too little experience in that area. Turkish organised crime evidently had its own tradition, which strongly deserved study.

This scientific research duly began – but in 1995 it was interrupted by a highly publicised scandal in the Netherlands that led to a parliamentary enquiry headed by the MP Maarten van Traa. What prompted the enquiry was the fact that several enterprising Dutch police officers and judicial authorities working for the North Holland/Utrecht Interregional Investigation Team had exceeded their authority in their fight against international drug trafficking. In fact, the police appeared to have organised their own covert cocaine and marijuana operations in order to lure real Dutch drug lords into a position where these could be caught. Politicians found such American tactics unacceptable under the Dutch legal system.

Four criminology professors were instructed by the commission to sketch a portrait of organised crime in the Netherlands. If new crime-fighting standards had to be designed in the Netherlands to combat organised crime, the parliamentary commission wanted to know its exact nature and scope. The criminologists found that organised crime appeared to be restricted to the traditional areas of trading in illegal goods and services, with drug trafficking dominant. Reassuringly, there was no sign of criminal groups having taken over legal sectors of the economy at a national or local level. There were cases of corruption, intimidation and influencing the media, but not to the extent where it could be said that the government or the press was controlled by criminal organisations. There were also individual cases of professionals such as lawyers and accountants who could be accused of 'culpable involvement' in organised crime but that, too, was insufficient to establish that those professional groups were controlled by criminals. The term 'octopus', which had until then been used to describe organised crime, was misplaced in the Netherlands.

In one respect, however, the portrait of Dutch organised crime was worrying. It proved to have taken root in a number of established immigrant groups – and in their country of origin, organised crime was fully mature. There, the interests of drug traffickers, political groups and even parts of the government were intertwined. Organised crime was looking for a safe opportunity to earn money from selling drugs on the market in Europe, where there was a big demand with great purchasing power. That applied to Suriname, where the coke barons smuggled their wares together with politicians and the top ranks of the army by using the infrastructure emigrants had created in the Netherlands. It also applied to the *Ras Kbir* (Big Chiefs), the prominent hash traders in Morocco, who, with support from the military and government officials up to the level of the Moroccan royal family, used the transport routes and distribution channels migrant workers had built up in the Netherlands. Morocco is easily the world's largest producer of hashish.

Part of the Turkish and Kurdish community in the Netherlands also proved to be involved in such collaboration with their country of origin. This situation was extremely difficult to oversee, as there were underworld connections with both ultra-right wing and ultra-left wing politicians and with individual politicians and civil servants at the centre of power. Turkish drug trafficking turned out to be an integral part of the armed struggle between the Kurdish PKK movement and the Turkish government. The similarity between the course of affairs in Suriname, Morocco and Turkey was that, directly or indirectly, the government in those countries had become partially dependent on the European drugs revenue. Some wondered whether the label of organised crime should not be replaced with another criminological offence category in this case, that of *state organised crime*.

The criminologists' findings for the Parliamentary Investigation Commission on the involvement of the Turkish government were initially received with disbelief. Further research more than a year later, however, confirmed their conclusions, for which the events in Susurluk became symbolic. Susurluk is the town in West Anatolia where, on 3 November 1996, a luxury Mercedes 600 crashed at high speed into an old truck that was just easing out of the exit to a filling station. Three of the four people in the car were killed in the accident. The sensational news, however, was who was actually in the car. The party included a police chief, a beauty queen with known mafia connections and a Kurdish member of parliament who was fighting the Kurdish rebel PKK movement with a kind of private army of village militia. The most surprising passenger, however, was Abdullah Çatli, a top figure from the world of the *ülkücü*,* a political activist from before the coup in Turkey on 12 September 1980 and a drug trafficker who had been involved in the attack on the Pope, in Rome, in 1981. This proved, in no uncertain terms that there were close links between the Turkish mafia, the police and the government. Since then, it has even become normal to speak openly of the mafia in Turkey.

At first sight, the term 'mafia' is not entirely correct. The mafia is an Italian – or rather, Sicilian – criminal organisation. The Turkish under-world has its own characteristics. The meaning of the word has already been stretched considerably in common parlance. The Sicilian mafia emerged from an agricultural economy within a feudal society without any effective state authority. It is characterised by certain cultural codes and initiation rituals. The Turkish mafia only emerged in the 1970s and manifested itself in international trade. It appears not to have any codes of honour. Additionally, Turkish and Kurdish groups concentrated largely on drug trafficking, while the Italian mafia, in principle, controlled all the criminal sectors in southern Italy.

---

* *Ülkücü* literally means 'idealists'. They are secret, ultra-nationalist troops, often also called the Grey Wolves after Asena, a legendary ancient female wolf that led captive Turks to freedom.

During our research, however, we became convinced that there were many similarities between the two groups, due both to the history of the Turkish underworld in rural areas and in cities and to the international position it occupies today, and so we use the word 'mafia' without qualms. Like all organised crime, the Turkish mafia has a fundamental effect on the two great monopolies of the modern state: the exclusive right to use violence and the right to levy tax. The term 'mafia' implies an extensive network of criminal organisations that originates from extortion and smuggling and manifests itself these days primarily in international drug trafficking and in personal violence such as that which took place in Rotterdam and alongside Lake Brielle in 1992.

The fact that organised crime has, at the same time, come into close contact with the ordinary citizens of a large Western European city can be seen from a story told by one of the Dutch detectives, which you will not find in the report on the Lake Brielle case. The building being used by the gang, where there was a continuous coming and going of drug traffickers, was under observation for several months. A lookout post had been installed behind an upstairs window of the house directly opposite, from where police officers continually watched the building through binoculars and took photographs. When spring arrived, the trees came into leaf and observation became impossible. Local authority gardeners were asked to prune the trees, but all the other trees around the park had to suffer the same fate, otherwise it would have been too noticeable. The area's residents saw this and organised a demonstration. The campaigners against this 'senseless destruction of the environment' never actually knew what it was all about.

*

Turkish journalists have distinguished themselves in their study and discussion of the mafia. Yet their books and articles have rarely filtered through to international literature on organised crime. This is due to three barriers. Firstly, virtually all this work has been published in Turkish and little has been translated into English or indeed any other language. Secondly, there is a political barrier. For authors living and working in Turkey it is extremely difficult to venture beyond the boundaries of politically correct discourse of state ideology, Kemalism. There is a vast array of both right-wing and left-wing writers in Turkey, but certain subjects are simply not open to discussion. The spiritual heritage of Mustafa Kemal Pasha, Ataturk, in particular, does not lend itself to an open-minded exchange of ideas; the role of the military, other than as guardian of the 1923 revolution, is rarely discussed; nor is the undemocratic character of the most powerful body in the country, the National Security Council, which is dominated by the military. The superiority of the Turkish state and Turkish people is also a touchy subject. The dozens of writers and journalists languishing in Turkish prisons, according to Amnesty International, keep the memory of these taboos alive. These restrictions are also reflected in this book; as we based our work chiefly on Turkish sources, the role of the military mechanism is insufficiently described.

The third barrier is that criminology as a science hardly exists in Turkey and those practising other social sciences seldom write about crime. The investigative reporters who have carried out most of the empirical work in this field are not really interested in criminological theorisation. There has therefore been no comparison with other international criminal organisations and, in Turkish works, the mafia from that country is portrayed as unique. In some aspects that is true, but that insight can only be gained by a systematic comparison with other variations of the mafia or other forms of organised crime.

Conversely, the international criminological community, primarily in the United States, has shown little interest in Turkey. It counts as a Third World country and has never received any great criminological attention, even though that is where you will find a great deal of crime in all shapes and sizes, particularly in the big cities. The Americans only showed any interest in Turkish organised crime during the period when it was linked with their own, internal, national drugs crime. In 1972, under diplomatic pressure, illegal opium production was effectively stopped in Turkey, closing the chapter for the Americans; they now study cocaine trafficking from Colombia and Mexico and heroin importation from the Golden Triangle and Hong Kong. It is not so strange that criminological interest in Turkey within Europe is, on the other hand, flourishing: Turkish and Kurdish traffickers in drugs and humans – illegal workers, refugees – are attracting attention and the manifestation of Turkish political factions such as the PKK, the Grey Wolves and Islamic fundamentalists in Western Europe is sometimes accompanied by extortion and violence. Intellectual refugees from Turkey who have learned a Western Europe language and the second generation of Turks with a university education are keeping the interest in their fatherland alive and are making documents in the Turkish language generally accessible.

There is probably no form of crime so complicated or controversial as organised crime. What is understood by the term depends on the place and time and varies with the degree to which it affects social and political life. To describe the Turkish mafia in all its complexity is impossible; all-round descriptions are logically incomprehensible. Nevertheless, it is possible to reduce that complexity by distinguishing a number of facets to the phenomenon, and by recounting the same story but from different standpoints. Those standpoints, which correspond to the chapters of this book, look at the Turkish mafia as, respectively: an economic phenomenon, social history, an organisation, an object of resistance by the police, a political phenomenon, and a social problem. Only one chapter, the seventh, deviates from this. In it, a prominent *baba* in the Turkish mafia tells his own story. The various aspects come together in the actions of one man, offering a real-life illustration of what is revealed in the preceding chapters.

Those who interpret organised crime as an economic phenomenon (see Chapter 1) concentrate on the markets, in this case, illegal markets. In their view, criminals are nothing other than players in a market, whose actions are determined by the relationships within that market and how they change. According to the simple definition of one American author, 'Organised crime is simply the activity of business people that happens to be illegal.' There are two types of such a market: firstly, racketeering, or the extortion of business people working illegally, which assumes the form of protection or forced trading; and secondly, trading in goods and services that are themselves illegal, such as drugs.

In the case of Turkey, unsolved social and political problems invite the offer of 'protection'. The market behaviour of the 'protectors' is, in itself, rational, but that should not be exaggerated. It can be handy for bona fide businesses and civilians to receive protection, but naturally no one is looking for extortion. These are not business people who have chosen a product that, on closer inspection and to their amazement, turns out to be illegal, but criminals who create a gap in the market in an extraordinary manner.

Internationally, the Turkish mafia profiles itself first and foremost in heroin trafficking. The product Turkish traders offer is morally loaded and their activities are resisted by an international cooperation of police forces. Their activities have become the subject of and are limited by international politics. In those countries where drugs are manufactured or from where they are exported, politicians deny all guilt by pointing out the real cause of the problem: the existence of an affluent demand in the big cities of the United States, Canada, Europe and Australia. If that demand did not exist, the farmers would grow something else and the salesmen trade in something else. In their opinion, the cause of the entire drug problem lies in the 'First World', rather than the Third World. The governments of the consuming countries turn the argument around; if there were no supply of narcotics, there would be no epidemic of drug use and their inner cities would not degenerate. The revenue is flowing in the opposite direction and that makes the attitude of the governments in the production countries ambiguous: they desperately need the foreign currency for their economic development, even for waging wars. After all, the drug economy provides jobs. In those countries where money that has been illegally obtained and on which no tax is paid disappears, this financial movement is a problem that undermines the integrity of the economy and the banking system.

The Sicilian mafia, the Japanese yakuza and the American 'mob' in the big cities and a string of other criminal organisations in other countries, regions or cities are the consequence of a long history. In many publications, the Turkish godfathers (*babas*) appear to have emerged only recently and their appearance would seem to be the result of the advent of drug trafficking. That representation of the facts is incorrect. Long before drug trafficking existed, there were underworlds operating in the cities and gangs in the countryside engaged in other criminal, and also non-criminal, activities. The tradition of banditism in Turkey goes back to the beginning of the Ottoman Empire. This history has been poorly documented and the social role the bandits played is still far from clear. According to some historians, such rebels play a proto-revolutionary role; other authors, such as Anton Blok, see them as the henchmen of the local rulers. Who is right in the Turkish case? There are reports of Robin Hood-style characters stealing from the rich to give to the poor, but also descriptions of merciless thugs and gangs working with the police or other state authorities in maintaining order and exploiting farmers and tenants. The figure of the *kabadayi*, or urban knight, and that of the *eşkiya* in the mountains have become the best known in Turkey because their social protest lives on in literature and oral tradition, but in reality there is a whole array of different personalities and organisations. It is important to know something of this historic background to understand the actions of the old baba and new baba of today. In the underworld, too, there are rules for conducting business, settling disputes and the admissibility of violence. Understanding that is a necessary complement to the market behaviour described in the first chapter. In Turkey, such rules are rooted in the code of honour, the *racon*. It is striking to see how such traditions affect the current behaviour of crime bosses from Turkey throughout Europe, down to the districts of the cities where they operate.

The structure of the criminal organisation is the subject of Chapter 3. Our image of the mafia has been formed by a long list of documentaries, novels, feature films and television dramas. The most famous in that list, Mario Puzo's *The Godfather*, has become the standard. According to this image, organised crime is a secret society, consisting of 'families', led in a dictatorial fashion and with the characteristics of a military organisation, held together by both swearing a solemn oath of allegiance and the fear of disciplinary measures should the oath of secrecy be broken. This portrayal of the situation is so persistent that the police and the judicial authorities easily assume such an organisational structure in their investigations and even novices in organised crime themselves attempt to learn the trade by watching the *Godfather* films over and over again. The criminological counterpart to this portrayal is Donald R. Cressey's book *Theft of the Nation,* in which the mafia is presented as an alien conspiracy organised along military lines. The book and the three *Godfather* films have changed the underworld, the police, the judicial authorities and general image-forming drastically and irrevocably. Before the film was shown in Turkey, the underworld bosses were generally referred to by the term *ağa*, which means no more than chieftain, lord or major landowner. Since 1971, however, under the influence of the cinema, this has changed and they are generally referred to as *baba* or father. Literally, the word godfather should be translated into Turkish as *vaftiz babas*, but the concept of godparents is Roman Catholic and unknown in Islamic Turkey.

In fact, organised crime – at least in the United States – is quite difference from the Puzo portrait, as has been demonstrated by a number of criminologists. Some of the better detectives have realised this, too; what they say is that if such organisations, with such a military set-up, were to actually exist it would be relatively easy to round them up. After all, the members of the organisation behave so predictably, just as they themselves do within the police organisation. Well-organised crime is therefore actually poorly organised. In the Netherlands, too, the police have fallen into the classic trap and in major, long-term investigations into a Turkish-Kurdish group, portrayed the organisation as far more closely structured than is the case and estimated the number of gang members far too highly. How structured is the Turkish mafia actually? Is it or is it not organised as a 'family'? In answer to these questions, the Turkish mafia will prove to fulfil the characteristics of the organisation run from outside the country, in fact a loose, flexible organisational structure.

Chapter 4 deals with the 'reception' the Turkish mafia has received in the various countries of Western Europe. The Turkish baba and all other persons active in their various organisations operate according to their own pattern, but in this chapter it will become evident that they are treated differently within the different countries. Every country has its own (criminal law) definition of organised crime, implements its own drugs policy to some degree and has its own, unique tradition of investigation and adjudication. Criminal organisations respond to those elements and the Turkish mafia therefore also exhibits diverse traits. In police circles, it is generally assumed that the government adapts its methods to the changing face of crime, but the varied face shown by one mafia in different countries clearly shows that the contrary is equally true. The British criminologist Mary McIntosh is known for her theory that the actions of the police and other investigative bodies influence the nature and character of organised crime at least as much as the other way around. Government response is one of the formative forces of crime. On the other hand, internationally operating mafia organisations have a logistical head start on the national police forces, as the latter are only able to collaborate with difficulty. There are conflicts of interest between the Turkish police and the police forces in Europe and cooperation is hindered by cultural differences. We will show how mobile some drug traffickers are and how fickle and unpredictable their movement pattern is. No international detection system of police suspects can contend with that and arrests are therefore often due to chance. Police material is, without doubt, a major source of criminological knowledge, but inevitably generates an incomplete, one-sided picture of the Turkish mafia.

What motivates organised crime? Criminologists, and all of us actually, will generally immediately think of unbridled greed and hunger for power. It is possible to formulate the motivation of gangsters more abstractly: they make every effort to achieve spectacular social advancement, to gain the esteem and respect only enjoyed by the very rich. The social background of the most prominent figures in organised crime is humble and such motives are therefore quite understandable. Ideological considerations will play no role in their motivation. Certainly, these gentlemen sometimes do their utmost to demand justice, to eliminate social evils or support the poor, but in these circles you cannot expect to find any ideology in a broader sense, which demands sacrifices for a complex, abstract ideal or a political conviction; the lack of ideological motives is even included by some authors as a distinguishing characteristic in their definition of organised crime.

The unusual thing about the Turkish case is the unique relationship between organised crime and the state. In principle, the state and the underworld are antagonists. Indeeed, organised crime can be defined as gangs that threaten the two major state monopolies: the right to levy taxes and the right to use violence. The traditional mafia of southern Italy organises the economy by means of alternative taxation, in the form of protection rackets. The gangs of Saint Petersburg and other cities in the former Soviet Union supply private violence to regulate the new market. This produces a form of predatory crime: organised crime penetrates the legal economy and the political system by corrupting officials or using other counter-strategies against the authorities, or goes beyond national borders and operates transnationally. This form of organised crime flourishes in countries with a weak state mechanism, such as Colombia and various parts of Africa.

What is unique about Turkey, however, is the way a state that is, in itself, strong is covertly creating its own underworld. The state gangs assist in the fight against the Kurdish separatists and donate funds to the secret national treasury to pay for a war that has never actually been declared. It is equally unique that the discovery of these state gangs fails to lead to the perpetrators being brought to trial and convicted; it leads instead to a veneration of heroism on behalf of the state ideology. In the political analysis of this phenomenon, authors usually go back to the year 1952. The secret state organisation was later to be known by various names: the counter-guerrilla, the special war division of the army and, more recently, Gladio, which emerged in Italy in the late 1980s as a secret, illicit NATO organisation. Turkey joined NATO on 4 April 1952 and

Seferberlik Tetkik Kurulu, later called Gladio, was founded in September that year. It is clear from various sources that this was all done on orders from the United States. In 1994, there was also confirmation from the Chief of Staff of the Turkish Army, who indicated that the organisation would be active against enemies in the event of war.

The car accident in the little town of Susurluk revealed indisputable connections between the state and the dark forces of organised crime. These form the mirror image of the cooperation between a number of left-wing political factions and the underworld that has also existed for more than thirty years. Until recently, there was far more awareness of this latter connection, as this is the portrayal of the situation the Turkish government still presents. A large number of Turkish and Kurdish gangsters, however, are driven by considerations of patriotism and a longing for independence. It is possibly this element that distinguishes the Turkish mafia the most from all other organised crime. The connections between crime and politics, incidentally, are difficult to disentangle. Political organisations to both the left and right of the spectrum and parts of the Turkish state mechanism are connected with individual criminals or with entire gangs. Their function is clear: they fill the (black) coffers or carry out chores the so-called bona fide civil servants and politicians don't want to dirty their hands with.

The best-known historical example of such cooperation between the government and organised crime is the order President John F. Kennedy gave the CIA in 1962 to hire the notorious mafia bosses Johnny Rosselli and Sam Giancana to assassinate the Cuban leader Fidel Castro. The renowned American mafia expert Peter Lupsha quotes a whole series of political initiatives for using organised crime to eliminate political opponents. Chiang Kai Shek deployed the Shanghai crime triads to purge the party in 1927; the French government used the Corsican mafia against the French communists; the military occupational army and the United States military secret service, G-2, secretly concluded an agreement with the Japanese underworld, the yakuza, to establish their authority after World War II. In 1960, when President Eisenhower was about to pay a state visit (which he never did) to Japan, yakuza member Kinosuke Oke, 'Tokyo's Al Capone', was put in charge of ensuring his safety at the request of the Japanese government. In other words, these are not initiatives by the underworld to bribe or blackmail civil servants or politicians, as is the usual assumption with organised crime. The mechanism works the other way around: the initiative to work together in shady business comes from the upperworld. In Turkey, such collaboration is based on tradition. Both in Ottoman times and in the era of the Republic, 'special units' were drawn from the underworld to carry out tasks not even the prime minister or cabinet were aware of.

This also applies to the deployment of criminal gangs for committing the war crime of ethnic cleansing, as the Serbs did in the war in Croatia, Bosnia and Kosovo. It is not uncommon, either, for oppositional political movements to use organised crime to raise funds for conducting their insurgent struggle, as in Lebanon, Ireland, Sri Lanka and numerous other countries. The direct or indirect involvement of the Kurdish PKK in smuggling drugs and, nowadays, also in human trafficking in southeast Turkey, illustrates this clearly. Chapter 5 deals with organised crime as a political phenomenon.

Until now, organised crime has largely been studied and described in Europe with the help of material gathered by the police. There is also a tradition in criminology that makes use of autobiography, which has generated quite a lot of new perspectives, particularly in the United States and Italy. We follow in this tradition, by means of an excursion to allow one of the major players, Hüseyin Baybaşin, to speak for himself in Chapter 7. He recounts a number of episodes from the history of the mafia that he knows better than anyone, such as the failed smuggling affair involving the ships *Kismetim-1* and *Lucky S*. The principal function of this chapter, however, is to provide insight into the world of the people involved and therefore sketch their psychological portrait. The interviews with the baba concerned were held in the course of 1996.

Criminologists have often been troubled by the politically unpleasant fact that ethnic minorities are prominently represented in organised crime. Was this not unnecessary stigmatisation of the most vulnerable in society? Was this so-called fact not the artificial product of the discriminatory investigative methods of the police? Was there not also a great deal of organised crime amongst the indigenous population, which was perhaps less noticeable? The word mafia, and later the term La Cosa Nostra, became increasingly popular in the United States in the 1920s, which shows that there, organised crime during Prohibition was considered to be an Italian affair. That was a definite exaggeration. There were also immigrants from other countries, such as Irish and Jews from Eastern Europe, involved in crime, and later, after World War II, there were black

Americans, Chinese and Cubans. Indeed, some would argue that organised crime was actually started in the USA at the end of the 19th century by the thoroughly American robber barons, who now represent the respectable business community. The same applies to other countries today. In the Netherlands, for example, Turks, Moroccans, Surinamese, Antilleans, Chinese and Nigerians are, without doubt, involved in drug trafficking in larger numbers than their share of the population would suggest, but there is also a gigantic homegrown drug market and some products (chemical drugs such as ecstasy and so-called eco drugs) are a purely Dutch, or at least 'white' European phenomenon. Nevertheless, we can speak of a serious second-generation problem. A weak socio-economic position, relatively poor integration into Dutch society and the factor of access to the drug market in their parents' land of origin make the second generation prone to involvement in drug trafficking. Revenue can be transferred without risk to the old country, where they can live in style. The question is, though, exactly how many people are we talking about and in what capacity are they involved? And in what manner is their own, legitimate business community used for this illegal trade? In Chapter 8, we endeavour to answer the sociological question of what the social function of organised crime is for minorities. The 'favourable' version would be the American situation; according to this model the second generation of immigrants is attempting to gain rapid social advancement by trading in illegal goods and services. The opposite theory, according to which the second generation is crystallising a difficult-to-integrate criminal subculture, is equally plausible. This latter option would correspond more closely with current experiences in the American black and Latino ghettos.

One theme best reflects our view of the phenomenon and best illustrates the particular character of the Turkish mafia. This is that the Turkish mafia does not constitute a large, closely interwoven, independent organisation operating in the seclusion of secrecy and government protection. On the contrary, it consists of many large and small, varying associations of criminals, operating openly and under the auspices of the government and political movements and fulfilling a string of social, economic and political functions for Turkey and the affiliated Turkish communities abroad. This book aims to illustrate the accuracy of the theory Robert J. Kelly put forward in his publication on international organised crime back in 1986: 'Organized crime is hardly a Sicilian or an American invention.

It flourishes in many different kinds of societies – those differ politically, economically, and culturally. And even with many variations in origin and form, organized crime is intimately linked with the political structures and economic infrastructures in those countries where it appears.'

Organised Crime in Turkey

Old and New Markets

The term 'mafia' is used in Turkey for a wide range of criminal activities. It does not necessarily suggest drug trafficking to everybody. For most ordinary Turks, drug trafficking hardly plays any role in daily life, but criminal networks such as the property mafia and the cheque mafia play all the greater a role. There is no section of the law stating that organised crime *per se* is punishable, but most offences it covers can be prosecuted on the grounds of conspiracy under article 313 of Turkish criminal law. For offences not concerning drug trafficking, the Ministry of Home Affairs' Directorate General for Security 'petty crime' department acts as the prosecuting body. Drug trafficking is tackled by the 'smuggling department' of the same Directorate General. While the key role of Turkish and Kurdish criminal factions in selling heroin to the European market and beyond is what has made the country's mafia infamous, it is impossible to understand them without examing the many other kinds of organised crime in Turkish life.

The 'cheque mafia' is the Turkish term for private collection agencies that collect monies under threat of violence. Businesses use their services, as the government is too slow and clumsy a mechanism for responding efficiently to their demands for market regulation. If business partners fail to pay on time and the high inflation eats up their claims in the meantime, to whom should creditors turn? Should they start court proceedings? There is little point. 'The country's legal system is old-fashioned and slow,' according to the magazine *Euromoney*. 'The courts are housed in hideous concrete buildings with tiny, badly-lit, smelly rooms and staffed by poorly-paid judges, public prosecutors and clerks slaving away at ancient typewriters. Judges and public prosecutors are formally civil servants and can be manipulated by whoever happens to be in power in Ankara. Their budget is limited. Istanbul's public prosecutor says he is only allowed to make local telephone calls from his office ... It often takes years for a judgement to be pronounced and that applies to even the simplest of cases. It takes months, if not years, to recover money from a customer who is unwilling to pay on time or who has bounced a cheque … There are people who get justice far more quickly from the local mafia, so debt collection has become big business for the Turkish mafia.'

All businesses linked to the Turkish economic system are faced with this problem, even if they are located in another country. A Turkish man serving a heavy sentence in the Netherlands for importing more than two hundred kilos of heroin told us how, years before, he had started a flourishing transport company operating to and from Turkey. But when one of his customers there continually delayed payment, he saw that what he had was due to go up in smoke, due to inflation of a hundred percent a year. He was afraid his company would go bankrupt. What could he do in such a situation? He had, indeed, approached 'them' and received his money almost immediately. Since then, however, 'they' had decided which exporter he was to work with in Istanbul and that was what had landed him in trouble.

Like related criminal factions who hire themselves out for violent contracts, the Turkish cheque mafia is renowned for the background of a number of prominent bosses. Before 1980, relations between the *ülkücü* and parts of the government and the military mechanism had been good, but after the military coup that year, in which generals took over from what they considered irresponsible politicians for the third time since Atatürk had created the modern Turkish state, a number of them were arrested and imprisoned. When this group was released, which happened quite quickly, a lot of them turned sulkily away from the state. These trained hitmen were now unemployed and decided to use the experience they had gained over the years to their own advantage. They formed small groups and offered their services as a collection agency. Alaattin Çakici, one of the most formidable *babas* of the underworld, originated in this circle.

The inheritance mafia, which settles the conflicts that can arise in distributing the estate of a rich man, has a similar background. Divorce disputes are also solved through the mediation of the mafia. The courts play no role there, either. 'Wherever there is a gap due to lack of justice, the role of the judge is fulfilled by the mafia,' says the chairman of the National Bar in Istanbul. That applies to hiring gangs, too. Clients can pay these gangs to do all kinds of jobs.

The contracting mafia works for contractors determined to be awarded specific contracts, primarily new buildings and roads commissioned by the government. Any other interested parties are discouraged from tendering by a visit from – as a governmental report by the Directorate General for Security rather drily describes it – 'athletic' persons. If the message is still not clear, then threats, kidnapping, torture and even murder can ensue. When all other tenderers withdraw, the remaining party can insist on an unrealistically high contract sum. Politicians are also involved in this, while a former infamous *baba* of Ankara, Inci Baba ('Pearl Father'), specialised in this method of eliminating competition.

Another form of crime is the sale of land vacated when the original inhabitants were killed or chased out of the country. After the mass murder of the Armenians in 1915, enormous swathes of land in the east and southeast of the country became free, which the local underworld managed to get registered in its name. In the 1960s, the same thing happened when the Turkish government banished the Greeks from the city of Istanbul following the crisis in Cyprus. All Greeks outside Istanbul had already been deported in 1923 in a great population exchange.

Throughout society, inefficient, rigid government has been unable to stem the turbulent economic growth that began in the 1980s and numerous related mafias have emerged in this period. Heavy urbanisation has put gigantic pressure on housing stock and land ownership in the cities. The *gecekondu mafyasi* began in the 1960s. This regulates the 'overnight construction of houses' for people migrating from rural areas to the city without accommodation. The unplanned settlements created in this way resemble the South American *barrio* and the South African shanty towns. The mayor of Ankara was in despair: the mafia calls the shots in his city and decides who can and who cannot build more *gecekondu*. The head of Istanbul's Architects Union went so far as to say that not only *gecekondu*, but all of Istanbul is in the hands of the mafia. The unbridled growth of tourism on the coast encouraged similar development. The methods of the cheque mafia are applied here, too. Mafia figures have 'bought' property in all tourist spots from those unable to pay their bills on time.

In May 1995, the former mayor of Kuşadasi, a tourist area on the Aegean Sea, was shot dead. To protect themselves from the mafia, a group of companies had placed a full-page advertisement in the newspapers pleading, 'Government help!' Further investigation revealed that the notorious Istanbul baba Nihat Akgün, who was affiliated with the *ülkücü*, was busy taking control of the entire neighbourhood. Baba Kürşad

Yilmaz, another well-known *ülkücü*, was acting as front man. 'Arguments over the distribution of the income was the cause of the conflict that led to the murder,' wrote the *Hürriyet*, 'but the people are too scared to talk.' It did not stop at Kuşadasi. That same summer, it was the turn of Turkey's next tourist destination, Bodrum. 'In Bodrum, too, you can hear the footsteps of the mafia,' was the title of one article.

Protection rackets target the hotel and catering sector and even department stores. They have also gained control of the parking facilities [in cities, especially Istanbul]. Districts and streets are divided up between various groups known as the *park mafyasi*. If you want to park in a random place in the centre, you should not be surprised if someone comes along and informs you that he will be looking after your vehicle to make sure no-one damages it; if you don't pay, then damage could well be what you will get.

There is also a mafia in Turkey that plays a major role in forming the criminal careers of the main characters in this book: the prison mafia. It, too, owes its existence to the necessity to manage overpopulation. Who keeps order in a remand prison? 'Arms and drugs are smuggled into prisons in an organised system. There is no way that high-ranking civil servants in the prison are not collaborating. Inmates carry portable telephones. The mafia does not neglect the prisons. If a prominent figure is visiting the prison, then the governor and even the public prosecutor stand to attention. They did so whenever the underworld boss of Ankara, Inci Baba, came to the prison, for example.' These are the words of the chairman of the Association of Court Employees to the critical journalist Neşe Düzel. A couple of months after his statement, the deputy governor of the most famous prison in Turkey, Bayrampaşa, in Istanbul, was arrested with two weapons and a mobile telephone in his pocket, intended for a prisoner. Two wardens were also picked up for smuggling in drugs. The night before he was to appear in court, one of them committed suicide in the police cell. The warder's family did not believe it could be suicide; according to them, he was killed to silence him. 'The laws of the mafia are valued higher than those of the government,' someone who worked at Bayrampaşa told us. In Bayrampaşa and Istanbul it is quite normal for mafia members to control the prison. The situation is similar in juvenile prisons.

International organised crime also includes trading in illegal labour. Illegal workers in market gardening and Turkish sweatshops in foreign countries are not a result of the spontaneous immigration of individuals. Transport and often forged papers are organised by criminal groups who supply workers to employers short of manpower.

Human trafficking entails the activities of criminal factions that organise the journey and the necessary papers for people wanting to flee various countries to Europe and who are prepared to pay a lot of money for the service. The news is constantly full of such reports. According to the German magazine *Quick*, the father of the 'asylum seekers' mafia' was supposedly a Turk named Muhlis Pinarbaşi. According to *Quick*, Pinarbaşi had reputedly smuggled three to five hundred people into Germany every week and received 3,500-5,000 marks per person. This internationally wanted man had apparently brought ninety thousand Kurds into Germany. Pinarbaşi was finally picked up at the border between Slovenia and Croatia. He had, apparently, been arrested a year earlier in Turkey, but had been released again. Germany, which had been criticised several times by Turkey for its asylum policy, called the incident 'strange'.

Turkey's central geographical position makes it an appealing stepping stone from East to West. Kurds from Turkey, Iraq, Iran and Syria, Arabs, Iraqis, Iranians, Afghanis, Pakistanis and Bangladeshis pay thousands of dollars to get to Italy via Turkey and Greece, where human traffickers take over. These days, people often go via Bosnia, as people coming from that area can count on sympathy in the countries of destination in Northern Europe. Human trafficking also includes trading in human organs from hospitals. There is also a 'baby mafia' which will have a living child registered as still-born and then sell it to a couple wanting a baby abroad. According to European police forces, Russian and Ukrainian gangs are gaining increasing control of human trafficking. In Italy, smuggling Kurds for money by ship or in containers leaving Turkey is big business. One organisation was rounded up because a customs officer standing next to a container waiting to be shipped on the quay outside the tax zone noticed an ever-growing pile of chewed olive pips.

Although it became easier after the presidency of Turgut Özal (1989-93), who privatized state sectors of the economy and improved relations with the Western world, obtaining a passport is still a problem, especially if you need a visa for a European country. Special groups have emerged – the passport mafia – who are pleased to be of service to applicants. They deal not only in Turkish passports, 'We have also arrested Turks with an English passport and an Iranian with a Canadian passport,' said one chief inspector. The introduction of the compulsory visa for European countries produced yet another mafia, wrote the *Milliyet*: agencies staffed primarily by former policemen were set up in the vicinity of consulates, where the required visa could be arranged. In the first six months of 1992 alone, the Istanbul police discovered nine hundred and sixty-one forged Dutch residence permits.

Then there is international uranium smuggling. 'The investigation of the century' *Milliyet* called it on its front page in 1993: three Iranian secret agents had bought two and a half kilos of uranium from Turkish suppliers. This time, the traffickers came from the highest circles in Turkey. More arrests were made later and, a year on, four times the amount was confiscated from smugglers bringing it into Turkey from the former Soviet Union. The weekly paper *Aktüel* reported that the uranium from Russia and Kazakhstan reaches the international market via Turkey. A year later, *Nokta* reported on the increase in smuggling nuclear substances.

Traditionally, smuggling antiques is the domain of the Turkish elite. One lady, Ayşegül Tecimer, received repeated attention in that area from the police and the media. Tecimer is the ex-wife of Asil Nadir, the disgraced tycoon who fled England for Cyprus in 1993 after the collapse of his Polly Peck business empire. Tecimer faced a four-and-a-half-year prison sentence for smuggling Turkish antiques abroad, but managed to flee to the United States just before judgement was passed. She later returned to Turkey and has since led a quiet life. The antique mafia is now a thing of the past.

*

What is evident is that the mafia in Turkey has had a functional role: crime contributes to maintaining social, political and economic cohesion. The mafia pops up everywhere where economic growth is turbulent and the government is unable to deal with the problems that causes. The mafia offers its services and is quite capable of providing a solution for these issues in the short term. It does, however, have to ensure that the problem it is helping to solve continues to exist; otherwise there is no longer any profit in it. Organised crime is therefore always conservative in the long term and stands in the way of real solutions to problems.

It is also, however, a question of morality. Organised crime only flourishes if there are people prepared to play a criminal role. The fact that there is no shortage of such people cannot be seen in isolation from the general economic and cultural changes that have taken place in Turkey since the 1980s. The lack of reserve amongst the middle classes in pursuing personal gain is linked to the radical-liberal economic course followed by the country for many years under Turgut Özal. During the elections on 6 November 1983 (the first elections after the coup of 1980), Özal's Motherland Party (ANAP) won with forty-five percent of the votes. Özal became a popular politician and, economically, Turkey had never had it so good as under his government. He permitted liberalisation of the economy, increased exports and encouraged the import of foreign currency. Many wealthy figures from the underworld saw an opportunity to become respectable businessmen during that period. For Özal this was a practical policy. He once said in a meeting, 'Our ex-smugglers want to become exporters. Well, the secret service has incriminating reports on them. If we say, "They might be smugglers, but give them the permission to export," then we think they should take the initiative themselves. Who is better suited to international trade then they? The fact that they are focusing on export is a necessary consequence of the requirements of our economic system.' Özal abolished the import duty on foreign cigarettes and alcohol, making smuggling in this sector impossible. Further on in the book, you will read how he also attempted to steer black money from drug traffickers abroad into Turkey.

The sight of prominent figures lining their own pockets or turning a blind eye to crime when it benefits the tax balance cannot fail to have a great influence on the entire population. Culturally, Turkey is becoming Americanised and the rise of the mafia is closely linked to the development of unbridled capitalism. Working class boys and girls who have made good in crime are admired. The Çillers (Mrs Tansu Çiller has been prime minister and minister of foreign affairs, Mr Ozer Çiller is a wealthy businessman) are the model for such social climbing. How did they become dollar multimillionaires? By her own admission, Mrs Çiller got her first half a million Turkish lira from her father, which she invested wisely in property in the United States. She later claimed to have also inherited a substantial sum from her mother. More in keeping with her reputation is the story that neighbours and acquaintances tell about her mother: that she was a poor woman without a pension. The popular interpretation goes on to say that the couple feathered their nest through politics – such as the illegal spending of government monies between 1993 and 1996 – and through their connections with the mafia. The couple are constantly under public suspicion but that has a political background, according to Mrs Çiller. The Turkish parliament proposed instructing the high court to investigate the truth of all these stories, but to the relief of the Çillers, this was outvoted.

Most Turkish residents simply assume that politicians use their position to get rich. That may be unjust, but it is also understandable. In Turkey, people who suddenly and inexplicably become rich are subjected to as little questioning as to the origins of their capital as is the case in the United States. In Turkey, this mentality also corresponds with a habit from the time of the Ottoman Empire, whereby unlawfully profiting from the government or impersonal institutions is seen not as a form of deceit or fraud, but as a sign of cleverness and daring. 'Together, the Turkish mafia groups are twenty-three thousand armed men strong,' said criminologist Mustafa Tören Yücel. 'Partly due to the influence of the media, these days people in Turkey think you have to get rich, one way or another. Those who join the mafia earn the admiration of the people. They are seen as clever.' This mentality is reflected in a Turkish saying, 'The state's wealth is as great as the sea, he who fails to profit from that is as stupid as a pig.'

Opium, Heroin and Poppy Diplomacy

'Unlike conventional combat, in which the capture of a great general or leader is tantamount to victory,' writes Alfred McCoy, 'the war on drugs is being fought against a global commodity – controlled not by humans but by invisible market forces.' The scope of trafficking in any drug is determined primarily by supply and demand. In this model, government regulation, prohibition and penal intervention play no role other than that of 'environmental factors', with the paradoxical consequences that they make it more appealing for traffickers to combine supply and demand, as they can incorporate the risk they run from their illegal goods in the price.

The economic interests are great. According to the 2006 *United Nations Drug Report*, five percent of the world population (aged 15-64), or 200 million people, use illicit drugs annually. Sixteen million of these are addicted to opium. Seventy-one percent of these, or eleven million people, are addicted to heroin. After strong growth in the 1980s and 1990s, the number of heroin addicts has stabilised since 1997. According to the same source – although the often-quoted figure is now ten years out of date – $400 billion changes hands in this trade each year, no less than eight percent of the total for international trade. Prices have since fallen drastically and the scope of international trade has risen sharply. That eight percent is drastically out of date, but no one is sure how great the scope really is.

The regulation and penal approach to the use of opium are not much more than a century old. The substance has been used for millennia for medicinal or magical applications, and the Arabic scholars who possessed the formula for manufacturing opium from poppies did not divulge their secret. As a commercial crop, poppies were first exploited by the Dutch and British East India companies. In the 17th century, the Dutch imported opium from Java and sold this colonial product in China, where they taught enthusiasts to smoke it in a pipe (incidentally, the Dutch were to earn even more later from cocaine). The British grew opium on a large scale in the British East Indies from the end of the 18th century onwards and they, too, shipped it to Chinese seaports. In the middle of the century, they even fought two opium wars against the Chinese emperor, who wanted both to combat opium use and to retain control of its production. It remains ironic that two countries that can currently be seen as the most loyal of allies in the war on drugs, at least where the fight against trafficking is concerned, once earned massive profits from that same trade. When they met in the 1920s as members of the League of Nations, they were both still opposing the conclusion of treaties against drug trafficking, or only reluctantly acquiescing. That earlier opposition to such agreements by countries with colonies did little to help convince countries at that moment dependent on income from opium, such as Turkey, to limit their production.

The consumer market in the West became interested in opium at the end of the 19th century. In 1898, the German pharmaceutical firm Bayer marketed heroin as a cough medicine and, initially, the substance seemed to belong to the same category as the painkiller they had launched a year later, under the name of aspirin. The firm did what was expected of it: advertising, setting up points of sale as far as China and lobbying to ensure that the substance was not placed on the prohibited list. The cough remedy proved, however, to cause more dramatic effects than the company claimed and, what's more, it was scientifically established that it could actually lead to addiction. The American and international temperance movement, a primarily religion-inspired organisation aimed at banning the consumption of alcoholic drinks in American saloons, found British Protestants and even Chinese opponents on their side when they took up the fight on moral grounds against the non-medical use of opium. The first resolution to introduce international regulation was taken in 1909 at the opium conference in Shanghai. Of the countries invited, Turkey refused to turn up, as did Austria-Hungary. The international opium conference in The Hague, the resolutions of which were only ratified after the end of World War I in Versailles, had to do without the signatures of poppy producing countries such as Turkey, Persia and Russia.

A further step was taken by the League of Nations, which met in 1925 in Geneva to try to implement the resolutions of The Hague. Although it did not prove easy to restrain production, as the producing countries did not cooperate, it was possible to make a start in the consuming countries.

How much opium should each country need annually for strictly medical purposes? A special advisory committee set to work and a central supervisory board set up in Geneva began checking the annual reports on the scope of incoming and outgoing flows of drugs per country. Consulting these documents in retrospect, it is not difficult to see what went wrong: the trading volume of opium was measured, but all kinds of derivatives, such as opium powder and morphine, were not counted, apart from which an awful lot was able to leak out into the black market. The factories producing refined drugs were located chiefly in Germany, France and Switzerland – Paris was number one and Basel second – and from the discrepancies measured between import and export, one cannot conclude otherwise than that the underworld was being supplied outside the national quota in order to satisfy the, now illegal, demand.

*

Turkey traditionally produces extremely high-quality opium. Half of its poppy production originally came from the area around the town of Afyon (which means opium, incidentally) in Mid-West Anatolia, where opium is still – and for good reason – referred to as 'brown gold'. It provided the farmers with an existence: in the Ottoman period the export of opium was one of the major sources of income for the 'High Gate', the inner court of the Ottoman dynasty. In the period between the two world wars, Kemal Atatürk turned opium into a state monopoly, with the official revenue ploughed back into the pharmaceutical industry. The farmers, however, kept their best quality for selling secretly to other buyers who, unlike the state purchasing agency, paid cash. In that way, an amount equally as large as the official production disappeared illegally into Europe. Even stewards aboard the Orient Express smuggled opium to Paris.

To understand the standpoint of the Turkish delegation in Geneva in 1925, one has to realise that the Ottoman Empire had lost a substantial amount of its territory after World War I and the remaining part had become relatively more dependent on opium farming. Turkey was the biggest opium producer in the world and wanted nothing to do with the restrictions imposed by the League of Nations. Three factories had been set up in Istanbul by that time, which, already in the first year, together produced 2,300 kilos of morphine and 4,300 kilos of heroin and the country demanded a 'fair quota', based on its earlier production volume.

The cosmopolitan character of these activities, and of the city of Istanbul, can be no better illustrated than to point out the origins of these factories' directors. Oriente Products Co., in Taxim, was established in 1927 by two brothers from Japan who had managed to obtain a permit from the Ministry of Health. Two firms were being run by Frenchmen and one factory was in the hands of Armenians, a Turk and a Frenchman. The biggest market was in France and, in the 1920s, Paris was the centre of illegal distribution. But in other countries, too, all kinds of signs of smuggling were to be found. Forged papers were used; the shipments came from imaginary firms; they operated through a corrupt department of a legal company; bills of lading were forged and the contraband was ingeniously hidden; first the shipment was sent from Istanbul to an 'unregulated' country that was not party to the convention, to then be sent on; the first clandestine factories were set up. A League of Nations commission drew up a blacklist of smugglers and cooperating companies. According to this list, the illegal opium traders came primarily from Yugoslavia, Greece and Bulgaria, countries that had just extracted themselves from the Ottoman Empire. They were supplied from Turkey, France and Bulgaria.

Amongst the known smugglers on the 1936 list were a striking number of Jews and Greeks. The same observation was made sixty years later by the Observatoire Géopolitique des Drogues in Paris. The minorities involved come from towns and cities and are part of global ethnic networks. For that reason, they have good connections for conducting all kinds of trade. Their networks are difficult for outsiders to penetrate and the family links generate reliable trading partners.

A report from 1933 by the newly formed National Federal Bureau for Narcotics in the United States (the successor of the agency that had supervised observance of the law against alcohol) showed that forty per cent of international drugs smugglers detected in China were of Greek origin and the rest came from communities of Eastern European Jews, Serbians, Bulgarians and Armenians. The network the Armenian businessman Zacharian ruled from Cairo in 1925 was a good example. He pretended to be a carpet dealer, but smuggled heroin, together with a Greek. Zacharian maintained relations with business partners in Zurich, with a dealer in the Netherlands and with the management of a factory in the French town of Mulhouse. He formed a partnership with a pharmacist in Tel Aviv and went into business with two Jewish Polish brothers in Cairo. The 1996 atlas by the Parisian drugs research institute OGD portrays an equally impressive network, that of Elie Eliopoulos and his brother Georges, who operated from Paris and were the first in the Middle East to turn their attentions to the United States.

*

Opium is produced in border areas that are difficult to access, in those places where there are mountain ranges or plains without any good transport connection, in areas where the state authority is not effectively exercised and local leaders rule the roost. The transport of contraband over national borders is safest when a people, tribe or ethnic minority has ended up on both sides as the result of what for them is an arbitrary political territorial division. The trade in opium, and the associated chemical processing, acquisition of credit from banks and export over sea, is typical of big seaports: Istanbul, Smyrna (Izmir), Beirut, Alexandria and Marseille. The import and export companies are also often run by ethnic minorities. From the 1970s onwards, towns alongside major transport roads have also been included in these trade networks, as have towns near to airports from the 1980s, but up until World War II, transport was by sea. Legally imported opium is bought by the chemical industries in the western countries and opium, morphine or heroin is consumed as a stimulant by the large urban populations in those same countries. In the 1950s, Persia (Iran) was also included. Unlike Turkey, this drug-producing and exporting country had a major addiction problem, with more than a million people using regularly. This created a new consumer market for Turkey. In western countries, the use of drugs began among artists and bohemians, but also among minorities such as the Chinese and within certain professions with easy access to the substances – doctors were a high-risk group. The mass use that followed spread via a social pattern. It started with middle-class women and ended with lower-class men; it started with parents and spread among young people and it spread from whites to blacks and other minorities.

The traded volume of 'mind-expanding' or narcotic substances depends first and foremost on supply and demand. Demand is determined by the number of and purchasing power of consumers and is presently primarily dependent on young people. It is also highly determined by trends. Finally, governmental policy regarding the use of drugs is also significant, although it is not at all easy to establish how this influences the market. It depends whether the government policy is strictly symbolic or whether the prohibition of the use of narcotics is actually enforced. Apart from which, the question is whether the repression of drug use, toleration or even legalisation actually affects the consumption level.

The supply is created by entrepreneurs who spot a market and are prepared to invest in the new product. Supply is also influenced by the wholesale organisation and the willingness of retailers to act as pushers. So far, the market is not really any different from that for other products for which there is an international demand. This is, nevertheless, a product that was been declared illegal since World War I. In describing the history of the heroin trade, from that point onwards we have to take into consideration both that extraordinary factor and the consequences of making products illegal.

*

Between 1920 and 1940, Turkey and Yugoslavia actually occupied a monopoly position in export. As opium products were prohibited for consumer use, a black market evolved and trading became the domain of the international underworld. Paris was initially the distribution centre, but that changed at the end of the 1920s when the police there closed the heroin factories. This caused a relocation effect: the demand for and supply of the product remained, while the now functioning traffic was obstructed or interrupted by prohibition. The trade had to find an alternative. When Paris fell, Marseille rose. The market was also expanded by crossing the Atlantic.

The connection with the American market had existed since the gangsters there had sought a new illegal product after the prohibition of the manufacture, import and sale of alcohol was lifted in 1933. In innumerable books (both fiction and non-fiction), films and television series on the history of the mafia in the United States, a clear line is drawn between the good old days, when the underworld still had a code of honour that forbade the exploitation of narcotics (and prostitution) and the modern period of the Cosa Nostra, which began long after World War II and during which most gangsters did not hesitate to trade in drugs. Historical research also shows that connections existed between the Jewish and Italian mafia since far before the war. Racketeers such as Legs Diamond,

Dutch Schulz and Bugsy Siegel had linked up with the network of the aforementioned Eliopoulos brothers and, according to one reputable source, there were also connections with the Purple Gang in Detroit and the underworld in Cleveland, Saint Louis, Minneapolis, Philadelphia and Chicago.

Lucky Luciano, the great organiser of the American mafia, was the first to make connections with the Corsican underworld in Marseille. His illustrious companions there were François Spirito and Paul Carbone, who had forged a career in the 1920s operating a brothel in Cairo. After the two Corsicans had been deported from Egypt for trading in white slaves, they had decided to try their luck in Marseille. As early as the 1930s, they were given permission by the fascist deputy mayor of the town to set up a heroin laboratory in exchange for support from their gang in beating up left-wing demonstrators in the streets. And so the infamous French Connection was born. This entailed opium being transported from Turkey to simple laboratories in Syria – Aleppo is just twenty-four kilometres from the Turkish border – and Lebanon, where it was converted into a morphine base. This product was transported from Beirut in packages of three kilos by ship and sometimes by plane to Marseille. The chemists in France turned it into its most refined form: heroin number four. This substance, which can easily be transported undetected in small quantities and which is vastly expensive weight for weight, was then transported to the United States. One estimate calculated that there were eighteen links connecting the harvest of Turkish farmers with the users on the streets of New York. That is a lot for an illegal product and the organisation of this traffic flow demanded tremendous knowledge and talent.

After the war, a number of Italians, who had been serving sentences for serious crimes, were deported from the United States. Lucky Luciano settled in Italy in 1947, in the vicinity of Naples. Frank Coppola and Serafino Mancuso chose to live in Palermo. The first time the Italian police had dealings with heroin was in the 1950s in Milan: Luciano had managed to convince a chemist at the big pharmaceutical firm of Schiaparelli to sell him a total of seven hundred kilos under the counter over a period of four years. When that was discovered, the Italian government responded by introducing a better control regulation, but by that time this no longer affected Luciano. He had already set up his own network of laboratories together with a number of Corsicans and controlled the smuggling route between Tangiers and Marseille.

It would have seemed more obvious for the Italians to shift the focus to Italy, as the repatriated gangsters had the right family contacts for smuggling safely to America. The Sicilians were not yet very active in Italy. They proved incapable of managing laboratories where heroin could be refined. During this period, the Sicilian underworld underwent a major transformation (it moved its activities from the countryside to the towns, for example), which entailed mutual disputes generally referred to in literature as the 'mafia wars' and led to a series of arrests.

Marseille remained safe, as the well-organised local underworld ran the ports and maintained a kind of symbiotic relationship with the local government. On the orders of the Marseille *caïds*, as the drug traffickers there were referred to, a hodgepodge of Turks, Corsicans and Sicilians sent ships to the Côte d'Azur. Underwater, these ships were towing a hundred-metre-long rope, to which the little bags of contraband were attached, which nobody would find when searching the ship. French fishermen landed the bags at night: the risk was immediately spread. The French police started an investigative offensive against the laboratories, but they claimed it was extremely difficult to dismantle the concealed workshops.

It became clear that Turkish organisations were again smuggling overland to Marseille in 1972 when the Turkish senator Kudret Bayhan was picked up with his driver by the French customs in Menton with a hundred and forty-six kilos of morphine base in the boot. He claimed political immunity with his diplomatic passport and declared that he had only travelled to France to buy a new hat for his daughter's wedding. When questioned by the French police, his driver, however, told how he had already crossed the border by the same route twice that year with other smuggling Turkish politicians, Hilmi Işgüzar and Orhan Özçelik.

*

In 1961, at a United Nations conference, the Single Convention on Narcotic Drugs was concluded, the crowning glory for those who had begun their crusade against the non-medicinal use of drugs at the beginning of the century from the United States. On the grounds of this convention, the United States informed the Turkish government that the production of opium had to be stopped. This was the beginning of ten years of 'poppy diplomacy'.

In those same years, links were discovered between the Turkish drug traffickers and the Sicilian mafia. Following expensive, labour-intensive investigation, the Americans uncovered a drug ring that they were later to dub the Pizza Connection, which has gone down in history as the first proof of connections between the Sicilian and American mafias. The Sicilian Badalamenti and Salmone families dealt in heroin supplied by figures such as the Turkish baba Avni Musullulu. The connections ran from Burma over Turkey to Sicily and on to the United States. The revenue returned to Switzerland and Singapore and the actual settlement took place in Bulgaria. For those days, all this implied a high level of organisation and intelligence.

How was the Turkish government to respond to the increasing pressure from America? The then-prime minister, Sulëyman Demirel (later president of Turkey from 1993 to 2000), had to take into account the economic interests of literally hundreds of thousands of families working in the cultivation and production of heroin, and the members of parliament for the Province of Afyon resisted fiercely. The American pressure was entirely contrary to the predominant opinion in Turkey, where heroin poppies were seen as an economic resource and not in the least as a moral or criminal problem. Premier Demirel was from a farming family himself; he came from the province of Isparta and, as a child, had taken part in the poppy harvest. He tried to buy time, in the meantime limiting the number of provinces where opium was grown. In 1971, President Richard Nixon began his famous 'war against drugs' and stepped up political pressure even further. The United States switched to buying its opium for medicinal purposes from India. They offered $3 million aid to set up a seven hundred and fifty-man narcotics squad, as well as money for research into possible crop substitution and help in more efficiently organising the Turkish Marketing Organisation. When none of that worked, in 1971 the United Nations imposed a boycott on Turkey.

That same year, the Turkish military 'eliminated democracy' by removing the government in a coup. It was the second time since the end of World War II that the military had taken over at a time of unrest, when in their eyes civilian politicians threaten the secular political legacy of Atatürk.* One of the first measures the subsequent Erim government

---

* The first such coup was in May 1960. There would subsequently be two others, in September 1980 and in February 1997.

introduced was the full-scale prohibition of poppy growing. This measure was extraordinarily unpopular and was seen by right-wing politicians as a sign of weakness, as they had given in to foreign pressure. In turn, Turkish left-wingers blamed the brutal face of imperialism. After all, it wasn't the Turks who had created the problem of illegal drug use, was it? At that moment, at least, the country still had no drug addiction problem itself and felt America should get on and solve its own problems. When democracy was restored and Bülent Ecevit came to power in 1974, one of his first acts was to reverse the decision. And when the same Ecevit again became deputy prime minister in the summer of 1997, he decided to repeat that popular act of almost a quarter of a century earlier: on 7 August 1997 he told the daily newspaper *Sabah* that he was proposing to expand the acreage in Turkey for growing opium.

The cultivation of opium is currently limited to ten provinces and takes place under strictly controlled conditions. On 3 March 1997, a reporter from the *Turkish Daily News* wrote an article on a special information day for journalists. A coach took them through the red fields of poppies in Afyon, which were blooming behind high fences, and they were shown around the Alkaşan factory, which currently produces a third of the total annual world requirement of morphine: seventy-two tonnes, or thirty-two percent of the total two hundred and thirty tonnes. This generates $25 million a year, a pittance compared to what it would fetch on the black market. As on the outbound journey, the coach was heavily guarded on the way back.

*

The end of Turkish production again provoked a gigantic relocation effect, which hampered the desired effect of the American war against drugs. Production transferred to the Golden Triangle, the border area of Cambodia, Laos and Vietnam where 'white heroin' comes from, and to Mexico, and new consumer markets emerged: Europe and Australia. The first white Asian heroin found in the Netherlands and other European countries dates from around 1970. Chinese underworlds in Hong Kong and Bangkok had invited the Chinese communities already established in Europe to import and distribute their merchandise.

For decades already, Chinese sailors had been smuggling small amounts into the Netherlands for a few opium dens in the Chinatowns of

Amsterdam and Rotterdam. From there, small amounts were sold on to a handful of Dutch opium addicts. That changed in 1970, when the Amsterdam police started shutting down these establishments and arresting the dealers. A shortage of opium ensued, which was suddenly followed in 1972 by a plentiful supply of extremely cheap heroin. The market had to be 'prepared' for the change: a certain unwillingness amongst Dutch opium users had to be conquered to convince them to switch to heroin.

Chinese communities were to be found in England, France (particularly in Paris) and the Netherlands. Due to the central location of its major ports, the Netherlands was the most suitable distribution centre. The Dutch police started coming across larger and larger batches; in the first three months of 1973 alone, eighteen kilos were confiscated in Amsterdam. Amsterdam had also attracted a great deal of attention in the 1970s with two spectacular murders resulting from the struggle for the market between various 'triads', actually a far looser structure than the hierarchically organised, quasi-military organisation described in triad literature. In 1969, Hong Kong's 14K triad is reputed to have decided to make Chung Mon of Amsterdam its European contact for Chinese heroin. He was murdered on 3 March 1975 and, exactly a year later, his successor Chan Yuen Muk suffered the same fate, after which the 14K, weakened, moved over to The Hague, Rotterdam, Antwerp and London.

In all countries in Western Europe, the number of heroin users rose rapidly. With the risk carried by its injecting – the transmission of diseases such as hepatitis B, and later the HIV virus, through needle sharing – it was quickly branded internationally as the most problematic drug of all. There were also concerns that, proportionally, a lot of young people from ethnic minority groups had started to use it. Everywhere in Europe it was established that heroin use and addiction led to 'acquisition crime' such as burglaries and the theft of items such as car radios and bicycles, and heart-rending stories appeared in the press and in books about young people coming to grief and girls prostituting themselves: Christiane F. in Berlin, Floortje Bloem in the Netherlands, and others. Action by the authorities appeared to have little effect. Border controls traced only tiny amounts and the police had the greatest difficulty in penetrating what for them was the strange world of the Chinese. In general, the wholesalers who were arrested failed to fit the stereotype the police had of underworld bosses in any way. They included dealers who led a secluded life in a respectable part of a big town, whose neighbours would never have dreamed that they were drug traffickers. One police detective, who got to know the Chinese in the underworld well, characterised them to us as 'invisible'. The Chinese are still currently active in the European heroin trade.

The Rise of 'Brown'

From 1980, the market throughout Europe was to change entirely: the Turkish dealers appeared on the scene with their brown heroin. They, too, engaged in a special kind of marketing: the quality of the merchandise they supplied, which is determined by refining, purity and degree of cutting, was so good that, for a few months, there were suddenly many deaths as the result of overdose.

This is, again, the result of a relocation effect. After production in Turkey was halted, the countries that together form the Golden Crescent – Afghanistan, Pakistan and Iran – had emerged as production areas. These days, Turkish and Kurdish drug traffickers make use, first and foremost, of the strategic geographical location of their country. They buy raw opium, morphine base or morphine with a low number (a low grade of refinement) in the East; they make use of their chemical knowledge by setting up laboratories and finally they sell it on to the West via the Balkan route to Western Europe. Here, too, they make use of the transport of goods and people that has come about between Turkey and those western countries with Turkish communities following a long period of recruiting foreign workers in the 1960s and 1970s. Turkey has also evolved from a production area into an international trading country.

No-one knows the full answer to the intriguing question of why the ethnic group that controlled a certain part of the black market handed it over just like that. Why did the Chinese disappear so easily from the scene? A battle for the market in the underworld is generally accompanied by dispute, violence and war, but here it appears to have happened without a blow being struck. It may be that the Chinese took a step backwards but continued nevertheless in a less noticeable manner. On the other hand, for the past thirty years almost all the heroin confiscated in Western European countries – on the street in any event – has come from Turkish dealers. Another factor was the pressure the police put on the Chinese community to discourage illegal practices in restaurants and gambling joints. In 1980, a lot of Chinese who were in the Netherlands illegally were deported. Around the same time, a number of major investigations were successfully completed there. A number of dealers appear to have moved to the United States. What's more, the Golden Triangle had a bad harvest in 1979, so there was not enough competitive supply available. There was not yet a buffer stock of drugs in the market in those years, which steadily reduced the price over the years that followed, regardless of failed harvests or successful action by the drugs squad. It could also be that the Chinese dealers simply avoided the battle, as they would only have made themselves visible. In any event, it was clear that Turkish criminals would not have balked at an armed conflict. One detective who has experienced the transition from the Chinese to the Turks in the heroin market tells us that the subjects of his investigation transformed almost overnight. 'Peasantish, much rougher types' he calls them, after his earlier experiences with the Chinese.

*

The main chemical substance required in the refining process for heroin is acetic anhydride. This, itself, is a legal chemical product, but from the moment that it dawned on the police and the judicial authorities in Europe and America that large quantities were being shipped to the Middle East to manufacture heroin, various governments regulated its export via a permit system. Chemical companies in Germany, Scandinavia, the Netherlands and Belgium were keen to sell it, but even in those countries a black market evolved due to the legal restrictions. In 1996 a Dutch driver was arrested at the border with Turkey with an entire lorry full of acetic anhydride without the necessary permits.

Drugs for which a consumer market has recently developed also find their way from the West to Turkey. Cocaine is still a typical fashion item in high society in Istanbul and Ankara and there is a demand from young people for chemical drugs, such as amphetamines and ecstasy. The use of heroin is also a recent phenomenon in Turkey. Until a few years ago, the theory was expounded that the history of opium in their country and more than twenty years of experience in trafficking had shown that the population was well aware of the dangers of addiction and had not been tempted. At the United Nations congress in Vienna in 1988, where the last international Convention against Illicit Traffic in Narcotic Drugs was signed, the

Turkish delegate were pleased to be able to declare that his country was free of drug abuse, not only of heroin but also of the hashish coming from southeast Turkey.

In 1991, the United Nations commissioned Professor Doğu Ergil, of the University of Ankara, to carry out the intriguing task of discovering why this problem had not arisen earlier in Turkey. In 1992, Ergil interviewed several hundred people who did use drugs, to find out about their personal and social background, and delivered his initial findings to the U.N. Since then, however, he says the situation has changed. 'The number of heroin addicts in cities such as Istanbul has risen dramatically,' he says. 'Evidently it is true that if you play with fire, you get burned.' According to the Istanbul drugs squad, in 1995 twenty-four people died of overdose. Research was conducted in the same city amongst schoolchildren, of whom seven percent said they had tried drugs at some time. Turkish television reports regularly on the great rise in drugs use amongst the Turkish youth; the demand is increasing along with the purchasing power and westernisation of young people.

The drug traffickers in Turkey have tapped a new market. In the course of the 20th century, Turkey's function in the development of the world market for opium and heroin shifted from a production country up until 1972 to a transit country and from there to a consumption country.

*

The European market has grown considerably. Since the fall of the Berlin Wall in 1989, the number of inhabitants of Western Europe has increased to six hundred million. Prosperity in Western countries ensures increased purchasing power amongst young people. The young people of the former Soviet Republics present a new target group for international drug trafficking.

The heroin and cocaine markets in Europe expanded enormously in the 1980s and 1990s. Judging by the quantities of drugs confiscated and the number of seizures by the police, these markets have been doubling every year, though it difficult to tell exactly what the significance is of those confiscations: are controlling bodies paying more attention to the problem, are they working more efficiently or has the volume being traded actually increased so spectacularly? Between 1980 and 1993, the Netherlands appears to have intercepted the most hard drugs of all

European countries and the largest shipments. Does this mean that the investigative methods of the customs and police in the Netherlands are better than those in other countries, or that relatively more is done to trace drug trafficking? The latter may well be the case, as it is in the Dutch government's interest to convince the international community that it is more than fulfilling its convention obligations in fighting trafficking in the hope that this will reduce foreign criticism of the Dutch policy regarding drug users.

One overview of the price movement points in another direction, however. During the reporting period studied, consumer prices for both heroin and cocaine dropped sharply, which points to a greater availability of drugs rather than a rise in demand. In England and France the prices are still the highest, as those countries constitute the end of the market chain, where retail prices are charged. The fact that prices are low in the Netherlands has not so much to do with its drugs policy as with its function as a distribution country, so that dealers stay closer to the wholesale prices.

*

Most heroin imported into the United States at the moment comes from the Far East (Burma, the Golden Triangle) and Central and South America. The major production area for the European market is now the Golden Half Moon, or Crescent: Afghanistan, Pakistan and Iran. In the two latter countries, the home demand is so great that almost nothing is left for export. After the revolution in Iran in 1979, it did look as if an end would be brought to large-scale addiction among the population – Ayatollah Khomeini let there be no mistake that he saw drug traffickers as 'first-class traitors and a danger to society' – but the new Islamic regime took little in the way of concrete measures and did not place opium on the blacklist of forbidden behaviour, such as drinking alcohol. In 2004, the director of the anti-drug unit of the Iranian police declared on state television that the number of drug addicts exceeded two million. The year before, no less than 220,000 kilograms of drugs had been confiscated by the Iranian authorities. The deputy director of the drugs research unit at Tehran University has mentioned a figure of 5.3 million addicts in the country, where one gram of opium or heroin costs the equivalent of ten to fifteen euros. At the time of writing, in 2007, the Iranian government has started a programme for re-socialising drug addicts in empty villages.

The military rule of General Zia ul-Haq in Pakistan, under which opium production had initially been great, granted the Americans' express wish to reduce this drastically and, after deduction for the population's own use, there is nothing left for export. As of 2007, virtually all heroin comes from Afghanistan and a little from Myanmar (Burma).

Afghanistan acquired such a prominent position against the backdrop of the Cold War. From 1979 to 1991, Afghanistan was occupied by the Soviet Union. The Mujaheddin resistance was supported by arms supplied by the United States and others. In these conditions, warlords saw their chance to build up a position of power using the revenue from opium. With the aid of a secret CIA operation, the Americans put their money on a small group of Islamic rebels led by Gulbuddin Hekmatyar, which gave him every opportunity to evolve into an opium warlord.

Afghan opium is processed in laboratories in the border area with Pakistan. The Pakistani military uses the revenue for buying uranium, for example, in the republics on the southern flank of the former Soviet Union. For them, it is all about realising their big dream: manufacturing the atom bomb that will defeat the archenemy India. The disgrace of two earlier defeats in wars against India can then be put to rights once and for all.

The opium fields were traditionally located in the southern Helmand and Kandahar provinces and in the east in the province of Nangarhar. That pattern has changed. Nangarhar is no longer as important, but the opium has now spread over far more provinces and, in particular, in the northeast, in the province of Balkh. Production has risen spectacularly. While opium poppies were grown on a total of 29,000 hectares in 1986, by 2006 that had become no less than 165,000 hectares. There was one huge dip in this upward trend. The nationwide ban on opium cultivation by the Taliban in the year 2001 caused a massive cutback, to less than four percent of the preceding year. The land under cultivation shrank to 8,000 hectares. It is unclear whether the background to this decision was ideological conviction or a surplus stock in the storehouses that needed using up, but it demonstrated what the Taliban was capable of.

One of the objectives of the international aid supplied to Hamid Karzai, elected President of Afghanistan after the removal of the Taliban in 2004, is the eradication of opium. To date, that international aid, combined with the Afghan National Drug Control Strategy announced in

2003, which consists of crop destruction and arresting major drug traffickers, has had precious little effect. In 2006, Afghan poppy production increased by twenty-five percent, according to the U.N. Office on Drugs and Crime, and accounted for ninety-two percent of the world's heroin. The political problem is that the international community wants to disrupt the drug trade, whereas the Afghan government is afraid that excessive eradication may have a detrimental impact on security, governance and wider economic development goals, as it will confront powerful economic interests.

The import and export ports used to be located in the north, near the town of Mazar e Sharif – which means Tomb of the Saint – where, with the aid of the Russian mafia, arms and drugs are sent on to the neighbouring countries of Tajikistan, Uzbekistan and Turkmenistan and from there, by plane, to Russia and Azerbaijan. Then there is the infamous Balkan route. The routes shift continually and the access gates move as a result of territorial power shifts caused by war and politics.

As in all drug-producing countries with few resources aside from agriculture, an enormous number of people are involved in these activities. Under favourable market conditions, the poppy farmers earn ten times as much as they would by growing other crops and, moreover, the crop demands little care. Where the merchandise has to be smuggled over the mountain border of no less than five thousand metres in height, horses and donkeys provide the transport. Then there are the 'agents': young men from the towns who make the contacts between the farmers and the laboratories. They receive a percentage of the transaction in dollars. The roughly five hundred laboratories the border area boasts are managed by the local tribal chiefs.

The knowledge of the opium cookers is quite specialist and is transferred from father to son. Their workshops are no more than sheds hidden in the countryside, guarded by armies up to five hundred strong. From there, the drugs are transported by car and truck and sometimes by plane. Finally, there are the traffickers, generally Afghanis, who export the product. They maintain contact with people at a high level in political and military circles in the countries through which the export passes.

This opium economy is able to flourish in what constitutes the administrative territory of the 'free tribes'. The Pakistani constitution states that these tribes are not ruled by the authority of the government. No checks are carried out in the border area by the Afghani government, as there is no actual central authority there. The hundreds of tribes and clans in the border areas maintain good relations with the local governments in the big cities, based on the exchange of gifts. Not all tribes are involved in drug production and trafficking, by any means, but the leaders who are maintain strategic relations with the president. A well-known example was the Enwer family from Herat, a smaller drug-producing area in the west, of which the seven formidable brothers, who had amassed great wealth through opium, derived their power from such political relationships. The local population speaks disapprovingly of 'Enwer and the seven robbers'.

Big drug bosses arrange an average of two transports a year, but it can be four or five. They proceed according to a meticulously detailed plan, as there are a lot of people in diverse positions involved and all along the route the special corruption surcharge has to be paid to officers from the police, the customs and the army. A former member of the anti-drug committee under the chairmanship of the pro-Soviet former President Najibullah recounted a story firsthand to the present authors in 1997:

> These bosses sometimes have to start handing out gifts and money to important people as far as two years in advance of such a transport. He has to continually grease the palms of his agents the transport goes through. There are groups of various sizes in Uzbekistan, Prague and the Netherlands. All those little groups independently develop their local contacts, their own financial resources and their own communication channels. The boss has to wait for the optimal moment for action, which can take a whole year for a big transport of a hundred kilos. He can afford to, because such a transport earns him a gigantic profit. The bosses don't show themselves, they spend their time like a kind of absentee lord in five-star hotels abroad and, if anything goes wrong – a bribed policeman happened to be sick on the day of the transport – it is the little man who gets caught and he only loses his investment. No fewer than ten thousand couriers are currently languishing in Iranian prisons.
>
> When the drugs reach their customers, the bosses have to collect their money. Due to the [civil] war, there are not many contacts between Afghanistan and other countries and that makes the money transactions more difficult. The country has no central bank or

centralised financial registration and traffickers have to work with all kinds of currency. There is a busy black market in dollars and francs via Pakistan and the drug traffickers make use of that. All transactions are in cash or via a firm; cheques are avoided. The big organisations own whole strings of firms abroad, which officially import and export fruit or electronics but, in fact, consist of no more than a small office. The several thousands of refugees from Afghanistan who have been accommodated in various western countries offer wonderful new opportunities for these traffickers.

In 1996, the world was shaken by the rise of the fanatical Taliban. As these are fundamentalist Muslims, one would expect them to have rapidly brought an end to the production and export of opium – and for a brief period they caused export to drop slightly to demonstrate their goodwill to the world in an attempt to gain international recognition for their government. But when the desired recognition failed to materialise, the Taliban took the trade into its own hands. They reversed the usual prohibition ranking of soft and hard drugs: hash was strictly prohibited, as it was used primarily by Afghanis and was against the rules of Islam, but as opium was solely exported to the West, they saw no real necessity to forbid the cultivation of poppies. On the contrary, the Taliban treated opium producers with courtesy and they soon constituted one of the major sources of foreign currency.

The Balkan Route

In the history of international traffic, the trade route through the Balkans, also known as part of the Silk Road, is vitally important, as it links Asia to Europe. Turkey has always played a key role in it as a geographical node. Each year, more than one and a half million trucks cross the borders, plus a quarter of a million coaches and four million cars. The classic route, which runs north through Turkey via the E80 and south along the E90, meeting up in European Turkey, continues through Bulgaria, former Yugoslavia, Austria and Germany, after which it branches out to the other countries in Western Europe. Goods traffic between Turkey and Western Europe is primarily an economic exchange: fabrics go to Turkey and textiles come back, electronics go there, semi-tropical fruits come back. The large group of emigrants of Turkish origin in Western Europe has also generated an enormous transport flow of people and goods.

It is via this Balkan route that heroin has been transported to Europe from the Golden Crescent since the 1970s and now, therefore, chiefly from Afghanistan. The collapse of Yugoslavia and the war there have also created alternative roads but the smugglers have been continually moving and expanding their routes. The reason is not difficult to guess: they see themselves forced to go to great lengths to evade the police and get around the border guards. Three to three and a half thousand kilos of heroin are intercepted annually in Turkey in this way, according to the Turkish police, and in the rest of Europe another two to two and a half thousand kilos a year. What proportion of the total this represents and how many drugs actually get through is, naturally, unknown. The police like to work on estimations and say what they manage to intercept is ten percent, but that is no more than a shot in the dark.

In the year 2000, we did a round trip of the Balkan route by car with a friend, Kenan Cinibulak. As an outsider, you see very little of all the illegal activity along the route. In Hungary, Romania and Bulgaria, simple restaurants line the roads. Young ladies come from the villages in the area to offer the drivers sexual favours for payment. We struck up conversations with restaurant owners and Turkish travellers (without residence permits) everywhere, in an attempt to gain some information. Participant observation in this way generates nothing, however, except the impression of a tedious coming and going.

The theory that the action of the police and other investigative bodies influences the nature and character of organised crime as much as the reverse is illustrated by this route. New solutions are continually sought for the new problems raised by the police. Almost as soon as the police catch on to the fact that the drivers used are mainly from the border area of East and Southeast Turkey and start checking those drivers for that reason, they decide to deploy Western European drivers; if a popular hiding place for heroin, such as the tubes of a luggage rack on top of a van of migrant workers returning from their holidays in Turkey, is discovered, then they devise something else, such as hollowing out the rear axle. Once a route has been uncovered, a new one is found and so the Balkan route fans out. One Turkish man who has played at the mid-level of such an organisation told us that his task had been to report to Istanbul on Dutch news reports about the police and its methods. There is definitely contra-observation of police activities.

European police forces have built up considerable knowledge of the Balkan route over the years. Interpol has a Balkan team, maintains a Balkan route information system and has set up a Pro Balkan project. Every year, the German Bundeskriminalamt issues a thick report on smuggling along the route and the Dutch National Criminal Intelligence Service issues a special information bulletin on Turkey, largely featuring the latest routes. The Turkish narcotics division of the Directorate General for Security also devotes special attention to the subject. Balkan route conferences are organised annually. There are annual statements of the number of arrests along the route, with the quantities of the various types of drugs confiscated in various countries and even where they were found according to border town. Confiscated money and goods are also noted. The police gauge their success on the basis of such figures. The parties do contest each other's figures from time to time, suggesting that perhaps the police of another country have exaggerated the number of confiscated kilos, or they have given too high a figure for the total value of confiscated assets by counting them twice (by claiming everything confiscated in international campaigns in all the various countries nationally, for example).

Documents show that the most drugs are found in trucks, followed by cars, campers and finally coaches. The documentation is richly illustrated with photographic material, showing which hiding place is currently popular, but also how ingenious the smugglers are in continually devising new solutions. Increasingly, parts of the route are travelled by sea. A connection has been discovered between Istanbul and the Romanian port of Constanza and there are ships that take a route across the Mediterranean. Planes are used too, but this method is nothing like as common as in the cocaine route from South and Central America to Europe. Some Africans have been found flying as couriers between certain countries. Nigerians stop in at Turkey and then go on to Italy. A small amount of drugs has been traced in international trains. Throughout the material published, it is possible to follow the development of the dynamics between the drug bosses and the police.

*

The raw materials for manufacturing illegal heroin, for example morphine-base, are imported into Turkey and end up being sold to retailers in Western Europe. The value of the substance increases with each phase of processing and with each step on its way to the consumer. There are four phases to the processing. The first two take place in the country where the poppies are grown, Afghanistan; the last two take place in Turkey. Laboratories, which can sometimes better be described as kitchens, can be found in the far east of the country near Van and in the southeast near Gaziantep. In Başkale, half an hour from the border with Iraq, hundreds of heroin kitchens have been counted. Many refineries have also now been set up in Istanbul. The city functions as the distribution centre for destinations and routes. As the volume for the same monetary value of drugs reduces with each processing phase, at least up until the point where the drugs arrive in the country of destination, and as smaller volumes are easier to hide in transport, reducing the risk of getting caught, this relocation of laboratories is significant. The fact that the smugglers transport their merchandise another 1,500 kilometres from east to west in Turkey to have it processed there means they evidently feel far safer, despite the confiscations that do take place. They have neutralised the controlling bodies. Once in Istanbul, the smugglers are relatively safe. The road network is diverse and there are many ways of driving to the West. The port is also vast and difficult to oversee.

Police material clearly shows where the smugglers generally come from. The traditional old smugglers from the eastern and southern borders of Turkey, those with Iran, Syria, Iraq and Azerbaijan, are immediately recognisable. It is striking that those smugglers who have been arrested always come from the same areas and, sometimes, all from the same town, district or village. This is because there has to be a collaboration based on mutual trust, with the added ability to control the personnel in the field. Such relationships exist within groups of relatives and neighbours and that geographical concentration is reflected in the regional origin of the culprits. The province of Diyarbakir and, in particular, the little town of Lice, has the highest concentration of smugglers' nests. Then follow Van and Gaziantep, with a highly pronounced concentration in the little border town of Kilis; Hakkari with the town of Yüksekova; Adana; the province of Elaziĝ with the town of Palu and the town of Tunceli.

If the transport is carried out by truck, the merchandise is hidden in the fuel tanks, in the chassis, in the spare wheels, behind the bulkhead, in the driver's personal luggage and between the load. Generally, the drivers are working on instructions, but sometimes they and their vehicle are used without their knowledge. Certain car parks on one side of the border are renowned for packages being attached to the underside of the vehicle while the driver is asleep, for example, to be retrieved on the other side when he takes his next break. The driver therefore runs the risk without knowing it.

*

From Istanbul, the route branches out over the main road in three directions.* There is a primary northern route via Bulgaria, Romania, Hungary and Austria or Slovakia and the Czech Republic to Germany and the Netherlands. From there it continues to Belgium, France, the United Kingdom and Scandinavia. When it reaches this final destination, all the

---

* Four now that the Serbian conflict has ended and territories of the former Yugoslavia are once more passable.

borders have been crossed and the sales price is, in principle, at its highest. The volume of the drugs is also reinflated by cutting; for a long time a combination of the neutral substances paracetamol and caffeine was popular. The second northern route runs from Romania via the Ukraine and Poland to Germany. A variant runs from the Black Sea area through Russia to Poland. This Black Sea route has already become so important that the Turkish police, who concentrate on the Balkan route, are now confiscating smaller quantities of drugs. The third route runs along the southern flank of Europe through Greece and from there by sea to an Italian port, such as Bari, Ancona or Trieste. From Italy it branches out to the north to Germany, but there is a southern branch that leads through Southern France to Spain.

To allow trucks to cross the borders quickly and relatively unobstructed, the TIR system is used: controls are carried out by means of a bundle of carnets, the temporary export documents that eliminate the need for a Customs declaration at border points, which are only checked afterwards by comparing the stamps of the country of departure and destination. It is all a question of time. The smuggling organisers are acutely aware of the amount of time it takes to search their vehicles. Combing a car takes one or two hours, a coach two to four hours and a loaded truck six to eight hours. They endeavour to speed up the procedure at the border by arriving with perishable goods, such a cooled truck of flowers, in the hope that customs officers will be courteous. They also make grateful use of the frequent antagonism and mutual distrust of officers on the two sides of the border; if a customs officer notices something unusual, he will not often pass this on to his colleague on the other side of the border.

The bag of tricks is big. With a substantial transport the organisation can decide to sacrifice a small quantity of drugs in order to distract the attention from the real shipment crossing the border at the same moment. Drivers can work together by driving one behind another and letting the one behind know if checks are being carried out. If that does happen, the one following can feign a breakdown and wait with his bonnet open until the coast is clear. It is also possible to grease the palm of the border guard or customs officer beforehand or at the moment of discovery. 'Actually, it doesn't work without bribery,' one of the larger Dutch drugs barons told us. More than ten years previously, he had worked as a driver in Turkey. He always took several tens of thousands of German marks with him for on the way and, if a customs officer didn't trust him, he took out his wallet. Fortunately for him, that always worked, although he always had to wait and see whether the bribe would be accepted. A Turkish guard at the border with Bulgaria had once asked him what was in his big fuel tank. '"Diesel," I said, but he looked at me and shook his head in disbelief. I looked him straight in the eye, grabbed a few notes from my breast pocket and handed them to him. Thank God he accepted them, but further on I noticed I'd given him a couple of thousand marks, far too much.' On a trip like that by truck from Lebanon to the Netherlands he lost ten kilos in body weight through nervous sweat, he told us.

A lot of people are involved in a transport like that. First of all, naturally, are the couriers or drivers themselves. They are followed by someone in a car who keeps an eye on things – is there a threat of discovery? Is the driver going to take off with the shipment? – in order to take any necessary interim logistics decisions and report on how and why anything might have gone wrong: the controller. There are also the transport organisers, who map out the route and draw up the timetable. At the end of the line is the receiver, who receives the transport and distributes it to those who have invested in it, in proportion with the capital invested.

From the descriptions in police journals, one might get the impression that the thorough planning ensures that such transports go smoothly and without a hitch. The following passage from a Dutch police manual gives a good example.

The driver/courier transporting the heroin often does not know who he has to deliver to. He goes to a designated location where he is contacted, generally by the escort. The escort therefore plays a crucial role as intermediary between the courier and the organisation. The contact place is often a car park for trucks alongside the motorway. Striking is that, before the arrival of a heroin shipment, the members of the organisation come across as nervous. This is reflected by the way they pace up and down in front of the location where the organisation generally congregates. The telephone traffic also increases. Frequently, just before the arrival of a shipment of heroin, someone comes over from Turkey who is highly esteemed in the organisation. This is demonstrated by the respect shown to him by other members. To prevent discovery by the police, the organisation is cautious in its dealings. Permanent observation of the location is required. We recommend tapping the telephones at this point.

That impression that it is so simple, however, is mistaken. Things go wrong all the time; connections fail, the driver turns up days too late, there is a misunderstanding about the meeting place, and so on. Detectives who have been involved in operational investigations into such transports can recount vivid tales of things that have gone wrong in such a stupid way that nobody could have imagined it beforehand. That is partly because telephone communications always take place in secret codes due to the risk of tapping. Those codes are generally transparent to experienced police and interpreters, but the smugglers themselves often get confused. This is not exactly an advantage for the police, however. They have to plan their action well ahead, making sure the necessary personnel and resources are available and arranging sufficient finances. If the transport then arrives late, increasing uncertainty, that costs so much money that the whole thing sometimes has to be called off. It is actually so difficult to get to grips with 'organised' crime because it is so badly organised.

The police are continually drawing up profiles of suspicious transports and drivers for investigation. The Germans are the trendsetters, with their *Rasterfahndung* system, which boils down to testing transports based on all kinds of risk indicators. This is, in fact, the core of all police checks: noticing what doesn't fit into the normal pattern. Making a round trip without a load is suspicious. A car that has clearly just had work done on it can have been 'prepared' with storage space; new bolts are one give-away. A car that has been freshly sprayed is also suspicious. If the goods don't fit within the usual routes of origin and destination, that arouses suspicion, just as when the truck has an unusual driver; if there is vague or no advertising for the company on the sides of the vehicle; if there are any unusual documents, unusual packaging or an unusual route, or when a truck and a car with a registration number from the same place are driving one after the other for a long time.

The response of alert smuggling organisations is equally clear; all signs that might betray them are eliminated in the course of time. One of the most interesting measures for avoiding risks is the practice of storing large quantities of drugs in the countries along the Balkan route where the expertise level of the controlling bodies is low, such as Romania, by way of a buffer stock – in jargon, a stash. In Poland, a loophole in the law was discovered: transporting drugs was a criminal offence, but storing them in a stash-house was not. The reaction of the Western Europe Balkan route specialists in the police is again predictable; delegations are sent to Hungary, Romania and Slovakia to teach the authorities there how smuggling can be intercepted and to make collaboration agreements.

*

Those specialising in the Balkan route have learned that the smuggling bosses have a certain type of intelligence and an unusual mind-set. In Turkish they call it *köylü kurnazliĝi*, or craftiness.

Smugglers are generally people from a simple background without much education. They barely master the technology they use. But they are brilliant when it comes to finding loopholes in the system and thinking up elements of the trafficking process that can be manipulated. As soon as someone 'invents' something new or when a new police investigative method is discovered, it spreads like wildfire through criminal circles.

The police and the judicial authorities are forced to reason in the same way; they put themselves in the shoes of their opponents and try to anticipate the smuggling world's response to their next move. The police and the underworld continually influence each other's psychology.

Fighting organised crime by confiscating its proceeds only succeeds when three conditions are fulfilled. First of all, the fact that there is a problem at all has to be acknowledged in the country in question. Second, laws against it have to be passed – usually international rules that are then adopted by treaty by the country concerned. Thirdly, the government needs concrete authority with officials who enforce these laws.

Two important international conventions concern laundering drug money: the UN Convention of 1988 in Vienna and the guideline formulated in 1990 in Strasbourg on the way national states should confiscate illegally obtained assets. Turkey was not party to these conventions. That was initially because the problem simply did not exist there. All foreign currencies were welcome for the reconstruction of the Turkish economy and, in the 1980s, premier Turgut Özal openly encouraged money laundering to boost the free market economy. The racket of false export, where products of little value were exported from the country while a far higher value was indicated on falsified invoices and customs documents, dates from the 1970s. This justified income actually generated by drug sales, smuggled cigarettes and illegal arms trading. The nephew of a former president of Turkey, Yahya Demirel, a colourful figure who we will come across regularly in this book, is credited with having invented this system. The Turkish Central Bank rewarded all exports up until 1989 with, on average, a further fifteen per cent of the indicated trade value and that therefore applied to these fraudulent practices, too. Officials from the Central Bank of Turkey, who visited the companies in question to check for subsidy fraud, found dilapidated buildings and deserted industrial premises. When the bank reported their findings, these bothersome memoranda were shoved aside by Özal himself by means of a guideline whereby all investigation into companies receiving export licences was cancelled.

With its gigantic informal sector within the economy and poor governmental regulation, Turkey was and still is, in fact, a paradise for laundering criminal money. There is a sizeable offshore banking sector that makes it appealing for Turkish criminals to take their money to Turkey. A banker in Istanbul declared, 'I don't care who you are or how you get your money. If you arrive with a briefcase full of cash, then we will ask no questions. The law says it has nothing to do with me. I am not obliged to inform either the tax authorities or the Central Bank about your activities.'

Those countries that did sign the international conventions saw Turkey as an enormous leak in their system, in the same way as several Central American republics and the Channel Islands were. The group of the seven most industrialised countries had set up a Financial Action Task Force, which successfully demanded that Turkey should participate seriously and investigate all financial transactions above a certain minimum amount of roughly 10,000 U.S. dollars. The police forces in Germany, England and the Netherlands who were pursuing Turkish drug organisations realised that their national regulations in this field remained simply a formality as long as everyone was free to take his criminally obtained money to Turkey. They saw men and women with plastic bags full of uncounted money and later with entire suitcases, travelling to Turkey. It was also extremely simple to transfer money to Turkey via a joint account. What this system came down to was that, in Western Europe, money was deposited in a general bank account and the combined amount was then transferred as one sum to a Turkish bank. The original contributors were unknown and simply gave a false name; the only thing that was known was to whom which amount should be paid in Turkey.

The major reason why Turkey was unwilling to participate in the international anti-laundering legislation is that this money benefited Turkey's economic growth. The system of money transfers by migrant workers in the 1960s engendered a certain accustomisation to foreign dependence. Drug money that followed the same route went to the poorer parts of Turkey. There was therefore an influx of capital with which land was bought, houses were built, shops were established and investments were made in setting up hotels and amusement parks in those parts of Turkey where tourism needed to develop. Premier Özal encouraged this in exactly the same way as the South American governments who were unwilling to let the currency flow from cocaine escape; he even introduced a one-time general amnesty for people suspected of drug trafficking.

While this may have only been a defensive act, in 1989 Özal also actively attempted to raise money from drug traffickers for Turkey. Premier Özal went with two of his Turkish bankers to the Grand Dolder Hotel in Zurich, Switzerland, to convince the infamous Lebanese 'high king' of money laundering, Mamoud Shakarchi, to move his activities to Turkey. Wouldn't Shakarchi like Turkish nationality? he had asked. 'No, minister,' the laundry king replied. Would he like to own his own bank? There was one ready and waiting for him in Cyprus. That, too, was rejected. According to the newspaper *Sabah*, the Turkish laundry king Berber Yaşar was also present at this meeting. The premier's message was clearly understood by Turks abroad: money obtained from drug trafficking is welcome. In an Amsterdam coffee house in the 1990s, a drug trafficker was noted to have made the following remark: 'Özal has openly stated that he is in need of foreign currency. We will send money to Turkey.'

While unwilling to act, on the other hand the Turkish government could see that, unfortunately, such moneys were also used to support oppositional political factions, primarily the Kurdish nationalists of the PKK. The government would have liked to confiscate the drug money that ends up in that organisation. Although the idea of forfeiture of illegally obtained profits or advantages may have been unknown in Turkey for a long time, the police and judicial authorities of Western European countries who worked with Turkish colleagues in concrete cases sometimes succeeded in convincing them to participate on those grounds. Later, after 9/11, the risk of financing international terrorism occurred to people.

The international pressure on Turkey had been increased in the meantime and, in November 1995, the Turkish parliament introduced an act against laundering criminal money. The Convention of Vienna in 1988 was also ratified in February 1996. Finally, was the feeling, the quibbling was over, because Turkey had been promising for years that this would happen, but the decision-making again became stranded at the Turkish parliament's special money laundering committee. Minutes of the committee show clearly that the possibility of also fighting political violence by banning money laundering played a significant role. All money 'originating from smuggling drugs, firearms and knives, the sale of human organs, the sale of cultural and natural treasures and a series of criminal offences summarised in the penal law' – such as terrorism – is defined as 'dirty money'. The Americans were enthusiastic about the ratification, as can be seen from passages on the issue in the State Department's International Narcotics Control Strategy Report of March 1997. This established the second step in the process of effectively fighting drug trafficking: money laundering had been acknowledged as undesired and a criminal offence.

In the meantime, legislation regarding money laundering and financing terrorism was tightened up in 2005 and 2006 and, in 2007, the third FATF evaluation report on Turkey was discussed. Despite the goodwill on paper, hardly any concrete measures have been implemented for confiscating illegally obtained profits and very few suspicious transactions have been reported. That goes along with the third condition: the laws also have to be enforced. The evaluation report shows that judges and public prosecutors in Turkey are unfamiliar with this complex subject matter. The number of acquittals is striking. From discussions with financial investigators, we have also deduced that the investigative authorities have insufficient knowledge and experience. One of the underlying problems is in the unclear distribution of authority. There is a power struggle going on between the financial investigation committee, which answers to the Minister of Justice, and the police forces and that obstructs a great deal of action.

2

Urban Knights and Rebels

Highwaymen live off love and fear. If all they do is inspire love, this is a weakness. If fear is all they generate, they are hated and have no followers.

Yaşar Kemal

Revolts and Rebellion

'Once upon a time there were *kabadayi* in Turkey. They were men who protected a neighbourhood or district in Istanbul. Brave men with a good heart, strong men who knew how to use a knife, experienced men who went to prison again and again to pay for their deeds. With their experience, they were able to keep disputes from getting out of hand. They preserved the peace and kept their area safe. Whatever they said went.' Engin Bilginer, the Turkish journalist quoted here, is romanticising. Books like his *Symphony Of The Godfathers* tend to present a picture of the serenity of the old underworld, when 'real men of honour' were still in charge. Everything was so good and honest and nowadays it is all bad and dishonest. In these nostalgic accounts, the introduction of the firearms that democratised the violence is always the watershed. This is clear from the words of Köroǧlu, the hero of an old folk epic: 'The invention of the gun was what killed honesty.'

There is not a country in the world without an urban underworld and every language has a word with a similar meaning to *kabadayi*: the Mob in American, *le milieu* in French, *Ganoven* in German. All across the globe, people speak nostalgically of the good old days when 'honest men' fought with their fists. The *kabadayi* would settle a wide range of issues among the people of 'their territory', according to norms and unwritten rules. Their romantic image has a lot to do with their charmingly daredevil lifestyle. Literature is filled with stories of the long nights they spent with gorgeous prostitutes, their sumptuous meals and bacchanalian revelry and how they listened to exciting music and watched belly dancers. In Turkish literature, the *kabadayi* are presented as the immediate precursors of the contemporary crime bosses known as *babas*. Their world evokes associations with courage, lawlessness, honour and defending the weak.

Today's *baba* is only too willing to refer to this noble tradition to justify his conduct. Turkish books about the *kabadayi* do, however, also include passages that are considerably less romantic. Not that the misfortune they describe is met with by *kabadayi* themselves; instead it is the misfortune of the people they deal with. They might have been protective, but they were also violent extortionists and the residents of the territory they protected paid in blood, sweat and tears. Although the first impression of the *kabadayi* is far more enchanting, the second one is no less realistic.

*

In traditional accounts of kings, emperors and sultans, *kabadayi* are described as ignoble and unscrupulous men, rebels or separatists who are a threat to law and order and deserve to be officially or unofficially prosecuted and punished. There is no place for them in the 'history-from-above' about the powerful rich, the despots and the men who run the country. The rise of a variant social history that is now roughly half a century old and makes a conscious effort to describe the course of 'history-from-below', however, has turned rogues, bandits and the underworld into a topic of serious study. In the case of Turkey, it is instructive to go back in history to the time of the Ottoman Empire and examine the rebels and bandits who developed the cultural codes that still shape the conduct of today's Turkish mafia. This is no simple matter, as good sources are largely lacking, but Turkish authors have saved a few of these men from oblivion.

Like the empire of the Seljuqs (1040-1244) that preceded it in the Asian part of Turkey, the Ottoman Empire (1299-1923) can be characterised as a society of peasants administered by a court in the fashion of a patrimonial bureaucracy. Power was in the hands of the sultan and a strikingly small group of courtiers and administrators for such a large empire. The grand cultural tradition was preserved at court and, in the words of author Feroz Ahmad, the strong and centralised state that is identified in theory with the nation was 'viewed as neutral, as standing outside society and not as representative of any personal interest'. This tradition was a factor in shaping the ideology of the modern Turkish state, which can be expected 'to intervene if and when the national interest seems to be threatened by small self-seeking interests'.

Sultan Osman, after whom the grand empire that existed for six centuries was named, was one of the Islamic monarchs who fought the holy war against the Christian Byzantine Empire and emerged victorious. In reality, though, the vast area that stretched all the way from central Asia to Bosnia-Herzegovina was an infinite patchwork of peoples and tribes with their own languages, customs and 'small traditions'. The theory of one nation is ideology, says the political scientist Doğu Ergil in his numerous columns and lectures advocating a modern democracy for Turkey. In essence, the Ottoman Empire was the artificial product of military conquests. Despite the lengthy process of state formation and an all-encompassing assimilation policy in the modern period of the republic, one ethnographer similarly has no trouble compiling an ethnological atlas for the present-day smaller territory of Turkey with so many combinations of languages, tribal frameworks and religions that there are no fewer than forty-seven different ethnic groups. The distance between the small feudal administration apparatus and the eighty-five per cent of the population scattered over the vast countryside was enormous. The administration was extremely decentralised and local rulers were the ones who exerted the actual power. A social and political constellation of this kind produced weak links in the power hierarchy, which contributed to the emergence of rebelliousness and banditry. Who was there to defend the tenant farmers and peasants? Or whom were they keeping under control? Who was the connecting link between them and the large landowners and tax collectors?

In his book *Dissidents and Capital Punishment in the Ottoman Period*, Riza Zelyut summarises the structural conflicts that led to the rebellions. Firstly, material conditions played a role, such as exploitation by local rulers via a complicated system of land ownership, especially since there was so little to keep them from increasing the tax burden. Then there was the resistance to forced Islamisation. The circles that were the first to accept Islam as their religion consisted of prominent wealthy Turks who chose the Islamic movement most advantageous for them, the school of Hanefist law. 'It offered them the flexibility they needed for their administrative activities,' wrote Zelyut. The poor were not as quick to abandon their religions and customs. They did accept Islam, but in their own way.

The third structural problem had to do with the ethnic hierarchy that prevailed throughout the empire. In the Seljuq periods, the authorities viewed Georgians, Iranians and Slavs as the top ranking peoples and Turks and Turkmens as the lowest. Turkish was a language only to be spoken by people of humble descent and it is not difficult to find offensive and racist comments in the writings of Seljuq authors: 'Bloodthirsty Turks ... If they get the chance, they plunder, but as soon as they see the enemy coming, off they run.' Matters were not much different in the Ottoman period, even though the empire was governed by a small court elite which was itself Turkish. According to Çetin Yetkin, one of the major Turkish authors on the Seljuq and Ottoman periods, 'In the Ottoman Empire, though Turks were a "minority" they did not have the same rights as the other minorities.' In fact the term 'Turk' was a pejorative. One Ottoman historian Naima, who also wrote a book about the Anatolian rebels, used the following terms for the Turks: *Türk-i bed-lika* (Turk with an ugly face), *nadan Türk* (ignorant Turk) and *etrak-i bi-idrak* (Turk who knows nothing).

*

Authors inspired by socialism – such as Eric Hobsbawm with *Bandits* in 1969 – have tried to turn early modern rebels who rose up against the wealthy into noble rogues promoting the interests of the oppressed masses and therefore playing a proto-political role. Some authors have done the same with the mafia in Sicily; discussion about this criminal organisation contains the same themes connected with bandits in peasant societies. Particularly in the extremely decentralised Ottoman Empire, writes Hobsbawm, banditry flourished in the remote and inaccessible mountain regions and the plains where there was no network of good roads. The most sympathetic outlaw is undoubtedly the Robin Hood kind who is active in peasant societies throughout the world. Those in power might view him as a criminal threat, but he is a man who restores social justice and 'steals from the rich to give to the poor'. This kind of outlaw violates the law but obeys a higher law of good and evil. This noble rogue is expected to exhibit a fixed career pattern. He is a young man of humble descent who turns to a life of robbery after he himself is a victim of injustice and has to flee. No matter how notorious he is, the rules he lives by are still civilised. No one is ever killed except in an honest battle. This kind of Robin Hood is admired by the people, who are always willing to provide him with a place to hide. He is invisible and the authorities can never find him. He is protest incarnate against an unjust social order.

Anton Blok exposes this depiction as a purely romantic one. In his book about the roots of the mafia in Sicily, he describes the men other authors have referred to as 'social bandits'. He, however, views them as unscrupulous accomplices of large landowners and the troops who stifle the protest of the peasants. He demonstrates how the steward class of the large farming estates became independent in the second half of the 19th century and formed its own private armies.

Although the underlying economic and political causes of rebellion are the same in most societies – poverty, exploitation and oppression – there are two specific types of traditional Turkish rebels. The first is part of a social movement with prophetic aspects and a revolutionary nature. The force of this type of rebel lies in his ability to gather a sizeable following on the basis of a programme. The second type, the bandit, operates individually or in a small band of kindred spirits. In the city they are called *kabadayi* and in the mountains they are known as *efe* or *eşkiya*. With their individual agility, fearlessness and strength, they command the respect of all. The prevailing social movement requires its members to obey strict rules of conduct, but the bandits, insofar as they live in the city, opt for a worldlier lifestyle.

The rebel and the bandit are separate and do not represent successive stages in one and the same development, revolutionary or otherwise. Even though the authorities do view the rebels as a criminal group, it is the bandits who are the real source of the modern underworld. They are motivated by revenge – it is striking how often their careers begin with a vendetta – and a desire for esteem and personal wealth. They fulfil many roles in their community, but their basic activity is always extortion. In most accounts of the *kabadayi* and the *eşkiya* it is striking that, at some point in their career, they are bribed to start working for the authorities. Politically speaking, therefore, these predecessors of modern organised crime in Turkey would seem to represent a conservative rather than a revolutionary force.

*

The earliest sources on Turkey pertain to the Seljuq period. Accounts are scarce but invaluable. In the literature on Anatolia, a number of primitive 'criminal organisations' are described that are typical of the socio-economic situation in a peasant society. They always have a strongly religious aspect and can sometimes almost be described as prophetic movements. There were, for example, the Batinis, whose philosophy had its origins in the Sabilik sect and who were partially under Hebrew influence. They refused to accept the traditional concepts of heaven and hell. Their trademark was a small box of hashish on a string around the neck. Their famous leader Hassan Sabbah had a beautiful garden where they would smoke hashish and dance all day and night. Since they are viewed as the ones who introduced hashish to Anatolia, they are referred to as *haşhişin*, a term now used in Turkish for people who smoke hash.

The Ayars were picturesque; the only garb they usually wore was a loincloth and a headpiece made from the bark of a date tree, and they carried scimitars. The Kalenderis shaved their heads and the Haydaris refused to acknowledge any law at all. All these groups would attack the rich, plunder their homes and divide the spoils among the poor.

The popular uprisings named after the Babai sect, which helped end Seljuq rule, were the most important of all and the sect still has followers in Turkey today. Their aim was to promote the poor peasants against the usurpers, but there was also an element of religious protest. Babai could be recognised by their red headdresses and extremely simple attire. According to one authoritative study, they soon had numerous followers. In 1239 the Seljuqs attacked their leader Baba Ishak and his 50,000 followers and the battle went on for a year. Ishak's following in Anatolia grew from day to day and his followers believed he was immortal. The Seljuqs finally captured him and hanged him near the city of Asmasya at the bastion, after which they cut him up into tiny pieces and scattered them over his followers to convince them he was really gone. As was often the case with prophets, his followers did not want to believe he was dead and assumed he had just gone off to consult with God about getting help.

The Seljuqs won in the end, with the help of French mercenaries. Four thousand Babai followers were beheaded and 1,000 hanged. The movement nonetheless lives on. Poor villagers who could not read the Sunnite manuscripts written in Arabic and Persian – and did not wish to – would listen to Turkish translations of the texts. The Babai abandoned the strict rules of the Sunnites – they wanted to drink alcohol and dance and listen to music and pray to music. They did not go to the mosque and they refused to fast in the month of Ramadan or to treat women and children as second-class citizens. These are all more or less customs of the liberal Alevites, who now constitute about a third of the Turkish population.

*

In the period following the 13th century, there were also uprisings for religious, social and economic reasons. According to various sources, Bedreddin was behind the first important rebellion against the Ottomans. The renowned Turkish poet Nazim Hikmet, who was a communist, paid homage to him in a famous epic poem. Bedreddin had a plan for the future, a political programme based upon the principles of honesty and equality, which is why he is depicted in left-wing and intellectual circles as Turkey's first 'socialist' rebel. Bedreddin lived at the end of the 14th and the beginning of the 15th century and was well educated and respected as a wise man. He expounded his materialist philosophy in the book *Inspirations*. When he came to have thousands of followers in the area of Aydin and Manisa in western Turkey, the government in Istanbul grew concerned and decided to step in. Two attacks by the government were successfully warded off by the philosopher's *müridler*, or followers, but a third attack, this time on a larger scale, was not and the government troops hanged all his followers. Bedreddin himself was captured and hanged naked in the centre of Serez. In the memory of the local population, Bedreddin and his prominent *müridler* remain alive in many ballads.

The early 16th century saw the Alevite uprisings, including those led by the Islamic high priests Kulu, in 1511, and Sheyh Celal, in 1518-19. The followers of Sheyh Celal were called Celali, a term the Ottoman rulers later gave to all the rebellions. The most important of the Alevite rebellions was the one led by Pir Sultan Abdal at the end of the 16th century. He, too, still has followers in left-wing and Alevite circles, and in Turkey as well as Western Europe, there are associations, foundations and other organisations named after Pir Sultan Abdal. This leader of the people and poet, from the vicinity of Sivas in Central Anatolia, dreamt of a saviour who would liberate the common people from the Ottoman yoke. His hope was mainly focused on the spiritual leader Ali, the Prophet Mohammed's son-in-law and the fourth caliph, but in practice he sought the support of the Shiite regime in Persia. Pir Sultan Abdal was hanged in 1590.

There were other uprisings besides the Alevite ones. One was led by Karayazici Abdulhalim, and is now also called the Celali rebellion. Most of Abdulhalim's followers were poor peasants, but a role was also played by some prominent people from Anatolia, who had their own objections to Istanbul. The uprising began in 1598 and spread throughout Anatolia. The Ottoman Empire had no choice but to recruit troops to defeat Karayazici and the striking thing was that Anatolians were not allowed to enlist in the army for fear of their being Celali's followers. The wars between Karayazici and the Ottoman Empire went on until Karayazici died a natural death, but his brother, 'Crazy' Hasan, carried on the resistance with 30,000 men. Peace was finally established at the beginning of the 17th century and Hasan and his fellow warriors were given prominent positions at court. This did not mean an end had come to the political and social opposition in Anatolia. In any number of places, groups continued the opposition up until the mid-17th century, such as Kalenderoğlu's movement controlling the central region and Canbuladoğlu's controlling the south of Anatolia. The Ottoman grand viziers 'Gravedigger' Murat and, later, Ismail Pasha murdered tens of thousands of Anatolians and buried them in mass graves or pits.

*

After the 15th century, rebelliousness seemed to shift from the countryside to the cities. By the 16th century, bands of criminals were active in Istanbul, a vast city at the time in comparison with those in Europe. The Suhteyan movement has gone down in history as the first 'criminal organisation'. Suhte was a student at one of the religious academies, the *medrese*, and Suhteyan is the plural of Suhte. More students graduated from the academies than there were jobs for and, like modern-day students in so many developing countries, they protested and proclaimed themselves revolutionaries. They left the classrooms, formed groups that took to the streets and started plundering shops and homes. Their targets were the wealthy and the officials and 'accomplices' of the government. They not only stole material possessions but also murdered their victims and earned a reputation for being extremely cruel and amoral.

The social uprisings in the empire always targeted Istanbul, but there were also considerable class differences within the city and, as was the case in Anatolia, ethnic differences as well. The court itself also had a tradition of intrigues, which usually involved the military. Several sultans lost their lives in these armed skirmishes. The food riot of 1730 was named after its instigator, Patrona Halil, and another one was led in 1807 by Kabakçi Mustafa. In a later period, there were conflicts between the

Western-oriented reform movement Tanzimat and more traditional thinkers. In 1839, there was a Tanzimat victory and a mission statement was read out loud in public at the Square of the Rose Gardens, thereafter known as the Noble Decree of the Rose Garden. In the rebellion of 1876, a group of leading Ottoman politicians replaced the sultan with crown prince Murad. He did not hold this position for long, though, because when a constitution was enacted a few months later, the new sultan was declared insane and locked up at Çirağan Palace on the shores of the Bosporus, where he remained imprisoned for almost three decades.

The World of the *Kabadayi*

Mafia bosses like to talk about the kind of *kabadayi* we described at the beginning of this chapter. *Kaba* means crude and coarse and *dayi* means uncle or mother's brother. The word *kabadayi* had and still has a double meaning. It is a romanticised figure and, in this sense, the term has a positive meaning to people in Turkey. It also has a negative meaning, however, that implies just the opposite – someone who is unjustly demanding something of someone else: 'How can you be such a crude uncle that you would ask such a thing of me!'*

The *kabadayi* came from the rather innocent ranks of voluntary firemen called *tulumbaci* or *tulumbaci kabadayisi*. In Istanbul – one of the oldest and largest cities of the world – where there was and still is little space between the houses, firemen fulfil a vital function. Ergun Hiçyilmaz, a former police reporter and a fine storyteller, wrote some interesting books on the topic. He now sells knick-knacks at one of the covered markets in Taxim in Istanbul. Hiçyilmaz told us, 'Every district in the city had a group of *kabadayi* who worked as firemen. The people would pay them to put out a fire. They were known for their strength, their courage and mainly for the fact that they could run so fast.' These *kabadayi* usually did not go in for a career in crime; they were simply fulfilling a duty. There was a certain amount of competition among the various groups of *tulumbaci*. Who could run the fastest? Who could put out the fire first? Cevat Ulunay, the Turkish historian who is the best author on the *kabadayi*, calls it a kind of sport, not unlike soccer today.

To some people though, it did mean a career in crime. One important pillar of the Ottoman Empire had traditionally been the salaried Janissary

---

* A second category of *kabadayi* was called the *külhanbeyi*. They were the lowest ranking in the *kabadayi* hierarchy. Real *kabadayi* had only one fear: that they would be called *külhanbeyi*. People feared the *külhanbeyi*, but that fear did not entail any respect.

infantry corps, but by the early 18th century it had degenerated and engaged more in terrorising the local population than defending the empire. There were Janissaries in the capital who supplemented their income by extortion or by serving as superintendents who helped settle neighbourhood disputes. Some former Janissaries turned their sidelines into their main source of income and became *kabadayi* in the modern sense of bandits. Since these neighbourhood tyrants had lost the power base of the military status, however, new opportunities opened up for boys from the neighbourhood itself, who could do more justice to the social motif of promoting the neighbourhood interests. This abuse of power was one of the reasons for the thorough reorganisation of the military apparatus under Sultan Selim III in 1794.

The *kabadayi* were known for centuries for their costume – shoes with golden heels and black cloaks worn loosely over the shoulders, so they could quickly draw their weapon from their belt. It was hard not to know when they were around, since they would shout every so often to make their location known. Their special shout started with a long drawn out 'heeeeyt' followed by the message, so everyone knew which *kabadayi* was there.

The status of *kabadayi* was linked more to personal traits than membership of a group or gang. Each was an individual who had independently earned a reputation for fearlessness. To become a true *kabadayi*, a man had to have been known for acts of courage ever since his youth. This did not mean just stabbing someone or always getting into fights. A dauntless reputation involved performing courageous deeds and not pointless violence. A brave man could command respect if he managed to win a fight with a well-known *kabadayi*, but only if it was a totally honest fight in keeping with the code of honour. 'A kabadayi would never shoot someone in the back,' says Hiçyilmaz. And if shooting was not necessary, it would never happen. Knives were – and still are – only used to warn someone, or to cut off a piece of their ear, much as it would be done with a dog, the message clearly being that the victim was as low as a dog.

What was viewed as honest is illustrated in the following story about a big, black *kabadayi* called Reyhan the Arab.*

---

* In the Ottoman tradition, black people were usually erroneously referred to as Arabs.

One day, Reyhan was attacked by five men known to be skilled with their knives. To defend himself, Reyhan grabbed his chair and used it as a weapon and the five men ultimately ran off. But Reyhan had lost face and for two months he could not go to his favourite coffee house. His friends frowned upon him for not defending himself with his bare hands but using a weapon. A knife would not have been considered a weapon, since it was viewed as part of the body. Every good *kabadayi* had a set of special knives he could quickly draw and use with skill. Sometimes they also had pistols, but they served more as accessories. Prisons were their schools and the more experience they gained, the better. In the course of his career, a *kabadayi* would cross paths with the police again and again and usually serve a couple of prison sentences. Although the sentence might have been designed to keep the kabadayi from committing another crime, in fact it educated him in the rules of the underworld and helped him build up a reputation. Once his reputation had been established, the police would also be respectful and, whenever they arrested him, would even forego the usual torture, as they had good reason to fear reprisals. For other *kabadayi*, a reputation was mainly founded on the capacity to settle conflicts among others in a rapid and effective fashion. The same trait has often been described in connection with Sicilian Mafiosi. It is based on the personal authority the Italians call *prepotenza*, which always includes an element of intimidation, a suggestion of the threat of violence. Anyone who was able to settle an argument at the *gazino*, the ubiquitous Turkish music café, with one simple gesture was a real *kabadayi*.

There were *kabadayi* who did not drink alcohol, like Abu the Arab at the beginning of the 20th century, but most of them drank and liked to associate with female entertainers or prostitutes. They were supposed to be able to drink a lot and, at the same time, keep their composure and this was not an easy combination. More than in other urban underworlds, in Turkey the show element seems to be linked to relationships with women. There were women in Turkey's nightlife just as renowned as the most prominent *kabadayi*. For a price the women, who were Muslim and non-Muslim, offered their services to gentlemen. At brothels, the *kabadayi* associated as equals with rich businessmen and pashas. Matild Manukyan of Istanbul, who died in 2001 at the age of eighty-five, continued this tradition as 'queen of the brothels', a businesswoman and benefactor to the city's hospitals and universities. Everyone in Turkey knew her because for years she had been number one on the list of top taxpayers in Istanbul.

In addition to its own slang, the world of the *kabadayi* also had its own clear code of honour. It is this code that stipulated the etiquette of inter-personal relations. The ordinary man in the street came to the *kabadayi* with his problems, but to whom did the racketeer and the illegal problem-solver go if he had a conflict with a colleague or rival? The solution was to consult *kabadayi* who were older and wiser, called the *racon kesmek,* or parley. The members of the *racon* parley were elderly *kabadayi* who were retired but still respected. They could be found at certain coffee houses in Istanbul. The elderly men of honour would listen to both parties and then pass judgment. The judgment only consisted of a well-founded suggestion, since the board of wise men could not exert any sanction or enforce any decision. Usually both parties listened to them, but some-times they ultimately still disagreed with each other. If both parties disagreed with the decision, they could make that known and then all they could resort to was the crude method of settling a dispute, in other words, the fistfight. In the event that one party stated he was willing to accept the judgment and the other one was not, the sanction was that from then on all the other *kabadayi* would avoid any contact with the one who contin-ued to oppose the judgment of the council of elders.

The worst thing that could happen in the life of a *kabadayi* was to become *madra*, which is slang for losing face. Ergun Hiçyilmaz gave an example in an interview with the authors: 'There was also such a thing as a "phoney" *kabadayi*. Someone who pretended to be a *kabadayi*, but when push came to shove, the first punch would have him flat on the ground and he lost face in front of everyone. Then the only thing left for him to do was quickly get out of the neighbourhood.' In a case like this the *kabadayi* has become *madra*. The terms *racon* and *madra* are now part of everyday language in Turkish, just as many slang words have been incorporated into English or French, but their meaning is no longer the same. In the underworld, *racon* means rule or norm. *Madra* has been changed into *madara* and is now used for people who can no longer be taken seriously, people who have made themselves ridiculous.

The *kabadayi* have played the same social role for centuries. In the power vacuum between the administration and neighbourhood residents, they informally fulfilled certain administrative functions, which the local people appreciated because they did it in a more honest way than the authoritarian and repressive formal officials. The police were a state agency that, in principle, did not much more than suppress subversive activities. The police were seen as being 'against' the people and not as a body they could turn to with their problems. The *kabadayi* were the ones who were there to restore justice and settle disputes among neighbours. Willing to show the nice side of the underworld, Hiçyilmaz mainly views the *kabadayi* as problem-solvers: the referees of the street. 'If there was some kind of argument on one of the streets, the *kabadayi* would come and pass judgment. He would say, "You are wrong and you have to apologise." People would listen to him. So that was the good kabadayi.'

What we view as extortion can also be seen as a form of 'market regulation'. After all, businesses can only flourish under conditions of market predictability. If official bodies are unable to provide these conditions, it is only understandable that businesses should seek the protection of a patron. This is why kinder authors might think of the *kabadayi* as a kind of urban knight. For centuries there has been a modus vivendi between the *kabadayi* and the police that seems to work to both of their advantages. The *kabadayi* is allowed a certain leeway to 'regulate' matters in the neighbourhood as he sees fit, but in the event of a serious problem or a real threat to the political order he, in turn, is obliged to lend the police a helping hand.

There is no denying that, in the underworld, a great deal has changed as a result of the introduction of firearms. The unscrupulousness associated with international drug smuggling has also tarnished the heroic image of the old style underworld. But something of the code of honour has been preserved and the *babas* still like to rise up against injustice and help the poor by acting as the patrons of their less well-to-do clients. The most negative aspects of their own criminal activities are linked to this as well, since they are, in effect, providing protection against a threat they have caused in the first place. This is the classic protection racket. It definitely was not always the case that the victims were the rich who were being robbed to benefit the poor and that is still so today. Instead, the victims were likely to be the owners of coffee houses, brothels and restaurants, places where there was ample cash and where the owners were in a vulnerable position as far as their reputation was concerned. The *kabadayi* had his own men working for him, who would pick up a fixed amount on his behalf and, if the owners of the business failed to pay up on time, they could expect to be 'taught a lesson'.

In a political sense, too, the role of some *kabadayi* has been far from progressive. Some of them were unofficially in the employ of certain individuals at the sultan's court, such as pashas or ministers. *Kabadayi* were also used to infiltrate and spy on intellectual movements in the period of Abdulhamit, the last sultan. They were mainly Albanians and Kurds. There is much less information on their activities than on the 'nice' side of the *kabadayi* that has lived on in the popular romantic imagination and that the present-day underworld is so fond of using as a shining example.

All across the globe, the memory of rogues and bandits is kept alive by telling the life stories of individuals. There are innumerable books and films about 19th-century American bandits, such as Jesse James and Butch Cassidy, and their 20th-century counterparts from the urban minorities, such as Al Capone and Arnold Rothstein. Every segment of the Turkish population, particularly in Anatolia, has produced its own social heroes. Chrisantos and Abdullah the Arab both gained fame at the beginning of the 20th century.

Two Portraits: Chrisantos and Abdullah the Arab

Chrisantos was a champion of the Greek minority in Istanbul in the early 20th century but was revered by Turks too. He was a dauntless bandit who always managed to escape the authorities, thanks to a combination of guile, boldness and the unconditional support of the common people. His conduct is symbolic of the latent resistance of the entire populace to authoritarian rule. His nickname was 'Panaiyas', which means 'holy' in Greek and 'God' according to Turkish sources, and it was clear that he was expected to avenge all the injustice done to his minority. He was definitely no favourite of the Turkish authorities and contemporary authors consider him a murderer. Ulunay does not feel any need to include him at all in his acclaimed book on the *kabadayi*. Perhaps this is because Chrisantos deliberately shot and killed a number of Turkish police officers. Nevertheless, his life is extremely well documented, as Teşkilat-i Mahsusa, chief of the Turkish secret service at the time, devoted ample attention to him in his memoirs.

Chrisantos fulfilled all the requirements of a fascinating *kabadayi*, and he was a man who could find hospitality anywhere he wished in Istanbul – all doors were open to him. He was born in 1898 in Istanbul. His father left when he was twelve years old and he grew up with his mother and a brother and sister. His older brother worked as a waiter in a café and undoubtedly introduced him to Istanbul's nightlife. In the neighbourhood where he also worked at a café, Chrisantos launched a new career as an extortionist. He was only sixteen when he committed his first murder, slitting the throat of a shopkeeper who did not want to pay up. Chrisantos was arrested and sentenced to prison, but soon escaped. He then married Marika, who was to be his wife all his life, but his true love was Eftimya. Despite the efforts of other men to win her hand and the opposition of her brother Yani, Eftimya never stopped loving Chrisantos and remained faithful to him.

In one incident, officer Mehmet of the Taksim Square police station was chasing Chrisantos to arrest him for murder when Chrisantos put an abrupt end to the chase by shooting the officer four times. The Ottoman police set out to hunt him down dead or alive. But the police could not get their man and even attempts by the secret service were in vain. His adventures were the talk of the town and the reason why he was so hard to catch was probably because he would spend every night at the home of a different beauty. At any rate, he managed to remain out of sight of the police. A brave police officer by the name of Ismail wanted to personally take on the challenge and used the mafia method for luring his opponent out of hiding. Ismail told everyone around that he was going to find Chrisantos and kill him. When Chrisantos heard this, it made him so angry that he rushed to the police station where Ismail worked. No one could have predicted this bold step and after Chrisantos gave a short speech for whatever police officers happened to be there, he left the police station in style and did as he promised when he said, 'One bullet should be enough of a warning.' The Ottoman police were flabbergasted, the chief of the secret service later recounted.

Chrisantos was by now famous and the hero of the Greeks. Every time he murdered someone, they would shout, 'Fantastic! Bravo! He is knocking off the police.' Chrisantos used a different approach for a police officer by the name of Muharrem. While Muharrem was relaxing at a popular Turkish bath, enjoying a steam, it suddenly dawned on him that Chrisantos was reclining to his right on the warm stones. After a moment of hesitation, the policeman decided to interrupt his pleasure and dash outside. This was not a wise decision. The fact that he was in such a hurry gave him away and Chrisantos immediately reacted by following him. Chrisantos caught up with Muharrem on the street and asked him why he was in such a rush. 'I am not in a hurry at all,' the policeman replied, 'besides which I don't know you.' This was another error on Muharrem's part. He realised it was too late to carry out his original plan to get his fellow police officers to help. He was all alone and drew his pistol. But he was not fast enough to deal with Chrisantos, who first fired a shot in the air to extinguish the nearby light. With his next shot, Chrisantos killed Muharrem, his fourth policeman.

The police were enraged, but they were also powerless. Every time they thought they had Chrisantos, they would lose him again within a matter of seconds. It later turned out that Chrisantos was receiving information from inside the Police Department through his informer, Hulusi. This information was always enough for him to hazard some new operation. One evening he took a couple of friends to the Aynaliçeşme police station. There were six police officers there and a commissioner, who were all disarmed and taken to the detention room. 'The commissioner was the only one who refused to give them his gun. He felt it was too much of a humiliation to endure,' the chief of the secret service at the time recounts in his memoirs. Taking the only course open to him, Chrisantos killed the commissioner, too.

This picaresque story ended with an inevitable shoot-out, but this time our hero was hit. Not that he did not die in style. Chrisantos went to Eftimya, the woman who had been his first and only true love. This was not a smart move and he must have been aware of that. Perhaps he was tired and looking for a place to rest in peace. It was only a matter of a couple of days before he had to go out and look for a doctor, but he was already too far gone. By the time the police found him, he had virtually lost consciousness. The overwhelming turnout at his funeral showed how popular Chrisantos had been. This murderer was honoured as a *kabadayi* by thousands of mourners who followed the coffin, all clad in black mourning attire.

*

The story of Abdullah the Arab illustrates the function of the *racon*, the parley that passes judgment on the grounds of the code of honour. Abdullah did not know exactly what year he was born in, but he did know he was born in Suleymanie, which was part of the Ottoman Empire at the time and is now in the border area with Iraq. Judging from the peers referred to in the accounts of his life, his peak was in the late 19th and early 20th century. As an adolescent, he was sent to Istanbul to complete his education, but studying was not what he wanted to do. Every day, he would be at his regular spot at an Istanbul coffee house. His life was one of fighting by day and then enjoying the company of ladies of the night. It was not long before every other *kabadayi* knew how fast he could draw his knife. He spoke Turkish with a slight accent, which explains his nickname 'the Arab', and his friends called him Abu. Not that he had many friends or protectors, and he engaged in his extortion schemes on his own.

Hayk Anuş was an Armenian woman who worked as a prostitute. Abu had a fling with her, but they did not keep in touch afterwards. She went on to become quite a famous lady, known as Hayganoş, courted by Istanbul's finest gentlemen. This rekindled Abdullah's feelings for her and he proposed picking up again where they had left off. But it was too late, because a man by the name of Necip, who had inherited a fortune, took Hayganoş to his home to 'make her his own'.*

This impossible situation only served to intensify Abu's 'love'. He went to Necip and said, 'This is not the way we do it in the world of the *kabadayi*. You are living with Hayganoş now, but I had a relationship with her before you did and you know the rule. In that case no other *kabadayi* can live with her.' Necip flew into a rage and said, 'I have no idea whether what you are saying is true. But even if it is true it doesn't change anything because I didn't know anything about it!' Abu's 'hands' (his knives) were itching to go and Necip's 'friends' (his pistols) were ready for action. But the two men decided to be sensible and go to the *racon* to let them decide. 'They are going to prove you wrong,' Necip sneered, 'but we will do it anyway.' This was not so much a romantic dispute as a question of honour.

At Poison Ali, a coffee house in the Tophane district, three older *kabadayi* were willing to listen to both sides of the story. 'Necip,' they concluded, 'in principle you have no right to Hayganoş, but first we have to know for sure that Abu really did have a relationship with her before you.' Necip protested that it didn't matter whether there had been a relationship in the past or not, as Hayganoş had been working as a prostitute at the time and could have had a relationship with anyone. The *racon* ruled that neither of the men could associate with Hayganoş unless one of them wanted to demand his right by marrying her. Neither of the men was interested in doing that, nor was either of them interested in obeying the ruling. The men at Zehir Ali managed to keep the two men from attacking each other, but a very tense situation was inevitable. First Abu sent a message to Hayganoş telling her to come and see him, but when she failed to respond he devised a cunning scheme. He had a letter written in Armenian, supposedly from Hayganoş's mother, telling Hayganoş that she had taken ill and her last wish before she died was to see her daughter. Hayganoş burst into tears and there was no way Necip could refuse to let her go and see her 'dying' mother.

---

* Women of this kind are called *kapatma*. Men do not marry them, but neither do they allow them to have relationships with other men.

On the way, it was not hard for Abu to stop her coach, threaten her guard and coachman with a knife and kidnap her. When she had been with Abu for two days, he threw a big party so everyone could see that Necip's great love was with him. Then Abu sent her back to Necip. The history books do not mention how Hayganoş herself felt about being manipulated this way, but it was a slap in the face for Necip. This was the worst imaginable insult to his honour. Necip nonetheless took Hayganoş back into his home, as he was really in love with her and, if she stayed with him, then in a way he would also have won to some degree. But even if he had wanted to forget what had happened, he did not get a chance to. Abdullah kept telling everyone what had happened and he even devised an unacceptable visiting arrangement whereby Hayganoş would come to see him once a week. Necip sought revenge and a chance to shut Abu's big mouth once and for all. Until that was done, he could not show his face. One day Necip and three of his friends ambushed Abu, but they lost the fight and one of his friends was killed. This turned it into a matter for the law and Abu had to appear before the judge and account for his action. He was counselled by an Armenian lawyer, who argued that it was self-defence. Abu was acquitted, but from then on, Hayganoş stayed with Necip.

The course of Abdullah the Arab's life is interesting for another reason. He started as the 'protector' of his neighbourhood but, after he was acquitted, this bold man who knew no fear was appointed by the Ministry of Home Affairs to head the Kawas (honorary guard), following which he rose to the position of pasha, the highest rank in Ottoman bureaucracy.

The *Efe* in the Mountains

For centuries there has been an Anatolian tradition of people wronged in some way taking up arms and heading to the mountains. There they organise a gang to combat social injustice. In literature and folklore there are always the same reasons for this retreat to the hills: an unfair decision on the part of some judge or other authority, or the intolerable exploitation of a labourer or tenant farmer by a landowner. There are many such stories. Often the person fleeing has committed a punishable offence, but always for a very respectable reason, for example to avenge the family honour. This is not the kind of thing the perpetrator is willing to go to prison for, especially as he was only doing his duty, so his only choice is to take to the mountains. Once there, fugitives have to fight off the government troops that come looking for them and they support themselves by extorting money from rich people or kidnapping them for ransom. These acts earn them a reputation in the vicinity and some even gain national fame. The local population are sympathetic towards them, due to the reason for their flight and because they leave the people in peace. The people feed the bandits and tell them about the area and the movements of the police.

These desperados were also considered folk heroes. They were particularly active in the border regions of the Ottoman Empire, where the power of the state was at its weakest. These are the predecessors of today's smugglers. Several of the *babas* now operating in Europe are from the border regions where these fugitives were most prevalent and, in fact, their own personal histories often include an episode as a member of one of these gangs.

In the western part of Turkey, especially in the region around the Aegean Sea, these men are called *efe*. The term is also used as a generic name for young men who are honest and brave. There is also some regional use of the term *dağlilar*, which means mountain people. Sometimes the authorities grant a general amnesty or allow certain *efe* to return to society. They surrender to the authorities and become *düze indi*, 'those returning to the plain', and are then recruited to preserve law and order. Hiçyilmaz refers to Çakircali Mehmet Efe as 'the most important and greatest' of these *efe* and Murad Sertoğlu has written two books about his life. It is clear from the foreword in one of them how difficult it is for the author to distinguish between the facts of Çakircali's life and stories traditionally told by the people. The author has spoken to numerous people and the soldiers who hunted him. He concludes that the existence of *efe* of this kind is the result of a centuries-old Ottoman policy that went against the interests of the peasants. 'Of course the villagers felt hatred and a desire for revenge against the [Ottoman] authorities, as all they did was levy taxes and plunder the people. This is precisely why the peasants were supporting a man like Çakircali who dared to stand up against the Ottomans.'

Çakircali Mehmet's career as a bandit in Anatolia peaked around the turn of the 20th century. His father was also an *efe* and when he surrendered via the usual amnesty procedure, it turned out the authorities had tricked him. The governor of Izmir had lured him to the plain only to have him shot. Mehmet was brought up by his mother, assisted by other family members, to someday do his duty and avenge the murder of his father. After serving a prison sentence, he decided to head for the mountains, where he soon gained fame. His first important act of revenge was to kill the Ottoman officer who had murdered his father.

Although he did not deviate from the tradition of stealing from the rich and helping the poor, the very sight of Mehmet struck fear in the hearts of one and all. There are thousands of stories about him, his biographer writes, and they recall far too many acts to have ever been committed in one lifetime, so no one any longer knows what is true and what is not. He would pop up all over the place, but still seen by no one. Not only the local authorities, but also the government in Istanbul became worried about Mehmet. After having chased him in vain for years on end, the government drew up an amnesty measure especially for him, including all kinds of guarantees. He accepted the terms and, as was the case with Abu, the urban knight, he was incorporated into the system. Çakircali Mehmet was given five gold coins a month and granted the title of *serdar*, or commander, in charge of a special corps formed to go to the mountains to track down the *efe*. Set a thief to catch a thief, the authorities thought. His departure for the plain now left room for the rise of new *efe*.

Çakircali Mehmet met his end quite predictably in what looked like the result of a vendetta. An act of revenge by the brother of an Ottoman officer whom Mehmet had killed made him leave for the mountains one last time. It was one of his own men who shot and killed him 'by accident'. The last command he gave from his deathbed was interesting. 'After I die, cut off my head and hands and bury them somewhere so the Ottomans won't recognise me and they won't be able to say they killed Çakircali.' But this was to no avail. The Ottomans identified him anyway after one of his wives identified him from a birthmark. His body was hung from the front of the local government building to serve as a deterrent to others. 'Çakircali's fifteen years in the mountains ultimately cost more than a thousand people their lives', was Sertoğlu's final conclusion.

In the region around the Black Sea, everyone is addressed by a nickname. As so many of the people of this coastal area work at sea, the nicknames are almost always related to some maritime function. *Kaptan* (captain) and the old word *reis* (captain or chief) are the most common nicknames. Topal Osman was the most famous robber and rebel of the region and his nickname was *ağa*. History also repeated itself in his case. Once a fearsome warrior and leader of a gang, he was appointed by Mustafa Kemal, Turkey's first president, to head the guards at his palace. *Ağa*, too, was to meet a sad end, through Mustafa Kemal's doing.

In eastern and southeast Turkey, regions mainly populated by Kurds, taking to the mountain was more of a tradition than anywhere else. *Eşkiya*, *asi* and *şaki* were only a few of the numerous terms used by local people and the authorities alike to refer to fugitives. The government saw them as a threat to law and order, but the locals looked up to and sometimes venerated them. Their story is very similar to the one of the *efe*. One of the leading Turkish encyclopaedias gives the following reasons for their leaving for the mountains: Kurdish farmers constituted an obstacle to the implementation of the [Turkish] administration's rules. In the exclusive tribal lifestyle of these farmers, they wanted to preserve their own standards and values. In addition to their tradition of smuggling, they wanted to go on breeding cattle and farming. The differences between the wishes of the Kurds and the rules stipulated by the authorities are what produced 'social rebels'. According to this encyclopaedia, thousands of people left for the mountains as recently as the 1960s to form gangs there. *Yön*, the popular opposition paper of the 1960s, once joked that, according to the gendarmerie's registration figures, there are 180 *eşkiya* even in a tiny town like Siirt. 'If every eşkiya has around five followers, then we are dealing with a whole town of nine hundred eşkiya.'

The most famous modern-day *eşkiya* was Koçero, who was shot and killed in 1964. Davudo and Kotto were similarly important. There were heated debates at the time about the positive and negative approach to the *eşkiya*. The authorities always viewed them as gangs, bandits and robbers, but there were also political 'obstructionists' and romantic souls who projected their wishes on to *kabadayi* and *eşkiya*. They have been the subject of many films, novels and short stories. The internationally renowned novelist Yaşar Kemal took sides with the *eşkiya* and his masterpiece *Ince Memed*, which translates as *Memed My Hawk*, is about one of them.

The three traditions of political and religious rebels, urban knights and the Robin Hood-type *efe* now survive mainly in folklore, ballads and stories, but many cultural features are still present in modern mafia families. Smugglers of drugs, especially heroin, traffickers of illegal migrants and various types of extortionist try to convey the ethos of the traditional *kabadayi*. They now fight with guns instead of fists and their business ventures take them all over the globe, but the old spirit is still treasured. However, the panorama of the Turkish underworld changed dramatically from the moment the news came out that organised crime groups have been drawn into the secret war of the state, with the help of the ultra-nationalist forces within the government, against first Armenian nationalists in the 1980s and then especially the Kurdish movement for self-government in the 1990s. The days of independent criminal mafia organisations are over.

3

Modern *Babas* and their Organisations

'The system is a whore. We are the benefactors'

Dündar Kiliç

The Resurrection of the *Kabadayi*

In 1968, hundreds of people congregated in Istanbul to pay their last respects to Oflu Hasan.* A heart attack had brought to an end the life and career of the man known as the mightiest *kabadayi* in Istanbul in the 1950s. According to the man we can now safely refer to as the 'president' of the current Istanbul underworld, Dündar Kiliç, Oflu Hasan was his *abi*, or 'big brother'. The Turkish press gave the funeral blanket coverage. While some mourners were deep in prayer in the garden within the walls of the mosque, others expressed their feelings by praising the deeds of the *ağa* and commemorating his honesty. 'It was in the 1950s that a disorderly band of Arabs in the Tophane district were fighting out a conflict with the equally rough Laz (an ethnic group from the Black Sea area) from the district of Galata. Goodness knows how many dead and wounded that conflict had already cost at the time. As Hasan ağa could stand it no longer, he invited both parties to resolve the situation via a *racon*. And successfully so.' According to the journalist Engin Bilginer, at that time he was what the Sicilians call the *capo di tutti i capi* in Istanbul, the chief of chiefs.

Newspapers reported on the funeral with bold front-page headlines. They gave plenty of attention to the unexpected composition of the mourners and to the visible fact that it was underworld figures who decided, according to protocol, who should be in which row. At the front were only men of honour, with their bodyguards. Behind them, twenty police chiefs were to be seen and then another fifty senior officers of lower ranks. It was less easy to decide the place for the Minister of Employment, but he ended up in the foremost row where he prayed, between members of the underworld, for the salvation of the departed's soul. What struck the media was one wreath amongst the many hundreds,

---

* His surname was Cevahir, not to be confused with Oflu Ismail; as far as we know, they are not related, but both originally came from Of, the little town on the Black Sea.

which had been sent by the son of President Cevdet Sunay. It was clear that the Istanbul underworld had entered a new era: the autonomous urban knight of half a century before had made way for the 'father' of an organisation that seemed to be connected with the most prominent authorities in the city and the country.

Abdullah the Arab and Chrisantos experienced their heyday as *kabadayis* around the turn of the century; Hasan ağa operated in the 1950s. In the intervening half-century, the urban knights appear to have disappeared from the scene – or at least historians devote little attention to them. In view of Turkey's highly eventful history from 1908 – the year in which the Young Turks initiated their constitutional revolution – up to and including World War II, the political conditions were not favourable for *kabadayis* to operate in. The effects of the Balkan war in 1912 and 1913, during which the European states drastically reduced the territory of the Ottoman Empire, those of the First World War, during which the country fought unprepared on the side of the Germans, and those of the war of independence against Greece, France and England in 1921 and 1922, had all been disastrous and led to depopulation – of more than twenty per cent in Anatolia alone – due to war deaths, ethnic deportations and emigration. The founding of the Republic in 1923, intended as an ambitious attempt to modernise the country in one fell swoop, was accompanied by the installation of the Kemalist one-party state or, to put it simply, dictatorship.

Dictators are rarely favourable to freebooters and rebels. Historians will immediately draw a parallel here with fascism in Italy under Mussolini, whose regime and social control had, after all, served as an example for the Turkish reformer Mustafa Kemal. Mussolini had seen it as his task to establish a state monopoly on violence throughout the whole of Italy and had personally travelled to Sicily to announce that the mafia would be eradicated, root and branch. He also sent 'iron prefect' Cesare Mori to Sicily with extensive penal authority, and his actions achieved great results. It is difficult to tell whether Turkey's totalitarian political system was really able to exercise its influence in every district and street of the cities. The comparison with the mafia doesn't hold water, in any event, where any targeted police action is concerned; they could count on far less resistance in Turkey, as these were primarily rebels operating individually, rather than close-knit organisations.

The fact that numerous other uprisings throughout the country were recorded argues against the assumption that such an episode in banditism during the period of the one-party state was simply not documented. Up until the mid-1950s, both the Kurds and the Sunnitic and Alevitic movements within Islam resisted the government in Ankara. In 1921 there was a Kurdish-Alevitic uprising in Koçgiri in the region of Sivas in Central Anatolia; in 1925 it was a Kurdish-Sunnitic uprising led by Sheikh Sait, in the area of Bingöl and Elaziz; in 1931 the Kurdish Ararat or Agri uprising took place and in 1937-1938 the Kurdish-Alevitic Dersim uprising, both in the east of Turkey. The Kemalist regime put down all of them with much bloodshed.

The heavy period of wars and, afterwards, the one-party state between the revolutions of 1923 and 1950 generated many rebels, who took to the hills. Unlike other farming societies that experienced a revolution, such as Mexico, Russia, India and China, Mustafa Kemal did not appeal to the masses for support. On the contrary, the farmers saw the nationalists not as a counterbalance to local rulers, but as representatives of the state, with whose support exploitation and arbitrary government were exercised. In World War I, and later in the fight against the Greeks, soldiers were recruited from among the people to fight on distant fronts in Eastern Anatolia, Gallipoli, Palestine and Mesopotamia. Banditism and desertion from the army were their way of protesting.

Things did not go well for many gangs, but in the period of the fight for independence, some rebels chose the side of the nationalists and, in the period of the one-party state, some cooperated with the government in Ankara. The best-known of the latter was Topal Ottoman, a Laz from the Black Sea region, who, with his gang, worked with Mustafa Kemal and was later appointed as chief of presidential security.

It is odd that after 1950 – the year in which a certain degree of liberalisation was introduced – the *kabadayi*, the *eşkiya* and then the *baba* suddenly reappeared in the Turkish press and in documentation. In the 1950 elections, the slogan of the Democratic Party was '*Yeter! Söz milletindir*', or, 'Enough! It is time for the people's voice.' This was accompanied by a more reserved attitude on the part of the national police towards the rural population and a reduction in the urban police force. The Democratic Party emerged as the clear victor of the 1950 elections. The emergence of modern organised crime, following in the traditions of urban knights and rural rebels, appeared to be the price Turkish society had to pay for more democracy and openness.

The face of organised crime today is, however, different from that of a century ago, which is one of the reasons why the concept can never be defined once and for all. In Turkey, in any event, the element and threat of violence is a constant. Bravery and a quick gun are still absolute conditions for being taken seriously.

*

The great Turkish-Kurdish drug trafficker Hüseyin Baybaşin took us through the history of the Turkish underworld during a series of interviews in 1996.

'Kabadayi?' we asked.

'Ah, my dear scholars,' replied Baybaşin, 'that is really something from the past. The only one of that type still left alive now is Hasan Heybetli. He is, indeed, a kabadayi, a real criminal. The police have put pressure on him to work for them, but he has always refused to do so. Hasan is a little older than me. He deliberately shot Yahya Demirel [a nephew of the president who was involved in underworld business] in the head in the Mahsun *gazino*. But they couldn't touch him. He got a really short sentence.'

Heybetli is the son of Hüseyin Heybetli, an underworld boss from the 1950s, and his lifestyle is a solitary remnant of the tradition of urban knights in our time. Hasan is said to have built his reputation with his own fists, but it is also said that he continues his father's tradition. Everything appears to revolve around honour and his violence rarely seems instrumental.* He gained national recognition through his love for a famous Turkish singer, Muazzez Abaci. She sang classical Turkish music of the type that once would have been heard in the Ottoman palace. Early one morning, Abaci saw that the road where she lived was filled with roses. The gift was from none other than Heybetli. Their romance turned into a serious affair, far from the brief, non-committal flings such as men in the underworld have with film stars, fashion queens and models. As soon as it became known that Hasan Heybetli had fallen in love with Muazzez, all the other men became terribly aware that they had better not stand too close to the stage, nor listen too enthusiastically, nor applaud her too

---

* Criminologists differentiate instrumental and expressive violence: gangland killing over turf is instrumental, honour killings are expressive.

loudly. Anyone unaware of Hasan's tacit ban ran the risk of a bullet in the leg. In 1978, Hasan had a disagreement with the owner of a tourist complex in Sarikamiş, in the east of Turkey. His salvos subsequently cost two people's lives. He shot at a truck because the driver did not recognise him and had not moved aside. The *kabadayi* from the Beyoğlu district had not shown him sufficient respect, which earned him a bullet in the foot. In both cases, the victim didn't even know the culprit. Even in his later convictions, Hasan followed his father's example; one of his men served the prison sentence.

After that, he moved abroad with Muazzez, now his fiancée. The couple were picked up in Amsterdam, together with another figure from the Turkish underworld. According to Engin Bilginer, they had no fewer than thirteen guns on them. 'Thirteen guns! It looked as if they had declared war on the Netherlands.' The Dutch authorities extradited Heybetli to Turkey. For several days, the wedding of the famous *kabadayi* and the famous singer, which was conducted in prison, attracted the attention of the gossip press. The fact that the marriage then failed to last long appears to have had less to do with a lack of affection than with Abaci's inability to keep up with her spouse's punishing pace of life. Later, after they'd split up, Abaci was taken into hospital. Despite the fact that Heybetli was wanted by the police, he still turned up in broad daylight to visit her there and was arrested on the spot, for the umpteenth time.

Hasan Heybetli built up a thick file with the Turkish police. It includes extortion, assault and battery, murder and, naturally, escaping from prison. He disappeared from the prison in Tekirdağ by walking out of the prison hospital with a bribed guard. In March 1995, Heybetli again made the national press. He was in Edirne on the border with Bulgaria, where he was 'negotiating' the take-over price with the owner of a restaurant. When things didn't go as quickly as he would have liked, Heybetli grabbed his gun and shot a member of staff. Police arrived immediately and ordered him and his men to lie on their stomachs so they could search them. 'Just like in American films,' reported one newspaper. 'This is the way they arrested Kabadayi Heybetli.' Heybetli objected strongly to the method of arrest and to the media coverage: that was no way to treat a *kabadayi*. He wanted to put two things right with journalists. First of all, he complained, 'We aren't PKK people, so they shouldn't make us lie on the ground.' Secondly, for the record, 'The police did not catch us; we gave ourselves up.'

Modern *baba* Huseyin Baybaşin summed up the life of the last real *kabadayi*. 'Hasan has been very lucky not to have been murdered so far. Really. He never makes any secret of where he is and he always wears his firearm more or less openly. He is a courageous young man and can shoot extremely well. It's a shame he wasn't able to get a good education. Then he might have ended up in an environment where he could have helped people. He takes far too may risks, but he can defend himself well and he is a real kabadayi.'

*

The old underworld of the Ottoman period was largely engaged in extortion, and from 1950 onwards, extortion again played a major role, at least initially. The career of Hüseyin Heybetli, Hasan's father, who was primarily active in the 1960s, started with extortion and protecting people or companies against other extortionists. Heybetli senior, who came from the town of Siirt in the extreme east of Turkey, found work as a porter at the Eminönü market in Istanbul.* He didn't take long to make his name as a bruiser and inspired such awe that he succeeded in controlling first the markets and then other sectors of the economy in Istanbul. He collected a number of henchmen around him for that purpose. Naturally, this brought him into conflict with the other *kabadayi* and their men, and a war quickly broke out with another feared boss, Çilli 'Freckles' Burhan. It cost Burhan his life and Heybetli was arrested for murder. He was quickly released, however, as it seemed more prudent to the police to arrest one of Heybetli's men than him. The sum of 120,000 Turkish lira laid out as a bribe is now worth roughly forty pence, but in 1972 it was still a lot of money.

After 1950, trading in illegal goods and services became far more important. The first illegal service was the operation of gambling joints. Gambling was officially banned in Turkey, except in a few special places such as international hotels, but in practice it went on in every coffee house. From 1950 onwards, more luxurious establishments emerged too, purely for the commercial exploitation of gambling. For Dündar Kiliç, illegal gambling joints were a major source of income.

---

* Kurds often use an abridged version of Turkish/Arabic names. Mehmet become Memo, Hüseyin become Huso and so forth. Heybetli became known as Kürt Huso, 'Kurdish Hüseyin'.

Smuggling also became important to the underworld. This fitted in perfectly with old traditions of trading in border areas, where trade was regularly conducted with Beirut, Damascus, Aleppo and Baghdad. Up to the start of the 20th century, the Ottoman Empire was so great that no borders had to be crossed for trade. Smuggling in its current form only emerged when borders were drawn between the modern nation states. The borders of the new Turkey often cut right through areas where certain peoples, tribes or ethnic groups lived. The levy of customs provided the local population with unexpectedly appealing opportunities for profit when they continued to trade within the seclusion of family circles or neighbours. There were clearly three regions in Turkey where those new national borders led to such smuggling: the border with Europe in the area of Istanbul, the southeast border with Syria, Iraq and Iran, where Kurds lived on both sides of the borders, and the northeast area by the Black Sea, which bordered with the former Soviet Union and where there were a lot of shipping connections.

Every country has villages and towns famous for smuggling. In the southeast of Turkey those were Gaziantep, Hakkari, Van and Agri. In the northeast, on the Black Sea, there were also Gümüşhane, Artvin, Trabzon and Rize. It began with tobacco and spirits. Rural peasants exploited the introduction of a government monopoly on tobacco. The quality of the tobacco the farmers sold the government was poor and cigarettes were expensive. Many tobacco farmers secretly retained the best part of their harvest, which they could then sell at higher prices. That good quality, illegal tobacco was not only smuggled abroad, but also sold in Turkey itself. At night, groups of smugglers transported the tobacco from village to village on the back of mules. Smuggling was part of everyday life in the southeast. Entire villages knew when they would be arriving and by which road. This illegal trading even became romanticised in literature.

Up until World War II, smuggling was not actually treated as criminal. From the end of the war, however, Turkish governments started applying a strict regime in the border areas. This was partly for the political purpose of keeping out the Kurdish movements from neighbouring countries such as Iran and Iraq, and partly because the government wanted to integrate the trade into the national economy. The population took sheep and other livestock abroad from Turkey and, in turn, carpets, coffee, tea and knives and forks came back. The Kurds initially failed to understand why they now suddenly had to have a passport to visit close family members, but once they got used to the idea, they were unwilling to relinquish smuggling as a source of income, which resulted in a confrontation with the authorities. The major clash took place in the summer of 1943, when thirty-three smugglers were arrested in the area of Van and subsequently executed in the middle of the night on the orders of General Muğlah. In response to this event, the Democratic Party included measures in their election manifesto for 1950: General Muğlah would be court-martialled. Under pressure from public opinion, in 1949 the general was indeed tried by the military court and sentenced to twenty years in prison. In 1956 a parliamentary inquiry also investigated the affair. The famous poet Ahmed Arif wrote a poem on this event, entitled *Thirty-three Bullets*, which was reprinted fifty times. In 1975, something similar took place when, according to rumours, nine smugglers were shot dead after being arrested. This time it led to little more than a student demonstration in protest.*

The area by the Black Sea is where the Laz originate. They lived on the fertile slopes between Sinop and the border with the Caucasus Mountains and spoke a Southern Caucasian language. The national stereotype of them says they were funny because of their clumsiness. They had a reputation for being fearless, which meant arguing was better avoided, and they were known for manufacturing arms. Guns were transported in and out of the area and tea was smuggled.

From the 1950s onwards, there was a lively smuggling trade in western goods in the city of Istanbul: foreign alcoholic drinks, American cigarettes, gold and many other goods. The ağa of the underworld formed groups and approached the illegal import systematically. Up until the late 1980s, when Premier Özal's government introduced a free trade policy, the import of foreign alcohol and cigarettes was forbidden. That there must have been a tremendous amount of smuggling can be seen from the fact that anyone looking Western was offered Lucky Strike, Kent and Marlboro brand cigarettes on the corner of the street, even by children. Arms smuggling was also lucrative. Uğur Mumcu claimed that hundreds of thousands of weapons and millions of bullets were brought into Turkey in the 1960s and 1970s.

---

* The co-author of this book and human rights activist, Yücel Yesilgöz, was one of the main speakers at the protest meeting, in Silvan in southeast Turkey.

The increasingly busy market demanded organisation. In disputes between smugglers, a third mafia boss with a respectable reputation would be asked to mediate, or it would be submitted to a council of wise men who would decide a *racon*. The solution often entailed a 'nephew' from one organisation going to work for the other, creating peace due to conflicting loyalties. Anyone harming the interests of the other party was now also harming his own man. Conflicts invariably concerned unpaid debts, and a double-edged settlement of the dispute entailed hitting the debtor so mercilessly hard that no-one else would dream of not paying their debt. If a mafia boss proved incapable of collecting his outstanding claims, this was seen as a sign of losing power and incompetence at keeping opponents in check. The same primitive law rules organised crime today. A higher level is attained when territorial agreements are made between the leaders and when the bosses appoint a council to which conflicts can be submitted. This situation has been reached at a regional, if not national, level in our time. Parts of cities are also controlled by the local mafia. Ankara, Istanbul and other cities have increased in size by fourteen times in the space of twenty or thirty years, which itself has generated governing problems. The residential areas of Akasary, Laleli and Beyazit in Istanbul are now, for example, controlled by several different mafia bosses.

*

Another type of boss emerged in the 1960s. More clearly than before, the modern bosses of the underworld were seeking social esteem. They strove to become part of the elite. These bosses are referred to as *baba*, a title derived, as mentioned earlier, from Mario Puzo's book and, in particular, from the subsequent film *The Godfather*. Just as in that film, the new guard is doing its best to build up and retain an image of respect. Gossip magazines, but also the more serious media, provide the *babas* with the opportunity to establish their names. Here 'the role of the media should not be underestimated: they present the mafia bosses as heroes'.

In the transition period of the 1970s some *babas* publicly declared that they had never been guilty of smuggling drugs. Hüseyin Uğurlu, another Kurdish agent who had worked his way up, declared in an interview with an investigative reporter, 'Certainly I smuggled whisky and cigarettes in the past. Young people wanted those types of goods, our country needed

THE RESURRECTION OF THE *KABADAYI*

those things. But there are two things I have never done. One is dealing in heroin and the other is arms dealing.' They are also keen to adopt the role of benefactor. The same Uğurlu stated through his lawyer that he wanted to change his title. The lawyer declared, 'He is not a baba, but an ağa. If we still call him baba, in other words father, then he is rather the father of the poor. He helps people who are starving and he is having a mosque built in Pötürge.' (Pötürge was – typically enough – the little town in the province of Malatya where Uğurlu was born.) Uğurlu was, incidentally, later accused of smuggling arms and drugs, but was eventually acquitted and, once back in society, continued his struggle for respectability. He bought a school where lessons were given in English, French and German and appointed the senior guard of the prison where he had served his sentence as director of his school.

These days, successful underworld bosses such as Uğurlu venture into philanthropy. Sponsoring football clubs, in particular, is popular. The drug trafficker Halil Havar, who was arrested in the Netherlands but managed to escape from the Marwei prison in Leeuwarden by helicopter on 18 February 1991, used to be the chairman of the Gaziantepspor football club. Nurettin Güven, who was wanted by the Turkish and French authorities for drug trafficking while living in an affluent area of London, used to be chairman of Gaziantepspor. Turan Çevik, the chairman of the Malatyaspor football club, is hailed in the Turkish press as the king of the fake export companies described in Chapter 1. Hasbi Menteşoğlu, chairman of Samsunspor, is similarly known. According to at least one journalist, the Turkish press has repeatedly written about the mafia relations of M. Ali Yilmaz, who was chairman of Trabzonspor and later even rose to become Minister of Sporting Affairs. In a photograph in *Hürriyet* on 22 June 1994, the minister was shown firing a gun in the air in Istanbul's Çirağan palace during the circumcision celebrations for the son of the known mafia boss Nihat Akgün.

Another chairman was discredited following the Susurluk incident in November 1996. Apart from the car that crashed and a car full of bodyguards following it, apparently there was another car, loaded with heroin destined for a board member of Türkiyemspor Berlin, a German amateur football club drawn from the Turkish immigrant community. Initially, the chairman of the club admitted that he knew of that connection, but later he denied all involvement. 'We are the number one football club creating publicity for Turkey,' he said. 'It is unseemly to express this kind of accusation and it plays into the hands of the separatists.' In March 2007, Nedim Imaç, founder and ex-chairman of the similarly named Dutch club FC Türkiyemspor, was shot dead in an Amsterdam restaurant from a passing minivan.

Only at the funerals of underworld bosses does the philanthropic network of the deceased become really apparent. On 7 December 1993, Mehmet Nabi, nicknamed Inci Baba (Pearl Father), was killed. He had become rich and powerful in the world of building contracting and was the undisputed boss of Ankara. His good deeds were innumerable. His relationship with the film star Filiz Akin, who was later to marry the Turkish ambassador in Paris,* was much talked-of. According to reports in the Turkish newspapers, he was friendly with President Demirel. At his funeral, not only Inci Baba's son and daughter were present, both of whom were studying in the United States, but also all the figureheads from the underworld.

Babas also demonstrate that they continue to adhere to the old code of honour. In principle, women and children are never shot at and guns are left untouched at parties to celebrate weddings or births, as well as funerals.

Striking, too, is the Americanisation of the Turkish underworld from the 1970s onwards. It is as if the *babas* are acting, in any event in their presentation to the outside world, like mafia godfathers or rather like the American actors who play them in films. A mafia boss in Istanbul, Nihat Akgün, is nicknamed 'Al Pacino'. A famed public prosecutor, who incidentally turned out to have mafia connections himself and has in the meantime been murdered, called himself 'Marlon' Cemal, after Marlon Brando.

---

* The ambassador later became head of the secret service.

Dündar Kiliç

The definitive anecdote about the top *baba* of the 1970s takes place some-time early one morning in the lobby of the prestigious Hilton Hotel, on a hill in the northern part of Istanbul. Dündar Kiliç was at the zenith of his power and mixed easily in elite circles in the city. That morning he was accompanied by a lady. 'After you,' he had said to her as they walked to the reception desk.

He recalled, 'I was impeccably dressed, by the way; I even had a tie on. We had to wait a long time at the desk; you can take it from me that it took at least a quarter of an hour. Then a member of staff came up to us and said, "It's no use waiting, brother, this is a hotel for Americans."' Evidently, Dündar had not been recognised, even though he continually made the front page of the papers at that time.

'What do you mean, for Americans?'

He could, of course, lodge a complaint for discrimination and conduct himself as gentleman, but when the staff member went on to call him 'arrogant and uncivilised', it was just too much for him. He drew his gun, ordered the entire staff of the hotel to assemble and gave them a brief speech. It would be wise, he considered, if the staff realised that they were in Turkey and that they had more reason to be of service to Turks than Americans. After these words, he turned courteously to his lady compan-ion with the words, 'After you,' and hailed a taxi. That afternoon, Dündar Kiliç reported to the police to explain his actions.

Kiliç enjoyed the reputation of being a gentleman, as well as 'the godfather of godfathers'. He always attracted media attention and famous television presenters waited from dawn to dusk to arrange an interview with him. His office was full of ordinary, common people coming to seek his help. He made a calm, unpretentious impression on the media, except that he had a tendency to fix his eyes on one spot, which helped him to concentrate. The things Kiliç got up to were suffi-cient to send him to prison thirty-eight times, not counting brief arrests.

Several times he was accused of offences for which he was shortly after-wards acquitted. One minute he was being arrested by generals, the next he was being accused of conducting illegal business with those same generals. One minute he was being tortured day and night – at least according to his account – and the next ex-president Özal's wife and children were turning to him for help.

In 1940, when Dündar was five years old, his family decided to move from Sürmene, a small town in the province of Trabzon, to Ankara, in the fallout from a vendetta, still common in the area by the Black Sea. His father, Ishak, was a baker in Sürmene and he continued his profession in Ankara. Dündar first fell foul of the police when he was fourteen, for possessing a knife he carried according to the tradition in the Black Sea region. 'The knives in Sürmene are good. But the government was of the opinion that I should not carry such a big knife. Luckily, it wasn't long before I was released again. But my parents thought it was awful. I got used to it later on and I always carry this knife.'

His second brush with the police was less innocent. 'Some children were playing football. This Erci, who was a boxer, was bothering the children and took the ball off them. He smacked a kid who asked for the ball back. That man was twice my size and height and I was really scared of him. But I had to stand up against such injustice.' Sixteen-year-old Dündar Kiliç, who had witnessed all this from his chair in front of a coffee house, grabbed the knife lying next to him and stabbed the boxer until he looked like 'an Emmental' cheese. Erci was taken to the hospital and Dündar to jail. He was sentenced to six months and twenty days in prison.

After he had served his sentence, Dündar opened his own so-called coffee house, where the main activity was gambling. By that time he had got in with extortionists and *kabadayi*. Dündar saw himself as a *kabadayi* too, and had no intention of paying a cent to his 'protectors'. Together with his men and a famed *kabadayi* called Kemal from Diyarbakir, the extortionist Çavdaroğlu went to Dündar's coffee house to hold it up. They had a rude awakening; Dündar put up such formidable resistance that he seriously hurt his attackers while escaping without a scratch himself. It was only then that Dündar started to make a name for himself, both with the police and in the world of the *kabadayi*.

That fame brought problems with it. At the time, Kurd Cemali was the king of the Ankara underworld and he didn't feel like sharing his gambling revenue in the city with Dündar. One of the two had to go, because *bir çöplükte iki horoz ötmez*: 'two cocks can't crow on the same dung heap'. A fight was unavoidable. There followed a series of clashes, culminating in Cemali's murder.

Dündar Kiliç swore he didn't shoot Cemali dead himself, but he later withdrew that denial in a letter to a military court in Diyarbakir. He was, however, convicted of the murder. Inside prison, he faced the threat of reprisal; Cemali's men paid a prisoner to kill him. Dündar was told in time by the other prisoners. The upshot was knife wounds to the face of the hired killer and another three years added to Dündar's sentence. Overpopulation of the prisons in Turkey was relieved by means of general pardons, and Kiliç was released in 1963. In the meantime, songs were written about the life and murder of Cemali. As Kiliç recounted, 'Everyone who drank raki and listened to those songs grabbed a knife or a gun to knock me off after a couple of glasses.'

Finally, his mother took control. She sold everything she had and the family disappeared to Istanbul. On arrival, Dündar opened another coffee house with the intention of operating it in the same way. But Cemali's men tracked him there and hired killers made a string of attempts on his life. 'You can put up with having enemies – you know the people, you know what they're going to do and how,' said Kiliç. 'But contract killers are the worst. You don't know them, you don't know if they're sitting next to you right now or if they will come from behind. They've negotiated, they've got their money and they suddenly come at an unexpected moment to shoot you, stab you with a knife or something else, you don't know. On top of that, the one who kills me is extra motivated, because he knows my death will make him famous.' He always managed to evade the contract killers, but one time he had a narrow escape. 'A car stopped across the street. While I was watching it, I suddenly felt something burning on my back. I dropped to the ground to draw my weapon from that position. Now they were shooting at me from the car, too. I looked around for the man who had caused me so much pain. I shot once.' With that one shot, Kiliç hit his assailant in the middle of his forehead. Then he aimed at the car, putting those attackers out of action. A judge later acquitted him on the grounds of self-defence.

Dündar quickly became an important man in the Istanbul underworld. He allegedly racked up three murders and at least fifty cases of grievous bodily harm, together resulting in a sixty-year stretch inside, which he again ended prematurely by means of a pardon. He ensured peace and security in the city, particularly in the district of Beyoğlu, the centre of the entertainment world. 'Dündar's men stood at the door of all the entertainment venues and the owners paid readily and without grumbling for what actually meant protection,' reported the newspaper *Hürriyet*. Even though his men were everywhere, it was very important for the underworld boss to demonstrate now and again that he was still a *kabadayi*. So when someone called him and threatened, 'I'm going to have you strung up by your legs. If you're a real man, you'll come personally to my coffee house,' Dündar responded by arriving on the spot in less than ten minutes. It was a coffee house frequented by the police, which was why the owner had felt secure enough to challenge him so boldly. 'I drew my gun and aimed right at the head of the man who had threatened me. Nobody could do anything. With my gun in my hand, I explained everything to those present and then I left the coffee house,' said Dündar later. That afternoon, he reported to the police station to tell them what had happened. 'Well, what else could I do? He said I had to come if I was a man.' The next day, the affair was in the newspapers in all its details.

'I've spent twenty years of my life in prisons,' Kiliç told a journalist from the weekly paper *Nokta*. He evidently belonged to the category of people the police chief in the film *Casablanca* was talking about when he said, 'Round up the usual suspects.' In two of the military coups that marked Turkey's post-war history – on 12 March 1971 and 12 September 1980 – he was arrested along with the other *babas*. It was at that time that he also got to know left-wing intellectuals who had been arrested. He became friendly with the Turkish authors Yaşar Kemal and Sabahattin Eyüboğlu and the film star Yilmaz Güney. 'I learned a lot from them,' he told an interviewer. He also got to know leaders of left-wing organisations, trade union bosses and student leaders, such as Deniz Gezmiş, who was hanged in the early 1970s. From then on he was registered with the secret service as a 'left-wing baba'. He didn't consider that new title acceptable. 'I was in prison with both left-wing and right-wing guys for five years and in all those five years I never took sides. I told them, "You're young people, you can't expect me to protect one side more than the other."' However, Kiliç had earlier supported the ultra-nationalist MHP financially.

More recently, he reflected, 'I've always been true to humanism, the philosophy based on loving thy neighbour.' A striking remark for a man with his criminal record. When he was arrested in the 1980s, he says he was tortured a lot, four seasons long. 'Who does something like that? A beast of prey or a crazy person? They tried out all their torture methods on me.'

The last time Kiliç was arrested by the police was in April 1984. This time he was accused of trafficking in arms and drugs. He denied everything. Nevertheless, the public prosecutor demanded the death sentence. A well-known criminal lawyer, Burhan Apaydin, who acted as lawyer for the former Turkish premier Menderes when he was hanged after the military coup of 1960, took Kiliç's case because, as he said, 'You can see from the file that he has to be innocent.' During the first hearing, the lawyer reminded the court that, according to the basic rules of the secret service, the organisation was not authorised to interrogate people. After a number of hearings, Dündar Kiliç was released and later acquitted. He attributed the arrest to his two enemies: the head of the Turkish police's smuggling department, Atilla Aytek, and the senior secret service officer, Mehmet Eymür. 'Their aim was to eliminate me. That would have been good for their careers and it would have enabled the two of them to take over the Istanbul nightlife themselves. They thought it rained gold in Istanbul and I was standing in the way of their ambition.'

Kiliç was left in peace for some time by both the authorities and the media. He transformed into a businessman – he owns an advertising agency – and philanthropist, righting social wrongs with his donations. He supported diverse people in need: prisoners, people unable to pay their debts (he precedes his gift with an investigation into the accuracy of the story) and the sick. He also devoted a great deal of time to his four children from three marriages. His oldest was his daughter Uğur. She, too, was to gain national celebrity status in the media, not only because she too became an underworld boss, but also due to her marriages. Her last husband was Alaattin Çakici, one of the most notorious underworld figures from the ultra-nationalist *ülkücü*.

After a shootout in Istanbul on 20 September 1994, the names of Dündar Kiliç, his daughter Uğur and son-in-law Alaattin dominated the media again for days. Live discussion programmes were organised in which prominent figures from the underworld, experts, politicians, journalists and – via the telephone – members of the Kiliç family and their son-in-law, who was in hiding, and the right-wing *baba* Çakici exchanged opinions. The Turkish public, no longer surprised at such a sensational turn of events saw all kinds of accusations of mafia connections being levelled at prominent politicians and rich families. This affair ended in the shocking murder of Dündar's daughter Uğur on Çakici's instructions.

'I haven't been reading much the past two years, only forty or fifty pages a day,' Kiliç said in 1988. He told the *Nokta* reporter he had been planning to set up a reading library, in which he wanted to make the book collection he had built up by that time available to the public. His arrest in 1984, however, had prevented him. The surprised reporter noted that his book collection, which contained no fewer than 8,000 volumes, included works not only by famous Turkish writers but also by Steinbeck, Solzhenitsyn and Dostoyevsky. He added, 'I can't speak English, but I've made sure my wife learned. She has been reading and translating all the important articles in *Time* and *Newsweek* for me for years now.'

The *kabadayi* would have liked to become an intellectual, but his style proved not to have changed where his reputation was at stake. When, during a television programme, his daughter's name was mentioned unfavourably, he called the presenter responsible, 'Listen, my lovely. You've got a prominent position there. But I am entitled to protection of my honour. This is not a threat. You shouldn't take it like that. But you people should be defending my honour.'

Kiliç died of a heart attack at the American Hospital in Istanbul on 10 August 1999.

The Conference of the *Babas*

Less than four months after the coup in Turkey on 12 September 1980, a conference was organised in Sofia, the capital of communist Bulgaria, that was to drastically change the nature and organisation of international drug trafficking. The secretive, repressive Bulgarian state was vying for power in the region and, with all the heads of the big heroin smuggling organisations gathered in the Vitoshya Hotel, the reins were given to the Turk Oflu Ismail, the son-in-law of Dündar Kiliç, who came from the coastal area of the Black Sea and who was the up-and-coming man in the international underworld. In his opening speech, Ismail expressed the Bulgarian government's wish that all those present should move to Bulgaria, that they could use Bulgarian banks for their financial transactions and that all activities would be organised in mutual consultation from a central point in Sofia. The country had ambitions to be the logistics centre of smuggling in and out of Europe, in order to restore its depleted national budget, and created appealing opportunities for the long-term accommodation of foreign smugglers and for setting up empty limited companies, fake companies and so forth.

Such top-level conferences constitute historical climaxes in the history of organised crime; other have taken place at the Hotel Palme in Palermo in 1947, at Appalachin in New York state in 1957 and at the Intercontinental Hotel in Cali in 1991. They almost always take place in the pleasant surroundings of a five-star hotel, where discretion is guaranteed. The gentlemen participating tend to have volatile natures which can be neutralised in the dignified atmosphere of the luxury hotel. More important still is that communication can take place through personal contact, instead of by telephone, telex and fax, which can be tapped and, moreover, leave traces. Additionally, the agreements made are easier to enforce, as the 'men of honour' themselves were present to witness the decision-making.

It is safe to assume that not all such summits are known about, but we know of the one in the Vitoshya Hotel from an extensive statement by the major Kurdish drug dealer Cantürk to the Turkish secret service. He was not personally present, but because the decisions in Sofia were significant to all the big dealers, everyone was well informed. During a later meeting in Switzerland, two of the main players at the conference, Doğan Çelik and Fikri Kocakerim, briefed him in detail. We can't be sure how completely and accurately the secret service passed on his statement, as he later withdrew it, saying it had been forced out of him under torture. There were no Kurdish families present. A political reason for excluding them is unlikely, as in 1980 the PKK had not yet embarked on its armed struggle against Turkey. Oflu probably initially invited his own, trusted network. Apart from that, it is striking that the list does not include any political figures. Were they not there, or did the secret service delete their names?

'The majority of those present came from the Black Sea area, from what I heard, and the rest were Turks,' explained Cantürk. 'Aside from these people from Turkey, there were also Syrian, Albanian and Italian smugglers at the meeting and the directors of several Bulgarian companies. The meeting was chaired by Ismail Hacisüleymanoglu, who is called "Oflu". The region his heroin trading covered was the Netherlands. Oflu used to smuggle arms and the last I heard was that he is trading in precious stones.'

Others present included:

- Hasan Conkara, better known as Crippled Hasan, arms smuggler and close colleague of Oflu Ismail.
- Enis Karaduman, who trades in heroin. He works with his cousin.
- Abdullah Cantürk. He is wanted for murder in Turkey.
- Hikmet Uzun, the partner of the big smuggler Ottoman Cevahiroglu, who comes from the Black Sea region.
- Hikmet Sevcan, who deals in arms and heroin and owns the road restaurant on Londra Road in Istanbul.
- Doğan Çelik, also from the area around the Black Sea. Arms smuggler, works with his brother Ismail.
- Fikri Kocakerim, a big man from the Uğurlu family.
- Ahmet Uğurlu, also at the meeting on behalf of the Uğurlu family.
- Ali Açmak, arms dealer. He is responsible for transporting arms in the Black Sea region.

THE CONFERENCE OF THE *BABAS*

- Bekir Çelenk, very prominent smuggler.
- Ilhan Sağlamer, from Samsun (Black Sea) and an arms dealer.
- Şaban Vezir, a really big smuggler from Syria. He lives in Bulgaria.
- Avni Karadurmuş was invited to the meeting, but wasn't present.

Additionally, there were representatives from the Savar and Çil families from Antep.

The meeting lasted two days. The major decisions were: to exercise more caution, as Turkey had a new military regime; to go back to smuggling chemicals for producing drugs; and to open up new markets in Iran, Iraq and other countries in the Middle East. The real aim of the meeting was different, however; the division of the European countries in which drugs would be traded. It was clear that Oflu 'controlled' the Netherlands and, from there, he would play a central role in the division and its enforcement. He portrayed himself as a 'soldier of Bulgaria' and an international smugglers' organisation was to be created under his leadership. But he was not to succeed this time. Those present might have pretended to agree to the plans, but as soon as the meeting was over, everyone returned to his home base, even those who had promised they were interested in staying in Bulgaria. The *babas* met twice more after that, as Oflu was eager to attain his goal. At each meeting there were fewer people, says Cantürk: 'Oflu Ismail (Hacisüleymanoglu), Dündar Kiliç, Hüseyin Gencer from Malatya. Apart from that, Dündar's man Doğan from Trabzon, who lived in Maltepe; he smuggled foreign cigarettes by ship and controlled the market in Istanbul. Oflu Ismail also smuggled cigarettes from Bulgaria, incidentally.'

It is doubtful whether binding territorial agreements were made at this meeting and it is not certain that Cantürk's account is a hundred per cent accurate. Cantürk himself was murdered in 1994. Oflu disappeared from the scene in 1987, when he finally ended up in an Italian prison, but that doesn't mean he was unable to continue his initiatives from there. What it does show is that the Turkish heroin smugglers – smuggling arms became less important – who were already operating internationally continued on a larger scale from the 1980s onwards and that they had the ambition to approach the business more systematically.

*

The 'discovery' of organised crime in America has led to the theory of the alien conspiracy. By organised crime, Americans mean the mafia; they had detected a secret conspiracy emerging from and inspired by the criminal organisation that had already had the island of Sicily in its grip for more than a century – and according to some interpretations even longer than a millennium – despite the fact that various powers had formally succeeded one another as rulers of the island throughout the course of history.

The Italian mafia families remained hermetically sealed as long as all members adhered to the sacred vow of silence, the *omertà*, which was confirmed with a simple but impressive initiation ritual. The idea of the family is a standard element in the American idea of organised crime. The more information the police in the United States obtained on these families, the more impressed they were with the huge power of their organisation and the efficiency of their operations. Over the course of more than eighty years, in various major investigations into the mafia by special commissions set up by local governments, the senate and even the president, the idea emerged that the mafia has developed into a strictly hierarchical organisation, most closely resembling the bureaucracy of the big companies or the military mechanism. It is always depicted as having a monocratic leadership, as delegating organisational tasks to an underboss, as having lieutenants to organise the activities and soldiers to carry out the day-to-day work. To assist the organisation legally in its contacts with the outside world, the boss generally appointed a consultative advisor, who was referred to, as befits the style, as *consigliere*.

This view of affairs doesn't apply solely to America. In other countries with a tradition of secret criminal societies, organised crime is also continually thought of as a strictly run organisation constructed in accordance with the pyramid model. The form and codes of conduct vary greatly: the Chinese triads are different from the Japanese yakuza, the Italian mafia is a family affair compared with the business cartels of Colombia and the Russian mafia has a more gang-like character than the Nigerian criminal networks. What all these societies have in common, however, is that they consist of a permanent collaboration held together by a hierarchical order. The archetype of this model is brought to life in the novel *The Godfather,* and the book and film were partly so successful internationally because people in the various countries recognised something of the national criminal organisations in them. The film also changed the underworld itself; underworld figures with aspirations to become leaders in organised crime apparently use films and books of this genre as a kind of educational and informative tool.

This model has been strongly criticised by other authors, however. Criminologists have continually pointed out that organised crime is of American origin, instead of being controlled from a far-off country like Sicily. Its organisations, whatever their ethnic origin, traditionally cater for purely American requirements, such as alcohol in the 1920s. Moreover, in their view the mafia consists primarily of the second generation of migrants from various countries, who were born on American soil. Adherents of the alien conspiracy theory, on the other hand, add that the American mafia in the 1930s received a powerful boost with the arrival of a generation of new gangsters from Southern Italy fleeing the pressure of Mussolini and argue further that the Italian and American-Italian Cosa Nostra started trans-Atlantic collaboration in drug trafficking in the 1970s and 1980s.

There is similar debate about the second characteristic of organised crime, the family structure. The logistical advantage of the familial organisation for clandestine activities would appear clear: the members are assured of optimal internal communication and great mutual loyalty. Others are of the opinion that the family concept only serves as a metaphor and that these are actually a number of unrelated criminals, bound by blood brotherhood; the actual relationship between the boss and the rest of the members of a 'family' is one of an employer and subordinates rather than that of fathers and sons, nephews and uncles. Yet others feel there is no primordial relationship or family at all, but simply collaborations between criminals who have joined up for purely commercial reasons.

The third characteristic, a hierarchical organisation of functions and people in a pyramidal structure, is also contested. Painstaking historical research by American criminologists showed as far back as the 1970s that the collaborations between the members of the mafia are changeable and flexible and that they also evolve along with the new opportunities within a changing economy and with the penal policy of the police and the legal authorities.

Since the end of the Cold War, there has been room for conducting serious research in Italy and taking legal action against criminal organisations and their entanglement with the political and business worlds. A

discussion similar to that which began in America about the real character and structure of the mafia has started between European social
scientists. Various authors described the mafia in the early 1970s as a
result of the mentality of the population and as a patchwork of patronage
systems. This refuted the predominant idea that had been continually
confirmed by earlier scientists, police reports, the media and films: that it
really was a secret society. In 1983, the most famous Italian mafia expert
at the time, the criminologist and senator Pino Arlacchi, analysed the way
the archaic remnants of the feudal system in the 19th century had transformed after the war – and after 1970 in particular – into a modern,
commercial crime structure. After a number of the mafia figureheads
were arrested as a result of heavy pressure from the police and some of
them proved to be prepared to break their vow of silence (since 1992 Italy
has had a law that enables cooperation between the courts and criminals
and promises the crown witness immunity and a reduced sentence under
certain conditions), Arlacchi held extensive discussions with a number of
repentants. On this basis, he changed his point of view: it really is a secret
society structured like family and run in a highly hierarchical fashion. His
U-turn was criticised by colleagues; one of the arguments was that
Arlacchi had let his opinion be swayed by what he saw in the files on the
repentants that the police had let him examine.

*

The Netherlands has played a major role in the development of the
Turkish mafia. From the moment the Dutch police and judicial authorities
were confronted with modern organised crime, and drug trafficking in
particular, they took the traditional American model of the strictly organised, monocratically run mafia as their point of departure. Typical is the
attempt by detectives from the Dutch National Criminal Intelligence
Services to measure the scope of organised crime by counting the number
of criminal groups that conform to certain characteristics: they have to be
hierarchically organised; the group has to be guilty of several types of
offence; there has to be an internal sanction system to prevent members
snitching; there has to be some incidence of corruption of civil servants
involved in the organisation; and a system for laundering criminally
obtained money has to have been developed. In 1987, a questionnaire
amongst all the police forces in the Netherlands showed that, in the view

of the police, almost two hundred organisations conformed with the police's minimum requirements, even though by far the majority of the groups possessed only one or two, or even none, of the required characteristics. Nevertheless, there were three that were so 'well organised' that they fulfilled all five characteristics, including one Turkish organisation: that of Oflu Ismail.

When operating outside Turkey, can the Turkish mafia be described as an alien conspiracy developed and run from abroad? Of course, such organisations would never be able to flourish if no affluent demand for drugs had arisen in the Netherlands or any other Western European country; as far as that goes, organised crime is a problem generated in the home country itself. At the same time, though, it is clear that markets cannot emerge if there is no supply and part of that supply is provided by criminal organisations. All kinds of traffickers in the Middle East were busy exploring new markets and finding suitable, reliable business partners who controlled the local situation in the destination countries or were at least well informed. The attempt in 1981 in Sofia to divide the market and the meetings of top criminals that followed argue for that theory. The fact that political organisations, prominent politicians and officials from the Turkish police, for example, were involved also supports this interpretation.

The big difference between the former situation in the United States and that now in Western Europe is the pattern of emigration. A century ago, the emigrants who had burned their boats and first and foremost wanted to achieve the American Dream of wealth and personal freedom emigrated to the United States. They used no resources from their country of origin to advance themselves in America and their ambitions were certainly not aimed at finally returning permanently to the country where they were born. The migrant workers who came from Southern Europe, Turkey and North Africa in the 1950s, 1960s and 1970s, on the other hand, came to make up a temporary shortage of labour. There was no immigration policy to begin with, as these were temporary workers and not part of a permanent immigration. The migrants saw their future in their country of origin, where they could build a good life with currency earned elsewhere. That migration movement is still underway. First, there was family reunification, then secondary family reunification – a Turk with a foreign residence permit or foreign nationality marries a partner from Turkey and settles in Western Europe; illegal Turks and Kurds came and still come and, finally, refugees arrived who often came from a far higher social level.

In the Turkish underworld, participation in drug trafficking often already begins with the first generation – and not, as in the US, with the second – and heavy criminals are sent to Europe hidden in the migrant flow, to build a bridgehead for crime organisations. In some cases, it is only the second generation that starts to move in criminal circles and the parents are kept ignorant, but the activity is still focused on Turkey and not only improving their position abroad. The means of existence is the sale of illegal goods imported from Turkey and a lively traffic of people continues to exist between the two countries.

Traditionally, the proceeds of the American mafia are invested in the education of their children; if they have gained a good, legal position in the American economy then, in retrospect, one could say that participation in organised crime was nothing more than a vehicle for social climbing. The majority of the money Turkish drug traffickers earn, on the other hand, is still sent back to Turkey and, for a long time, the Turkish government itself encouraged this. The currency is used for the dealers' personal economic projects and for the political purposes of the politicians and bureaucrats they work with in Turkey. The vast majority of drug traffickers exhibit little ambition to give the next generation a leg up to a higher level in the emigration country through education. True, many drug dealers say they would like to do so and sometimes they are ashamed to let their children know of their activities, but when it comes down to it, these same children are roped into drug trafficking in a subordinate function. All these considerations contribute to the American theory of the alien conspiracy insofar as the influence of foreign crime groups is great. The word 'conspiracy', however, is without doubt too strong, as this is not exactly a conscious attempt to undermine the economy or politics of Western Europe; they are simply taking advantage of the opportunities the market offers.

Is the Turkish mafia organised into a 'family'? The use of the term *ağa* or *baba* implies that people see the leader as a head of the family. Since *The Godfather*, some journalists and writers have had the tendency to use the term 'family' for criminal organisations in Turkey. But in the world of the *baba* himself, as in the rest of Turkish society, people reserve the term solely for relatives by blood or marriage for whom the head of the family is responsible. That responsibility primarily concerns protecting the family honour. Both the family of orientation – that into which you are born – and that of procreation – the one you create – are extremely important for understanding the Turkish mafia, but the term should not be used in the American way.

It is striking how many bosses have experienced a personal vendetta tragedy in their youth before beginning their criminal career. In the smuggling and organised crime nests described in the previous pages (the area by the Black Sea, Southeast Turkey), blood feuds and vendettas are still common; just as that applied to the *efe*, who retreated to the hills, and the *kabadayi* in the towns, most *babas* have such a background, including Dündar Kiliç, the two great bosses Alaattin Çakici and Behçet Cantürk, in fact all modern *babas* to some extent. They fled from the problem by going to the big cities and a number of them saw a chance of finding refuge as migrant workers abroad: the emigration motives of some Turks and Kurds are more complicated than simply seeking well-paid employment in an affluent country.

In 1989, one of the crime bosses in the Netherlands with 'Godfather' airs had a video made of his life, entitled *Proof*. He got professional actors to take the supporting roles, but played the main role himself. The idea was to let viewers see with their own eyes why he had had no choice but to do what he had with his life. The story begins in his childhood, with the cowardly murder of his father. One of his brothers sees the culprit appear in a dream and from that moment of revelation onwards, there is no alternative; they have to kill him. This is what happens, but as the other family is determined to take revenge, all the brothers are forced to seek refuge as migrant workers. One goes to France, four others end up in Amsterdam. A few years later, they get to hear on the grapevine that they have killed the wrong man and the real murderer of their father is still walking around free. They feel ashamed and draw lots amongst themselves to see who will revenge the family honour now. Mr X draws the lot. He returns to the shores of the Black Sea to do what is expected of him. This earns him the status of *kabadayi*, a just, retributive person. Back in Amsterdam we see how Mr X uses his newly acquired status to act as arbiter in disputes in the gambling world. Then he goes into business for himself. The way his sudden prosperity is portrayed in the film is amusing: one day, just as he is getting into his car, a motorbike roars past, pursued by the police. The hard-pressed pillion rider drops a bag containing thousands of guilders. From that moment on they are rich! When he then returns to the village of his birth to buy a house, he is arrested by the police for murder and vendetta, which carries a heavy penalty in Turkey. 'Ah!' cries A., 'How can we Turks be so stupid as to let ourselves be led by such stupid motives as vendettas?'

In actual fact, things finished badly for the family in question. The star of the film is in a Turkish prison, one of his brothers was gunned down in the Berlin underworld and the other is serving a sentence in a Dutch prison. Nothing is known of the fourth brother who went to France. What is striking, however, is that this true story concerns a dispute concerning the honour of a real blood relation and not, as in the vendettas between American 'families', a war between crime organisations.

When describing their leadership capacity or talking to others about it, the Turkish mafia boss's use of language is interesting. For his work, he is in the café with 'his friends', when he pays a visit somewhere it is with 'his men', but in the criminal context, there is no other designation than 'we'. Family life is kept apart from crime. If asked, the boss does not 'run' an organisation, but simply carries a certain responsibility for the people who need him. And there can, naturally, be a moment when he expects that help to be reciprocated. This all clearly indicates patronage, but the word 'family' is not used as a metaphor here. There is therefore little point in asking about the size of a particular *baba*'s family. The great status differences between the various *babas* do indicate a difference in their scope of influence, but not the subordination or superordination of their family members.

There is plenty of cooperation in the underworld. Interestingly enough, the ideological differences of opinion that can exist in the upper world between people with left- and right-wing political affiliations cease. In the event of a dispute, a committee is formed of *babas* of the highest esteem, which is entitled to gather evidence and indicate the guilty party. But this, too, has no similarity with a family tribunal. The *baba* employs people who are professionals in the underworld, but they are neither part of his family nor even of a kind of quasi-family. If anyone gets into trouble through the work and ends up in prison, for example, then the *baba* organises legal assistance and support for their family, as befits a good employer.

A Turk occupying a coordinating position in the mid level of such an organisation once told us how a cooperating group of criminals is generally structured in the Netherlands. He was talking about one of the larger suppliers for the Netherlands when he said, 'C. always has a small army of a dozen or so men around him. For such an organisation to function properly, you need certain people who are suitable for specific tasks. There are dealers, negotiators, violence specialists [here he used the term "marksmen"], guards, inspectors, exporters, suppliers, transporters and people in the government, who organise issues such as providing diplomatic passports, so you can cross the border with less risk.'

When drug traffickers talk about each other, they always refer to each other by their own names: A has a conflict with B and if they fight it out that is done by A with his men and B with his men, but family A does not get into conflict with family B. As far as we can ascertain, no secret words are devised for referring to 'the organisation', such as in the Anglo-Saxon euphemisms The Outfit and The Firm. The terms 'group' and 'gang' (*çete*) are, however, used in a derogatory fashion for units that allow themselves to be used for dirty business, such as carrying out liquidations on the instructions of politicians, but 'men of honour' do not talk of each other in that way within what we will here refer to as the classical mafia.

But even though the actual operationally collaborating units are more like an action set or crew than an organisation or a family, this does not detract from the fact that familial connections play an extraordinarily important role in the underworld. Firstly sons, uncles and nephews often work within the *baba*'s inner circle. If he gets into trouble, the eldest son generally takes over his responsibilities and there are also examples of daughters doing so. The April 1988 issue of the magazine *Nokta* featured an interesting overview of sons expressing their admiration for their *baba* fathers, including Kiliç and Kürt Idris. Additionally, real families in the underworld are often interrelated by marriage. We already learned something of the function of marriages between the children of various bosses; it ensures mutual peace due to the inhibiting effect of the conflicting loyalties. Famous mafia marriages include that between Dündar Kiliç's daughter and Alaattin Cakiçi, and that between Kiliç's other daughter and Oflu. Finally, there is evidence of a quasi-familial relationship with the family if someone is invited to act as the *kirve*, the man who holds the son during circumcision. This has also generated many strong ties in the underworld.

For the Italian mafia in America, the term family also serves to indicate a kind of continuity. In the United States, twenty-four or twenty-five families have been identified, which each control the underworld of their own town and which are named after the founding member. New York alone has five such families and they are the best known. Such families are decades old. They often stem from the Prohibition period and have seen four, five or six generations of bosses and lieutenants come and go. The successors are often no longer related in any way to the founder; at some point they are simply the boss or father of the organisation. The founder of the Gambino family, Carlo Gambino, was born in 1900 in Palermo and emigrated illegally to the United States in 1921. He became rich and powerful in the 1920s and 1930s during Prohibition and later, during the war, in the black market for rationed goods, such as petrol and meat. A family was named after him when, in 1957, he took over the organisation of Albert Anastasia, who was gunned down while being shaved by his barber. In 1975, Gambino died of a heart attack. His function was assumed by his son-in-law, Paul Castellano. He was shot dead in 1985 in front of the entrance to a restaurant in Brooklyn. The operation was then taken over by John Gotti, who was not related to the Gambinos but nevertheless became 'the boss of the Gambino family'. Such family legends do not exist in the Turkish mafia.

In 1973, American journalists for the daily newspaper *Newsday,* who wished to remain anonymous, wrote a book entitled *The Heroin Trail*, in which they gave a description of the heroin route from Turkey as it was in 1971 and 1972. At that time, the heroin still came from the Anatolian opium province of Afyon, just after the ban on the sale of opium had been imposed by America against the wishes of the Turks. The authors start their voyage in Turkey. Based on excellent contacts with an underworld boss there, they compiled a list of the fifty major heroin *babas* at that moment, to whom they referred, incidentally, as patrons. They described how these *babas* all invested money in their own hotel, as a safe base and meeting venue, and in places of entertainment; these days, it is still the same. With a little effort, it is possible to find documentation on a number of the men the journalists named in 1973, but – with the sole exception of the Uğurlu family – neither they nor anyone considering themselves to be their successors were on the list of fourteen prominent bosses who attempted to divide up Europe amongst themselves at the super-conference in Sofia in 1980. If we then compare the two lists with one the Turkish police provided in 1996 of the thirty-eight most important *babas* at that moment, only the names of Uğurlu and Çapan feature on both the first and last lists. There seems to be little continuity.

So what are such lists worth? The *Newsday* journalists, who won a Pulitzer Prize for their book, claimed that their informer was excellent and that the only name they missed out was that of the informer himself, as that was his condition for agreeing to a series of interviews. With the knowledge we have now, we would say that, in the early 1970s, the list should have included at least the names of Oflu, Kiliç (perhaps just too young) and Çelenk, and he missed those. This demonstrates strikingly little continuity. What is noticeable, however, is that the areas from which the most important bosses come, the Black Sea, the southeast – the smuggling village of Kilis – and the city of Istanbul, are still the same, but that there is little evidence of stable families.

Does the organisation of the Turkish mafia resemble a company, an army, or a pyramid? In the years following the first National Criminal Intelligence Service investigation into two hundred criminal groups in the Netherlands, more and more groups came to light and other researchers also started investigating the structures of criminal organisations. Their diagrams and drawings reflect the type of work a lot of crime analysts started doing from the 1980s onwards, which was an advance in investigative methods at that time. Firstly, the detective established a suspect's associates. That can be done reasonably easily by keeping an eye out for meetings and examining telephone bills to see whom the person involved calls. If the suspicion increases (for example because 'old friends' of the police turn up in the circle of those associates), under certain legal conditions the police are permitted to tap conversations. Tips from 'informers' from the criminal world and sometimes from undercover agents complete the information. All over Europe, 'graphical' representations of criminal organisations are produced based on such data, which are generally extremely alarming. A jumble of lines and people in diverse roles is created, which are always focused around one or two people who are assumed to be the leading figures. There has been a lot of criticism of this technique because, for example, the conclusion is too easily drawn that an organisation exists.

Virtually all investigations produce structures constructed around certain leading figures. Until recently, that applied particularly to Turkish criminal organisations: the figure of the *baba* as the absolute head appeals to the imagination and the impenetrability of the Turkish and Kurdish underworld for the national police forces makes it hard to correct that idea.

This portrayal is incorrect. First of all, police constructions of Turkish organised crime added up all the people who had had anything to do with drug trafficking in the entire process, from purchasing from the opium farmer in Afghanistan or Pakistan up to and including sale to the customer in a residential area of a Western European city. It was then assumed that all this was coordinated from one central point. That ignores the fragmented character of the trade and attributes far too much weight to one body. In a study of Arnhem's Spijker district in 1997, one of the present authors found a contradictory model based on the idea that the trade column progresses through various phases, executed by individually operating units. In the first phase, the product is transported from Afghanistan to North Pakistan and its northern neighbouring states. In this phase, the opium and heroin are smuggled by car, mule and horse from the source countries to Iran and the east of Turkey; this transport is organised by Kurdish groups working together with Iranians to regulate the passage through their country. There is therefore a separate crew for this movement. Then, a second party, independent from the first, transports the heroin by car, plane or helicopter to Istanbul or a coastal town on the Mediterranean. This is done by both Turks and Kurds. A third unit takes the heroin by car, truck, coach or ship to the final countries of destination. The most important link from the first phase onwards is, without doubt, the *baba*, who prepares, monitors and controls the matter with his men in Istanbul up until the end of the transaction chain. They organise the transports to Europe and the United States. The group that actually carries out the transport, however, consists of people quite other than the *baba*; these are Turks, Laz and Kurds.

Phase four starts once the drugs have arrived in Western Europe. The distribution in Europe itself is carried out by various organisations in the Netherlands, France, Germany, Austria, Italy, England, Spain and Portugal. Some organisations are based in interim countries, such as Bulgaria, or, more recently, Romania and Poland in particular. The organisations are formed by Turks from various ethnic factions; the individual small groups are generally homogeneous according to ethnic origin. Some organisations are responsible for more than one of the four traffic movements. There are therefore bosses who supervise both the second and third steps and groups occupied in the third and fourth steps.

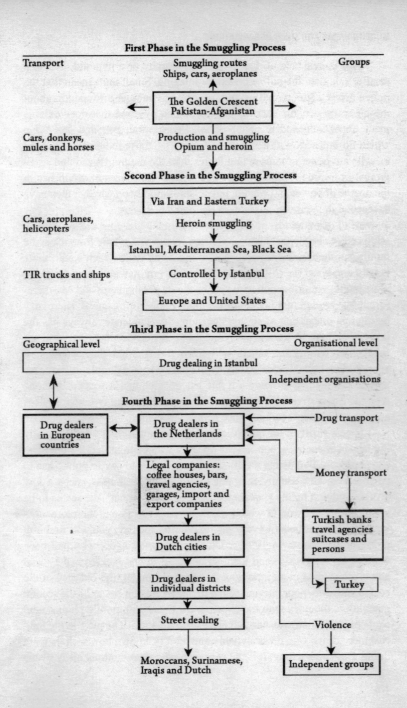

First Phase in the Smuggling Process

Transport | Smuggling routes
Ships, cars, aeroplanes | Groups

The Golden Crescent
Pakistan-Afganistan

Cars, donkeys,
mules and horses

Production and smuggling
Opium and heroin

Second Phase in the Smuggling Process

Via Iran and Eastern Turkey

Cars, aeroplanes,
helicopters

Heroin smuggling

Istanbul, Mediterranean Sea, Black Sea

TIR trucks and ships

Controlled by Istanbul

Europe and United States

Third Phase in the Smuggling Process

Geographical level | Organisational level

Drug dealing in Istanbul

Independent organisations

Fourth Phase in the Smuggling Process

Drug dealers
in European
countries

Drug dealers in
the Netherlands

Drug transport

Legal companies:
coffee houses, bars,
travel agencies,
garages, import and
export companies

Money transport

Drug dealers in
Dutch cities

Turkish banks
travel agencies
suitcases and
persons

Drug dealers in
individual districts

Turkey

Street dealing

Violence

Moroccans, Surinamese,
Iraqis and Dutch

Independent groups

There is evidence of a structure, a hierarchy or a pyramid, but on a smaller sale than the police generally imagine. Small units mean that the police arrest a group, cell or unit, no-one has enough information about the others to actually incriminate them. The pyramid that does exist is made up of independent collaborations, concentrated around one *baba*, which do business with each other. In Turkey, those independent groups or cells are better organised and larger than the medium-sized and small groups in Europe. The difference between the two sizes of group lies in the degree of power and wealth, but depends chiefly on whether they have succeeded in gaining a position in the ranks in Turkey.

Instead of pyramids, in Europe it would be better to speak of cooperating cells or beehives. Such a cell often consists of people from the same family. Yet there is indeed an absolute hierarchy within such a cell; there is only one boss. He will often be the eldest, but may alternatively be the most intelligent or the one who speaks the most languages and can therefore move around in other countries more easily for business. There may be internal discussion of certain decisions, but the leader always has the last word. He can't foresee everything, but this is accounted for. If something goes wrong, the others will learn from it, but they won't start complaining to the leader. Arrest by the police is an example: in that case no-one has made a mistake, but fate has decided that it was so. The one who has been arrested doesn't open his mouth under any circumstances and the leader takes care of those he has left behind.

It is very difficult for the police in Europe to work out who is actually the leader of such a group. To the western way of thinking, the one who ostentatiously flaunts his wealth and has the most to say in public has to be the boss. But usually it is not like that; the real boss keeps a low profile. Judging by his appearance – his clothes, his car – he seems to be a typical migrant worker who is currently out of work and therefore turns up to sign on for benefit every month. During the day, you will find him in the coffee house. In 1997, a Dutch undercover agent who had been working in the Turkish and Kurdish underworld and had learned by trial and error, told us in an interview, 'At first, I thought: the old men in the coffee house are poor, driving round in old bangers; it has to be the second generation, the ones with the expensive trainers and mobile phones who show off with their watches and drive a BMW 735csi. The guys in the long cashmere coats, who dress stylishly and let it be known how well they are doing. But I was wrong. It is the very man who gives nothing away by his appearance who is in charge. From my experience, there is only one boss per coffee house – and that is not, naturally, the one who runs the coffee house. The ones who really rule the roost often do so with no more than a nod of the head. And to work that out! Turks from the west of Turkey rapidly let down their guard and quickly get down to business. But those from the east are far more cautious; it can take months before they point out the man you are actually doing business with.

'I've learned that, in that world, it's all actually about honour and everything is a matter of rank and position. Where I went wrong, for example, was when I wanted to lend them my car because five Turks had to quickly pick something up somewhere. I gave it to the second man in the bunch! I'd passed over the one with the highest rank! It's just as important to know what you should do if you ask someone for a favour. If you do it the wrong way, then they'll turn away, insulted, and you can forget it.'

For the Turkish and Kurdish smuggling organisations, the process has not been completed until they, as wholesalers, have sold their merchandise to the retailers. At the end of the line is a Turkish and Kurdish infrastructure, in which coffee houses and bars, import and export companies, garages and travel agencies play a major role. This is where the logistics for the very last phase are organised. The European customers for the drugs and the rest of the population, too, have little idea of this culture and their chance of coming into contact with it is virtually nil. In the last phase, however, things are different. These activities take place in their own neighbourhood, behind the windows where tea is being drunk, or at the Turkish shop where you can get such nice delicacies, or at the travel agency where you book your next holiday to Turkey. There is nothing untoward going on in most of these places, but in some of them there is.

Right and Left in the Turkish Mafia

The classic Turkish mafia, with its own organisational structure, had its heyday in the 1960s and 1970s, when characters like Heybetli and Kiliç dominated the underworld and the mafia was not yet so controlled by politics. In the 1980s, that changed and the modern, politically aware type of mafia boss emerged. The best-known ultra-right mafia figure of our time is undoubtedly Alaattin Çakici. His lifestyle provides insight into the activities and etiquette in the world of the former members and current sympathisers of the Grey Wolves *ülkücü* movement.

Like many figures in the underworld, Alaattin Çakici comes from the area by the Black Sea, near the town of Trabzon. In his case, too, a vendetta was the reason why the family moved to Istanbul. As a young man, he joined the *ülkücü* movement there and took part in the 'street war' against the left-wing. In the battle against Marxist Dev-Sol supporters he lost, according to his account, both his father and his cousin, and his sister was wounded. He was part of a group of fanatical Grey Wolves who were sentenced to prison by the military court in Istanbul in a case against the Nationalist Action Party (MHP) following the coup in 1980. His group was convicted for the forty-one killings they reputedly had on their conscience. When they were released eighteen months later, the group was not the same. Disappointed because their patriotism and self sacrifice had been rewarded with a prison sentence, a large proportion of that generation of *ülkücü* developed independently after their release. Instead of executing political assignments in an organised context, they became professional criminals, who hired out their services for large sums to the political right-wing. Çakici's first assignment was the murder of Armenian ASALA activists in other countries, such as Lebanon. As leader of his own group, he subsequently became the most famous figure and *ülkücü baba* in the new cheque mafia branch.

Conflicts with Dündar Kiliç did not prevent him from marrying

Kiliç's daughter Uğur. He had told friends that he wasn't frightened of anybody and therefore not of Dündar, apart from which, he was 'sensitive and romantic'. This became the most famous mafia wedding in Turkey. The bride and groom, both of whom had been married before and brought children with them from those marriages, were followed closely by the press.

From 1993 onwards, wanted by the Turkish police for an impressive series of offences Çakici found himself forced to flee the country and go into hiding. There was plenty of speculation about his whereabouts. Some said he was still in Turkey, others that he was in America on a green passport issued to high-ranking Turkish officials or with the identity papers of a colonel, while others believed that they should look for Çakici in London or Amsterdam. Wherever he was, he knew how to reach the media. He let it be known that he was in Europe for a 'good cause', which consisted of liquidating prominent members of Dev-Sol and the PKK. Those organisations responded, in turn, by challenging him in the Dev-Sol magazine, calling him a 'slimy fascist' and expressing willingness to meet anywhere at all for a fight: 'he can bring a couple of ex-MHP dogs with him,' said *Hürriyet*. The following day, he replied in a letter sent to 'all newspapers and TV stations with the provocative text: "Those people already declared in 1988 that Amsterdam would be my burial place. I have visited Amsterdam repeatedly since that invitation, but have seen no-one from Dev-Sol. Now, circumstances dictate that I am in Belgium, Germany, France and England. They should leave me their address, instead of hiding like women."'

His marriage to Uğur Kiliç hit the rocks and, on 4 November 1994, was dissolved. Despite their divorce, Çakici insisted she should take care in what she said and should continue to demonstrate respect for him in her behaviour, because in the eyes of outsiders she was still under the care of his honour, his *namus*. Uğur stated in public that she was quite capable of looking after herself and that marrying him had been a big mistake. She would rather have married Abdullah Öcalan, the head of the PKK, she taunted, and concluded, 'He abused me throughout the five years of our marriage, but he is still in love with me.' Çakici sent a cassette recording to a TV station on which he said he would not appreciate them asking Uğur to comment in their programme. When Uğur heard that, she showed herself to be her father's child. She went to the TV studio and informed the astonished presenters, 'If you're scared of Alaattin, you should be scared of me, too!' then drew a gun and shot out all the windows in the room.

'I'm not a feminist and I'm not a man-woman, either; I'm just an average person,' she had said of herself, but the media did not share her view. With her chic clothes, long, black hair and strikingly beautiful eyes, she was a sought-after interviewee, but one not without risk. Ayşe Önal, an editor for the weekly magazine *Nokta*, wrote about Uğur that she was a female Casanova and reputedly lesbian, too. That cost her a threat that just missed turning out very badly for the journalist: Uğur was stopped from attacking her just in time, but shot two bullets into the leg of a fellow reporter who had backed up the challenged statement.

Uğur openly maintained relationships with all kinds of men. According to Çakici, one of them was the police commissioner, who was the second man in Istanbul: Kocadağ – the same man who became one of the victims of the car accident in Susurluk in November 1996 that turned the country upside down in indirectly proving that police and politicians had close connections with the mafia. For the more racy press, the intrigues between Uğur and her former husband made weekly fodder and, according to *Hürriyet*, Uğur's ultimate murder took place as follows: Çakici had called to tell her he wanted to marry her again. He had reserved accommodation for her in the winter sport complex in Uludağ. In the mafioso manner, however, Çakici had also charged her former private chauffeur, whom she trusted implicitly, with the task of gunning her down when she entered the hotel. Two children from her first marriage watched it happen. Uğur, who had not made it past the age of thirty, was buried the very next day. Her father Dündar's response was, 'I want a photograph of his body,' which in underworld language meant, 'I demand the immediate death of Alaattin Çakici.'

Çakici, however, remained alive and kicking and, in recent years, has made the news repeatedly. When his former friend Ağansoy turned against him, Çakici said, 'You have two months to live.' But it was more than four months before a shootout in a teahouse on the Bosporus between Çakici's men and Ağansoy's cost three lives. The extra, political tint to this shooting was that Ağansoy's guards included police officers and some of the Çillers' bodyguards. Later investigation showed that these same bodyguards were involved in other mafia activities.

*

The Turkish state has been at war with the Kurdish PKK movement for many years and drug traffickers supporting the movement with their revenue are shown no mercy by its leaders. At the end of 1993, the prime minister of Turkey, Mrs Çiller, announced in the Holiday Inn Hotel that she knew who these people were: 'Turkey has a terrorist problem that has spread and taken on an increasingly militant character. We know which business people and artistes* are behind this. We will settle the score with these people!' What Mrs Çiller said was actually no more than a reiteration. In April 1993, the most important state organ, the National Security Council, had already declared outright war against the PKK in so many words and, in June of that year, concrete measures were named. 'As the PKK is intensifying its struggle and needs arms and logistics services, it has contacted international drug traffickers, such as the heads of the Baybaşin, Polat, Aksoy, Koylan and Yildirim Kocakaya families.' As the most explicit enemy, Mrs Çiller consciously chose one person: 'According to an Italian police report from 1992, Behçet Cantürk is smuggling drugs to Europe and doing so in the name of the PKK.'

Cantürk had, without doubt, been one of the best-known figures in the Turkish underworld. His name was still mentioned in connection with the smuggling of arms, heroin, raw morphine and other contraband. As other gangsters are identified with ultra-right politics in Turkey, Cantürk stands for the left-wing. Before the coup of 1980 he was chairman of the Social Democratic Party in his town of Lice, the Republican People's Party (CHP), but like all political parties, this one was banned under the military government. In 1983, when politics was again liberalised, he was one of the founders of the new Social Democratic Party. In the years that followed, he focused primarily on the Kurdish struggle. He was one of the five owners of Ülkem, which published the pro-Kurdish left-wing newspaper *Özgür Gündem*, which was treated by the Turkish authorities as the official mouthpiece of the PKK.

Cantürk didn't talk to journalists as much as other *babas*, with one exception: he was prepared to grant Ayşe Önal from *Nokta* an interview, on the condition that it would not be published immediately. 'There will be a time for publication,' he said and, when she asked when that would

---

* She used the word *sanatçi,* the literal translation of which is artiste. The newspapers the following day showed exactly what she meant: she was talking about popular singers.

be, he replied, 'Who knows, perhaps if something happens to me.' There have also been various articles on him in daily and weekly papers and a book has even been written about him, largely based on his statements to the police and the Turkish secret service after his arrest in 1984. He withdrew these statements later, in court, as he claimed they had been made and signed under duress and after torture.

Behçet Cantürk was born in 1949 in Lice, in southeast Turkey. His father was a small trader, who travelled from village to village by mule as far as Syria and Iran. Like all inhabitants of this town, he was also a smuggler. As Cantürk later stated, 'The population of Lice is constantly dogged by bad luck. They started out selling cheap jewellery and then switched to smuggling heroin.' His father fell in love with an Armenian girl during his wanderings, whom he kidnapped and then, once she had converted to Islam, took as his second wife in the presence of the imam. Behçet was born from this marriage, which was not legally recognised, but he was not to know his mother; she died when he was a year old. His origins marked his life; the Turkish government registered him unofficially as a Kurd, but his mother had already registered him as an Armenian. As a 'committed' Kurd he became an enemy of the state. In his youth, he was teased about his Armenian mother, even by the Kurds, and because she had only converted to the true religion later in life, he was also despised as a *dönme*, a convert.

At the age of fifteen, by his own account, he 'accidentally' shot dead a school friend and went to prison, to be released only a year later in a general pardon. In 1969, Cantürk became embroiled in a conflict between two local clans. Although the circumstances were never entirely clarified, the conflict was attributed to a political difference. Wanted by the police, he chose the usual alternative to prison: he took to the mountains. In 1971, he was again involved in a dispute, this time with part of his family, and after a lengthy manhunt, that year he gave himself up to the police. To the other prisoners, he was an *iaki* or *eşkşya*, a hero from the hills. The following year, he was free again after another amnesty. He got married and set up a coach company.

In 1975, a major earthquake hit in the area of Diyarbakir, claiming the lives of 2,500 people. Cantürk lost his wife, son, brother and fifteen other close relatives. Like other *babas* from the Diyarbakir area, his political activism started with revolt against the Turkish government, which had left the victims of the disaster badly in the lurch. In the meantime, he devel-

RIGHT AND LEFT IN THE TURKISH MAFIA

oped into a formidable smuggler and, according to his biographer Yalçin, he was also active in the construction industry mafia. In 1979 he moved to Istanbul to internationalise his career in drug smuggling. He rapidly rose to the top in the underworld and his wealth became proverbial. Cantürk was an exceptionally good-looking man and the long list of conquests he chalked up kept him in the newspapers. On his arrest in 1984, several film stars were held for questioning, including the famous Ahu Tuğba.

As he had developed into a major opponent of the government over the years, with his donations to the PKK, Cantürk had every reason to take seriously warnings of his life being in danger. Just before Mrs Çiller's press conference in 1993, he was told by President Yahya Demirel's cousin, 'Watch out, they're after your head.' Others also warned him that he was top of the list. He took precautionary measures and only drove around in the latest bulletproof Mercedes. But it was to no avail. When he gave his chauffeur the order to stop at what appeared to be a routine check, he was arrested by people wearing jackets bearing the word *polis*. The 'police' found a weapon in his car for which he had no licence and he was taken to the station. From that moment the story is unclear. When he failed to come home, his family did everything possible to find him, including enlisting the aid of the Minister of Foreign Affairs, who came from Lice, but it was already too late; the next day his lifeless body was found just outside Istanbul with a bullet through the head. Twenty metres further up was the body of his driver, who had evidently tried to escape. Cantürk's wallet had disappeared, but he was still wearing his expensive watch. His visiting card was also found: 'Behçet Cantürk,' it said; no more was necessary. He was dressed to the nines in stylish clothes, according to his preference for European designers: Pierre Cardin and Davidoff.

The next day, the newspaper *Hürriyet* came up with three possible scenarios for what had happened: a mafia killing, a PKK killing, or a killing by anti-PKK forces. Cantürk's own newspaper, 'the newspaper of the PKK', and the family pointed to Çiller as the culprit and held the Turkish state responsible. Cantürk's murder turned out to be only the first in a series of unsolved murders of Kurdish underworld figures, legitimate business people and prominent lawyers, which makes the family's interpretation most likely. What's more, the victims of these murders were all kidnapped first by fake policemen, tortured and then shot. It was not until January 1998 that this latter interpretation was confirmed in a report on the Susurluk scandal.

4

A Police Problem

Immigration and Crime

The Turkish mafia has been able to develop in Europe as a result of the emigration from Turkey that started in the 1960s and 1970s and continues to this day. The commercial infrastructure these emigrants have built together in Western Europe acts as a network for drug trafficking and the various Turkish and Kurdish communities in Europe additionally provide the traffickers with a refuge.

The Turkish diaspora started with migrant workers, people who only left for a short period to solve a temporary bottleneck in the economy of affluent countries and who were generally only granted a work permit for one year. When the need for semi-skilled and unskilled labour continued year after year, the contracts were extended and extended again. The possibility also opened up to send for wives and children and so temporary labour migration gradually turned into permanent emigration. That doesn't mean to say that no labourers went back; on the contrary, globally it can be said that, in the more than forty years migration has been in motion, roughly as many people have returned to Turkey as have stayed. The Centre for Turkish Studies, in Essen, Germany, has gathered statistics on the number of Turks in the various countries in Western Europe. These figures are politically important for Turkey, as Turks living abroad have the right to vote and the total of three million Turks in Europe represent two million voting rights, which could theoretically elect twenty-nine members to the Turkish parliament.* The number of Turks in Germany is by far the greatest: more than two million; followed by France and the Netherlands with more than a quarter of a million each, Austria with 150,000; Belgium with 85,000; Switzerland with 79,000; the United Kingdom with 51,000; Sweden with 36,000; Denmark with 35,000 and Norway with 10,000.

---

* That voting right only applies to emigrants prepared to travel to the border of Turkey, where a ballot box is installed especially for them.

In all the countries of Western Europe where it has been studied, the position of Turks and Kurds on the socio-economic scale turns out to be unfavourable. True, the odd Turk or Kurd has managed to develop an extremely successful business career and an increasing number of students of Turkish origin go on to university, but in general the Turkish minorities fare badly in education, income and employment at the higher levels. This is partly due to a poor command of the language and a low level of education. The vast majority of the migrants come from the less developed areas of Central and Eastern Anatolia. After an initial period of active recruitment by representatives from the European business community, the phenomenon of migrant labour has spontaneously developed in accordance with the pattern of chain migration: the first emigrant convinces his family, friends and fellow villagers to come over. That explains why a striking number of Turks and Kurds from specific, limited areas of Turkey have settled in Europe. The people from the town of Afyon, for example, went to Belgium and those from Gaziantep to the Netherlands.

It is, in fact, misleading to talk of 'the Turkish community'; this expression implies a sampling of various communities from villages, districts and provinces all over Turkey. Many immigrant colonies in Europe mirror the original communities in their region or village of origin, forming transnational migration systems. The migrants marry partners from the same region, people from the same area meet at coffee houses generally bearing the name of that region – *Kara Deniz*, or Black Sea, for example – and now and again they demonstrate their solidarity with the village of origin in the form of a joint project; perhaps an ambulance is needed, or help after an earthquake. Mayors from their village regularly visit the Netherlands to 'remind them of their origin' and political and religious organisations are aware of how to extract money from the emigrants. Apart from that, there is strikingly little contact between the various Turkish communities; traditionally negative stereotypes on both sides and political division stand in the way.

If the migrant labourers were initially motivated by poverty and a wish to improve their individual lot and that of their children, from the moment the families were reunited, they found themselves in heavy competition for esteem, status and wealth within their own community. They place themselves not so much on the social status ladder of the country they are in, but rather compare themselves with other Turks. Which of the people from the same village or region in Turkey will be the first to buy a television or a car? Who will get rich? Whose children will obtain the highest qualifications? Earnings in Europe are largely invested in the village of origin in Turkey: houses are built, land is bought and shops are opened. The battle for prestige is fought on two fronts, both in the village of origin and in the village the emigrants form together in Europe.

Initially, things went well for migrant workers. The demand for their labour continued and their contracts were extended for a year or two. In the 1960s and 1970s, unemployment among Turks in Europe was virtually nil. However, the economic recession in Europe in the early 1970s, caused by the oil crisis, and the restructuring of the Western European economies in the 1980s that swept away a proportion of the job opportunities at the bottom of the labour market, hit migrant workers disproportionally hard. Some went back voluntarily or, in the case of Germany, were sent back, but among those who stayed, a serious unemployment problem suddenly emerged. Everywhere in Europe the Turkish unemployment percentage was at least twice that of the average for the country.

Added to this, there were negative stereotypes of Turks and Kurds and they were discriminated against when seeking work. Where socio-scientific measurements are available for the adaptation of immigrants, they show that Turkish migrant workers and their descendants have still failed to integrate to more than a low degree in comparison with other immigrant groups in those countries. This is partly a generation phenomenon; the immigrants themselves see their stay as temporary and look forward to retiring to Turkey. It is also the result of social circumstances; a deprived position in the labour market, the social isolation of living in the ethnic neighbourhoods, the children's poor educational results and so forth. Thirdly, it is certainly a conscious political choice, which can be a continuing preference for Turkey, which need not hinder integration in itself, insofar as people can act as 'ambassadors' for Turkey, but it can also mean a rejection of a 'society of infidels' in which you only stay temporarily for economic reasons – and that does reduce the chance of integration.

In summary, in the early 1970s there was a shift. A community that had been ensnared by mutual status rivalry was hit by economic adversity and had integrated into society to such a low degree that the step up to the status of a social middle class could not yet be made by the following generation.

Such a series of unfavourable circumstances easily leads to high crime rates. One would therefore expect the crime statistics for the Turkish minorities to be high. Yet for the first migrant generation, in general, they are not. That first generation has difficulty enough keeping its head above water and, moreover, is not yet familiar with the opportunities for successful criminal operation in the new country. According to the theory, it should be the second generation where this happens, if it is insufficiently integrated. It is therefore startling that a series of criminological studies on crime amongst minorities in Europe shows that, wherever the phenomenon has been studied, the Turkish ethnic groups are less involved in crime than one might expect on the grounds of their unfavourable socio-economic status. In Germany, their general crime level is equal to that of the Germans; that also applies in the Netherlands, where it is striking that the level of crime is far lower than that of young Moroccans, who demonstrate a corresponding socio-economic profile; in Belgium the low Turkish crime rate is equally surprising. If any higher rates than average are to be found, then these always apply to specific offence categories, such as drug trafficking or organised crime, or to the level of violence, which, for example, is far higher amongst Turks in Switzerland than the average, but this has little effect on the general crime rates.

Does this mean that Turks and Kurds actually commit few crimes, or do these figures rather reflect the selective methods of the police and the judicial authorities? In general, crime figures for all types of offences are added up together: violent crimes, property offences, violation of road traffic laws and so forth. Property crimes and, in particular, theft constitute the vast majority of all criminal offences that come to the knowledge of the police and on the grounds of which they compile their figures and statistics. There are well-founded reasons to assume that the Turkish population group scores extremely low where it comes to theft. Their standards and values are strongly opposed to such behaviour; in Turkish society, stealing means losing face. This powerful standard is applied when the internal social control of the group is strong. This is very much the case in local Turkish and Kurdish communities.

There are far less serious objections to certain violent crimes, and even the standards that oppose opium crimes have lost significance in recent years in Turkish circles. This should be reflected in the figures. That is not, however, clearly the case, which demands clarification. The first, theoretical reason is that drug trafficking, or more general organised crime, is harder to measure in figures and numbers than other forms of crime. Drug trafficking is a consensual crime, committed by parties with the same interests. One sells an illegal product, the other buys it and, in principle, there are no victims who are going to complain to the police. Theft demonstrates the opposite pattern: Almost all victims complain, even if only because they expect to be able to claim from their insurance, which generates substantial numbers, even when only a low percentage of crimes are solved. The second reason for the distortion of the image of Turkish crime is economic. Drug trafficking, like all commerce, entails a relatively small number of directors or managers and a large number of permanent and freelance employees at lower levels. Just as in the legal economy, in drug trafficking few business people reach the top and the largest number of accomplices and hangers-on find no more than a temporary favourable alternative to regular work. This does not discourage them, incidentally, as the few who do make it keep up the aspiration level of all the others.

This second interpretation, however, is also inadequate: the police and judicial authorities should, at least, notice the involvement of Turks and Kurds in drugs trafficking. They only notice consensual crimes, however, when they are specifically looking for them. In the latter instance, crime figures therefore always reflect the priority of the investigation.

That assumption is supported by the striking differences the police observe in specific crimes in the Turkish underworld in various European countries. In Germany and the Netherlands, drug trafficking is defined as organised crime and the major crime policy is to eliminate organisations by arresting them from the top. Whether this headhunting actually helps in a market where supply and demand simply continue to exist is a moot question. It does generate a small number of suspects, but they are the heavyweights. They let the lower level of minions and service providers go. The French system is quite different. Their view is that all those involved, from high to low, are equally criminal and all deserve to be arrested. For the police, in general, it is the street level of users, those users who also deal to support their habit and those who only sell drugs, who are the easiest to tackle. The French drug scene is in towns, at known locations and times, and French and North Africans are known to be involved, but few Turks. The Dutch and German approach, where the bosses are first identified, requires long-term police investigation, which largely has to be pro-active because, as we said, there is no preceding report of a criminal offence. The French approach, on the other hand, is reactive. If someone is arrested, then the police attempt to establish in their questioning who the dealers are and, from there on, endeavour to round up the company or gang from the bottom upwards. This 'fire brigade method', as it is sometimes derisively referred to by colleagues from other countries, does theoretically produce a large number of low-calibre culprits and that is exactly what the French statistics show. There, they see heroin trafficking as *trafic de fourmis*, an occupation of many thousands of ants, all smuggling in and dealing small quantities of drugs.

The low crime figures for involvement in drug trafficking are therefore deceptive and the difference in such figures in the various countries doesn't mean much, either.

There are, however, other convincing indications that, in most Western European countries, heroin trafficking is in the hands of Turkish and Kurdish groups and that quite a lot of people from these communities are involved. Virtually all heroin intercepted over the past thirty years in European countries has been brown, which means it comes from Turkish and Kurdish dealers. We can now assume that everywhere in Europe where there is an affluent demand for heroin and other drugs, where there is a Turkish immigrant community of a sufficient size to build up its own infrastructure so that a Turkish underworld can be created, and where the socio-economic position and level of social integration is such that a marginalised class can develop and/or people are driven by heavy mutual competition for status improvement, the chance of organised drug trafficking from Turkey succeeding is great. This has already been demonstrated in Germany, the Netherlands, Belgium, the United Kingdom and Scandinavia.

This 'rule' does not, however always prove to hold water. First of all, there is one country with a considerable Turkish community where the heroin trade does not appear to be in the hands of the Turks and Kurds, namely France. Judging by the white colour of the heroin confiscated in France, the home market there is still predominantly in the hands of the Chinese. It is not clear whether this is the result of the aforementioned French investigative method, where there is a relatively great chance of intercepting small shipments, while Turkish drug traffickers do actually control the invisible international wholesale market. It could, alternatively, be that the Turkish population in France lends itself less easily to involvement in drug trafficking because, proportionally, more intellectuals and fewer migrant workers and their children live there than elsewhere in Europe. There is one factor to which it cannot be due: lower heroin consumption, as this is actually higher in France than the European average.

The 'rule' also fails to apply to the logical opposite: countries without a large Turkish community, where Turkish drug traffickers have clearly managed to establish themselves. This applies to Italy and Spain, in particular. In Italy, the crime market has sufficient indigenous distribution channels, which means the Turkish wholesalers can suffice with importing. And in Spain, although it has hardly any Turkish community, the Turkish drug organisations have indisputably grown the most rapidly.

In Spain, the many-branched Çapan family is not just a household word amongst the police. It is here, too, that a new drug route was first discovered, running from Byelorussia directly into Spain. In this case, the dealers clearly sought out the internal market. The kilo price in Spain is exceptionally high. Spain also turned out to be interesting due to the investment opportunities for black money in the tourist industry; the investment pattern in the Turkish coastal towns is being copied. Additionally, Spain offers an operating base for the cocaine traffic from South America to Europe. Turks and Colombians exchange cocaine for heroin in Spanish territory (over the course of the years, four, three or two kilos of heroin for one kilo of coke). Snorting coke has become popular in fashionable circles in Istanbul and the police have arrested various popular singers for it in Turkey. Turkish dealers have also been spotted in South America, where they help set up the commercial cultivation of poppies.

One thing does apply to all countries where Turkish drug traffickers have been noted: they restrict themselves to refining, transport and wholesaling. This can be a major reason why the police in countries where they carry out their investigation at street level will come across little Turkish drug crime. This way of working is shrewd: it shifts the risk of prosecution to others. It can also be prompted by the aforementioned lack of social integration, because to succeed in dealing on the street, from a private house or in a café or coffee shop, you have to know the customers' language and demonstrate street savvy. The younger generation should, in principle, be more capable of that but, nevertheless, it doesn't happen. Street dealing is left to the members of other ethnic groups, who are considered more suitable for the task. During discussions with drug traffickers in Amsterdam, it dawned on us that the Turkish drug traffickers apply a racism here: 'Moroccans and Surinamese were created by Allah to be of service to Turks.' In Belgium, the police have noticed that the task of street dealing is allocated to the far better integrated Italians. In Italy itself, the drug shipments are taken over by the Italians and by Nigerians. Nigerians fulfil a similar role in England and Sweden. In Spain, the retail market is in the hands of gypsies and, in France, Tunisians and black Africans fulfil this function.

*

Drug trafficking is not the only problem among Turkish communities abroad. In various countries, the police are being faced increasingly with other forms of organised crime. For violent crimes alone, the Turks score relatively high everywhere. In all countries, the police have also observed an unusually high degree of firearms possession amongst Turks, even male minors. This does not necessarily have anything to do with organised crime; it can be explained by the cultural code that dictates that a man should at all times be able to prove his autonomy and defend his honour. If it comes down to a fight in Turkish gangland, however, then the consequences of the use of firearms are quickly more grisly than the police are used to from the underworld. There are also networks that help find work for illegal labourers from Turkey and those that are involved in human trafficking in other ways. In some countries, groups have also been dismantled that were engaged in laundering illegally obtained money, but this was often again an extension of drug trafficking.

One problem all police forces are finally confronted with is extortion of people and companies for political purposes. Increasingly, there are signs of intimidating behaviour by supporters of the PKK and Dev-Sol. It is hard for the police to tell what is a voluntary contribution to a good political cause and what is extortion; whenever they interpret violence as a sanction for default in payment, on further investigation other motives are always revealed. Appeals to the Turkish and Kurdish population groups to complain in the event of extortion generate disappointingly little result. The police's opinion that Dev-Sol is actually engaged in extortion and, in doing so, exercising little reserve is unanimous, but opinions on the PKK vary.

A drawn portrait of *kabadayi*. These so-called urban knights were the forerunners of the Turkish mafia and lived by their own code.

*Bıçkın Kozlucalı Tâhir ile Kahveci Lâz Mehmed
(Sabiha Bozcalı'nın kompozisyonu)*

A rare early 20th century picture of a group of *tulambaci*, the tough, fit, voluntary firemen from whose ranks the *kabadayi* are said to have sprung.

Dundar Kilic, the consummate *baba*, with one of his daughters. Kilic had close connections with leading politicians and the intelligence services. He died of natural causes in 1999.

Godfather Alaattin Cakici with Dundar Kilic's daughter Ugur. When their marriage hit the rocks, Cakici had her gunned down.

Above: The wreckage of the luxury Mercedes after the now notorious car accident at Susurluk in November 1996. The car hit the back of a truck on a road in western Turkey. Its four passengers, three of whom died, were revealed as a cross-section of the so-called Deep State.

Right: Sedat Bucak, member of Parliament for the province of Urfa and the commander of an army of village guards, was the only survivor of the crash.

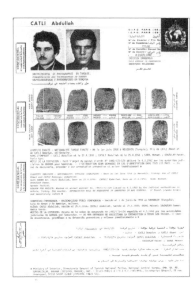

Left: Abdullah Catli, pictured here in court, died in the Susurluk crash. The Europe-wide heroin dealer and Grey Wolf leader, wanted by Interpol (top right), was a leading figure in the Turkish mafia. Also killed in the car were his girlfriend, beauty queen Gonca Us (top left), and a police chief.

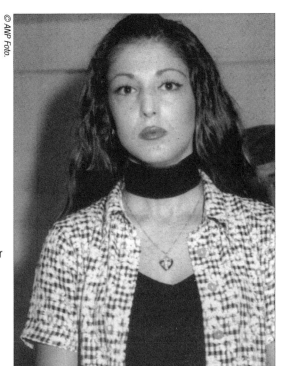

Dilek Örnek (see Chapter 8), the pretty young woman caught smuggling illicit cash for the Turkish mafia in the Netherlands.

Muazzez Abaci, a famous singer and former wife of the underworld figure Hasan Heybetli. Popular entertainers and the mafia often mix in the same circles in Turkey.

Left: Mehmet Ali Agca, the Turkish assassin who shot and wounded Pope John Paul II in May 1981. Jailed for life in Italy, he was later pardoned at the Pope's request, only to be jailed again on his extradition to Turkey.

Below: Fanatics display their 'wolf' hand signs at a demonstration by the *ülkücü*, or idealists, of the Grey Wolves, the deadly ultra-nationalist movement.

Above: A huge consignment of Turkish brown heroin hidden in the bed of a lorry stopped in the United Kingdom.

Left: Ingenious methods of concealment, such as this load sealed in a metal container, require painstaking search methods.

Below: The poppy fields of Afghanistan still yield the vast majority of the world's heroin, despite the recent invasion by Western forces.

Huseyin Baybasin (left), the most notorious of the Kurdish godfathers, and his wheelchair-bound brother Abdullah (right), who was sentenced to twenty-two years by a London court in 2006 for running a gang involved in blackmail, arson, firearms offences and conspiring to supply heroin.

Huseyin Baybasin and some of his clan in his home village of Lice. At the time of writing, he is serving a jail term in Holland.

European Police Discover the Turkish Mafia

The customs, police and security services of a number of European countries discovered the arrival of organised crime from Turkey in the 1980s and 1990s. It manifested itself differently from country to country, and responses varied too. This can be explained by the great diversity of penal systems in Europe, the difference in what is considered to be organised crime, a difference in investigative methods, the differences in national drugs policies and those in the form and style of politics.

In exploring Europe, the Turkish drugs organisations initially work in roughly the same way: They seek out the market, deploy transport resources, use the Turkish and Kurdish infrastructure for logistics and find themselves indigenous lawyers who can assist them legally if anything goes wrong. They find banks through which they can send the revenue to Turkey and accommodation agencies that can organise temporary housing for them. Europe was previously a fragmented entity, but with the increasing blurring of national borders, the drug traffickers also learned about the individual national legal environments: the risk of being caught, the punishments, the quality of the detention, the effectiveness of the fiscal investigation service. The Turkish mafia therefore diverged, but at the same time there was a certain harmonisation in the penal response in Europe. Drugs policy was brought more into line in a series of conventions, police authority was harmonised by the Trèves and Maastricht conventions and the battle against money laundering was consolidated in 1993 in a guideline from Strasbourg. And something akin to a miracle: from 1995 onwards, the Europol police forces have been attempting to cooperate.

Since the initial discovery of this mafia, cooperation has been sought with the police forces in Turkey. What happened there is a story in itself. In any event, the Turkish police started sharing some of their knowledge with the police forces in Europe. At an Interpol conference in 1995 in Lyon, they shared their insight into the methods of the most important 'family' with the European police. They named thirty-seven family names of organisations active at that moment and offered to work with European police forces if they would seriously get down to investigating in their country. No attempt was made to keep these names confidential; they were published in the Turkish press.

Until now, we have described the development of the Turkish mafia primarily from the viewpoint of the organisations themselves. Foreign police, however, tend to see the history of the discovery of Turkish organised crime in their countries as a series of cases and operations. Italy, the Netherlands, Germany, Belgium and the United Kingdom are among the countries where the police possess the most knowledge of Turkish organised crime, and here we turn to their experiences of the *babas* and their networks.

*

'Turks?' say two of the most experienced specialists in the Italian department of public security's Servizio Antidroga and the Guardia di Finanza, Colonel Rabiti and Inspector Fazio. 'In the beginning, we knew nothing other than the old wives' tales about them being people who ate their own children and that kind of thing. Now and again we came across a drug courier from Turkey, but we didn't [see] any more major organisation. We had heard of Armenians, but the first time we heard about the Kurds was in 1980 and only much later, when *pentiti*, or repentants, started to talk, did it dawn on us that drug trafficking was inextricably interrelated with politics in Turkey.'

Few, if any, specialists outside Turkey have as much insight and detailed knowledge as these Italian detectives; in the 1980s Colonel Rabiti had even served in Turkey as a liaison officer and learned to speak Turkish fluently. One of the reasons why the Italians took so long to recognise Turkish organised crime was that, in the 1970s, drug trafficking was aimed solely at the internal Italian market and was not connected with the international traffic to the United States, via Marseille or the heroin laboratories in Sicily. There was another, theoretical reason, however, why they failed to recognise this as organised crime. The Turkish underworld was different from the Sicilian mafia or the Neapolitan Camorra. To the Italians, the Turkish organisations appeared to be nothing more than a bunch of criminal groups and, in Italian eyes, that was quite different from the mafia.

The Italians did briefly wonder if their country was becoming the new centre of drug trafficking when, in a major case tried by Judge Carlo Palermo in Trente in 1981, connections were demonstrated between Turkish, Armenian and Jordanian traffickers and Roberto Calvi, the Vatican's mafia banker at the Banco Ambrosiano. But that connection did not survive. That was probably because no community of Turkish migrant workers had formed in Italy within which smugglers could hide.

Roughly 1,000 people of Turkish origin currently live and work in Milan, but these are business people and their community and infrastructure are too small – there is only one Turkish restaurant – to be used for drug smuggling. The distribution of drugs within Italy itself is organised by the local underworld and this criminal echelon is densely populated. The northern Italian city of Verona has been described as the hub of drug trafficking in Italy, for the very reason that there was no mafia there and because the local political culture did not constitute a good breeding ground for solving conflicts through violence. In the early 1970s, the heroin came from Amsterdam and was still of Chinese origin. From 1978 onwards, however, the market fell into Turkish and Kurdish hands. Drug trafficking organisations, such as that of the Kurdish Ay family, sought contact with the lower echelon of the criminal world in Verona to take over the distribution. The Veronian underworld was and is secure for the dealers from Turkey: it is not seeking to acquire real power.

The current route to Italy is partly by sea and partly by air. Milan is still the first clear city of destination, from where the flow branches out to the south. Another route runs to the Iberian Peninsula. With the sea route, the driver takes the truck in which the drugs have been concealed in Istanbul through customs to a ship. He then flies to Trieste to pick up the truck again. So many trucks with containers make this journey that they can never possibly all be checked. Some Nigerians started air courier services a few years ago. For the bosses, the deployment of such an interim chain is functional, as if the police intercept a courier they never get further than the Africans. As Africans are stigmatised as potential drug couriers in several parts of the world, however, they run a higher risk of being searched.

The greatest contribution the Italian police and judicial authorities have made to the fight against Turkish drug trafficking is fiscal investigation. The Italians are good at that, even though they often inwardly fume at the strict banking secrecy of countries such as Switzerland. The best-known case was a German-Italian co-production: Operation Mozart. The main characters were the Dilek family (including the father, Mustecabi), who ran a small office in Milan where, until 1994, they laundered the earnings from Turkish drug trafficking generated in Italy, Germany, Spain, the Netherlands and also sometimes Yugoslavia, England and Switzerland. In Italy, the great laundering king Mustafa Sakiroğlu also operated, while running a legitimate trade agency. Sakiroğlu, who comes from a prominent Turkish family, was initially unwilling to go into business with the simple Dilek, with whom all the heroin dealers did business. But his own network had come under pressure, as the war in Yugoslavia was obstructing transports and because, as he stated to the Italian judge, reliable money couriers were becoming increasingly difficult to find. Italian customers were also bad payers and one of his partners had been arrested in Germany. There was nothing for it but to start working from Milan with Dilek and with the West Star trading company in Munich. Sakiroğlu's right-hand man was originally a car mechanic and the transport of money from Italy in plastic bags, shoeboxes and suitcases took place in concealed compartments he had prepared. His partner Dilek was interesting because he made use of an ingenious laundering system, which is nowadays known as informal or underground banking. This system relied on trust within one and the same family at both ends, Munich and Istanbul, of all transactions and distinguished itself from other systems by having no written record, as no money was actually sent over. Debts to dealers and creditors were paid locally in cash.

In court decisions in Germany in 1995 and in Italy in 1996, eight people were convicted. Cleverly, Sakiroğlu took a cooperative attitude with the Italian police and provided them with just enough information to get away with it. It was through him and other crown witnesses that the Italian police and judicial authorities were gradually able to form an image of the Turkish underworld. They learned to recognise its major role in business and laundering in the Grand Bazaar in Istanbul, a popular international tourist attraction.

*

In accordance with the Dutch Data Protection Act, all police documentation and, in particular, information from the Criminal Intelligence Service on individuals in the Netherlands is destroyed after a certain time. From the point of view of privacy protection this may be justified, but for historians it is nothing less than a disaster, as there is no original material to be found in the archives.

When, in 1995, the Northern and Eastern Netherlands Interregional Investigation Team began a study of Turkish criminal factions, one of the objectives was to gather together all experience the police had gained in more than twenty years of Turkish cases. An attempt at an inventory had been made earlier, when it had become clear how much attention the police had already devoted to serious crimes in Turkish and Kurdish circles. In 1993, an inventory with the name 'Turkish criminal factions' by the investigation service in Rotterdam-Rijnmond had revealed twelve criminal groups that fulfilled the list of characteristics the police had used since 1987 to identify organised crime – and only sixteen of the twenty-five police regions had participated in this enquiry.

Since 1987, Turkish organised crime has been given high investigative priority in the Netherlands. That can be explained by three extraordinary circumstances. The first is that Turkish organisations generally deal in heroin and the police always take the hardest approach to this drug. As the wholesaling of heroin has been chiefly in their hands since 1980, the investigative bodies continually come across Turkish and Kurdish organisations in their investigations. Secondly, the level of violence in this circle is exceptionally high by Dutch standards. The number of murders and kidnappings is several times the rate that could be expected based on their proportion in the total Dutch population. An investigation into murders attributable to organised crime carried out by the National Criminal Intelligence Service in 1994 showed that, of thirty-one victims, nine were of Turkish origin – and in seven of the nine cases the Turkish culprits were known. The third reason is that Turkish and Kurdish organised crime sometimes also has a political aspect. The problem of extortion among Kurds, for example, is largely caused by groups seeking money for political or military goals and raises such cases to a higher position in the police's priority list. Some Turks in the Netherlands blame the relatively great attention on the distortion of all immigrant crime by the media or on racist prejudices among the police and the judicial authorities. To whatever extent that may be true, the three aforementioned aspects are enough in themselves to explain the relatively large police interest.

In 1996, the study by the Northern and Eastern Netherlands Interregional Investigation Team managed to discover no fewer than forty-two cases from preceding years, the first of which dated from 1985. Those cases sometimes concerned offences such as arms dealing, fraud and armed robbery, but they all entailed drug trafficking. The dealers and their organisations appeared to be active throughout the Netherlands, including all the provincial towns. A concentration of activities could be identified in provinces and towns where a lot of Turks and Kurds lived, but first and foremost they had sought out places where the market was established. This and other police investigations into drug transport and wholesaling, not retail, were given names such as Dragoon, Echo, Jan the Turk and Blue Fin.

The files from older cases have been destroyed, which makes accurate reconstruction impossible. But the detectives and members of the Public Prosecutions Department who were involved remember things. R.Weijenburg, who worked for the National Criminal Intelligence Service on many international drug cases and wrote a book about his experiences, tells how the Dutch police took rather a long time to notice the change in positions, as they were used to heroin being a Chinese concern. In the early 1980s, however, they finally realised that the Turks had taken over the business. From then onwards, Oflu Ismail (Ismail Hacisüleymanoğlu), the big boss who had been 'given' the Netherlands at the *babas*' conference in Sofia in 1980, was known to the Dutch police, after the American DEA sent them a report on him. The police in Tiel observed an international drivers' restaurant where a lot of trucks from Turkey called in. The owner was in contact with Oflu Ismail and his uncle, the big boss Osman, who alternated between homes in London and Amsterdam. Osman came from the casino world in Turkey, owned his own plane and ran a restaurant in Amsterdam. The British Intelligence Service also had some information on the contacts Oflu and his uncle had with the Grey Wolves, but at the Dutch National Criminal Intelligence Service that was covered by the terrorism department, which did not share its information with other branches of the police organisation. It therefore took a long time before anyone became aware of the true calibre of this *baba*.

One detective remembers that, in 1983, a team more or less by accident bumped into a group of people in Amstelveen that, in retrospect, turned out to consist of prominent figures from the Turkish underworld.

Oflu was among them, plus another well-known figure called Fevzi Öz. 'We had them all!' said this detective, but at the time the police didn't realise who they were and even less what a central role the Netherlands played in the movements of Turkish drug traffickers in Europe. A preliminary enquiry was started into Oflu's movements, which unexpectedly generated a surprising amount of material for the police. Oflu turned out to have started his activities in the Netherlands as far back as 1977, with his base in Amsterdam. The major investigative method at that time – as it still is – was tapping telephone conversations. More and more new international business relations came to light that no policeman in Europe had ever heard of. The police in Ede pulled out all the stops for this investigation: a team extra was set up including detectives from Ede, Arnhem, Renkum and Zwolle. From there, an international cooperation was set up with the German and Austrian authorities, who kept an eye on the part of the Balkan route in their own territory. As the headquarters of this team was in the border town between Yugoslavia and Austria, this was named the Spielfeld investigation.

Shortly afterwards, a national 'Turk team' was established, stationed in Utrecht, and it was decided to keep the preliminary enquiry open long enough to be able to develop new sidelines, which in turn led to separate preliminary enquiries. It is not permitted to keep a case open for three years without arresting the suspect or, at least, informing them of the investigation, but in those years, the judges let a lot of things pass without asking awkward questions and there were hardly any lawyers aware of what was going on who made any fuss about it in court. The impression the Spielfeld investigation left on the members of the team was one of a gigantic international organisation, in which an extraordinary number of criminals were involved. That was, incidentally, exactly the image the Drug Enforcement Administration in the U.S. had tried to get across in the Netherlands. Such a large organisation had never before been detected in the underworld of the Netherlands and those who had seen the descriptions of these Turkish organisations could do nothing but shrug in response to claims by criminologists who publicly declared that there was no organised crime in the country.

The Oflu case itself was closed unsatisfactorily for the Dutch investigative bodies in 1988. There was no evidence strong enough in the Netherlands to arrest him and Italy requested his extradition, as they had gathered sufficient evidence against him concerning, amongst other things, large-scale drug trafficking. On 20 February 1987, Oflu was arrested and taken to a detention centre in Maastricht. From there he was extradited to Italy, where he was convicted and is still serving a sentence in the prison in Milan, which will run, in principle, until 2012. In Italy, Oflu Ismail is known to police and the judicial authorities as an extremely sly fox. No-one doubts that he still exercises power in the underworld in true Mafia style from prison. He is now making grateful use of the opportunities Italian criminal law offers for cooperative witnesses to slightly improve his position.

So much expertise has gradually been acquired that, of all the European countries, the Dutch police have probably gained the most insight into the Turkish and Kurdish criminal organisations. In the meantime, though, the police were bothered by the fact that they were forced to pursue the same ethnic minority all the time in their investigation into organised crime. In daily practice, they saw that their efforts were to little avail, as the market for heroin simply continued to exist; the vacancy created when one dealer was arrested was rapidly filled by others. The mutual discussions of the situation led to 'Turk fatigue'. This malaise was brought to light when, in September 1995, during hearings in the Dutch Upper House, a team of criminologists led by Professor Cyrille Fijnaut testified for the Parliamentary Enquiry Committee on Investigative Methods on the relatively large involvement of some ethnic groups in the Netherlands in international drug trafficking. Having examined the large quantities of police material, which chiefly concerned Amsterdam, Arnhem and Nijmegen, the criminologists had been impressed by the number of Turks and Kurds involved in this trafficking. At the time, one of them (also one of the authors of this book), Professor Frank Bovenkerk, testified that, locally, 'several tens of percents' of the adult males in these ethnic groups were involved in drug trafficking. He went on to state that Turkish political movements and even people occupying prominent positions in the Turkish government also played a role in organised crime. This prompted heavy protest on the part of the Turks in the Netherlands and the Turkish ambassador lodged a complaint: he asked the Dutch Minister of Internal Affairs to silence this professor. Since then, however, there has been broad social discussion within Turkish and Kurdish circles in the Netherlands concerning this problem, as, however offensive Bovenkerk's announcement of the facts may have been, there was, indeed, a considerable problem.

Since the second half of the 1980s, police investigative work has been largely focused on other aspects of Turkish and Kurdish organised crime. Investigation has been carried out into the illegal employment of workers from Turkey in market gardening, for example, whereby the employers concerned are also arrested. It certainly made a number of Turkish illegal contractors rich. There is also a clampdown on Turkish textile companies that undercut because they deploy illegal workers, but in this sector hardly any connection has been established with organised crime and the police therefore don't really take the illegal sweatshops into account. Human trafficking, in the form of smuggling in people for payment, who then request asylum, on the other hand, is counted.

After 2000, organised crime reared its head in trading in women and prostitution. It seems to have started in Germany. This involves higher-level organisation; few brothels are owned by Turkish criminals and even fewer pimps are Turkish. The latest development, in the period since 2005, is that Turkish criminals are now specialising in the debt-collecting sector for Dutch drugs crime networks and investing criminal proceeds in property. They take advantage of their violent reputation in the underworld, which has since become multicultural.

The big problem is, above all, how the police, the judicial authorities and the National Security Service should tackle the criminal manifestations of Dutch branches of Turkish political factions. The left-wing Dev-Sol movement commits extortion and its victims are afraid to complain. The PKK manifests itself similarly: it also demands financial contributions. Right-wing political factions also commit violence. And they are involved in drug trafficking. Investigative journalists Stella Braam and Mehmet Ülger wrote a report on the Dutch branch of this international movement, which attracted a great deal of attention because the authors were obliged to go into hiding after threats from those same Grey Wolves.

In 2001, this prompted the Amsterdam police to conduct a large-scale investigation into the nature and scope of the Grey Wolves in the Netherlands. Their violent conduct had been demonstrated earlier in a police investigation in 1992-1993 into heroin trafficking and arms deliveries involving Servet Yilmaz, a gym owner, and Tahsin Kesici, a former policeman from the Dutch force in Utrecht. These same two were now threatening journalists. In 1999, the political branch of the Grey Wolves, the MHP, had joined the coalition in the Turkish parliament and this caused a resurgence of popularity among young Turks in the Netherlands. On 28 November 2000, the Grey Wolves' political organisation, which had adopted the name Turkish Federation in the Netherlands, was dismantled by the Dutch authorities; eighty-seven suspects were arrested. The organisation proved to be only part of a network throughout Europe involved in various crimes: murder, extortion, organising prostitution, human smuggling, political infiltration, kidnapping, embezzlement of subsidy funds, marriages of convenience, mortgage fraud and organising bakery cartels, to name a few. One meeting point was the clubhouse of the Turkiyemspor football club in Utrecht, whose founder, Imaç, was to be murdered in 2007, most probably because of a drug deal that went wrong. The leader, Yilmaz, was sentenced to a long stretch in prison, but managed to escape in 2006. His father had died in a hospital in Turkey and the judicial authorities let him go if he would return voluntarily. Which he did not.

*

In January 1997, the president of the seventeenth criminal division of the Frankfurts Landsgericht in Germany, Rolf Schalben, made the striking remark that some minor heroin dealers he had just sentenced were protected by the Turkish government. In his judgement, Schalben stated that the Senoğlu and Baybaşin families more or less controlled the heroin trade in Germany and that this was partly made possible due to 'excellent connections with the Turkish government and even personal contact with a female minister'. The latter could only be one person and, when asked, Schalben named her: Mrs Çiller. Mrs Çiller immediately responded with a categorical denial and a high-ranking civil servant in Ankara expressed the threat that the cooperation between the Turkish and German authorities in their struggle against the drugs mafia could be seriously damaged by this kind of rash statement. The case also received attention on German television, showing a map of Turkey in the background with the star, the half-moon and a heroin syringe. The response from the government in Ankara was 'We will not allow the respect of our state and our flag to be trampled underfoot.'

The German police forces had been aware for some time of the existence of extensive drug networks and the political connections that played a role in them. In 1979, a senator for the Islamic Justice Party, Halit

Kahraman, was arrested in Duisburg; his drug-smuggling earned him eight years in prison. In this case, there turned out to be a drug route to the 'heroin king of Berlin', Ismael Zakir, and his cousin Niyazi. Back in 1979, one writer had already provided an overview of the 'Turkish ants' who imported drugs, which showed how much was already known at that time about the political connections. His article was accompanied by a photograph of Necmettin Erbakan, the later prime minister of Turkey, with a caption stating that he was suspected of drug trafficking. The leit-motif of this piece was that all political parties in Turkey who needed money for activities that wouldn't bear examination had started engaging in drug trafficking. Nothing has ever been proven against Erbakan.

A German operation in 1984, dubbed Corncob, revealed for the first time that Turkish organisations were also becoming organised in Europe. In the same operation a number of prominent Grey Wolves who were officially wanted by Turkey, including Oral Çelik and Abdullah Çatli, turned out to have appeared on the scene in Europe as heroin traffickers. Various police reports indicated that such groups also maintained contact with people from the Turkish diplomatic service.

In the 1990s, Germany became aware of the dangers of political extremism. Among the two and a half million people in Germany of Turkish origin, all kinds of political tendencies to both the left and right emerged, giving the impression that internal Turkish political relations had been exported in a polarised form. In September 1996, the Polizeillicher Staatsschutz department of the Bundeskriminalamt in Meckenheim produced an overview of potentially dangerous organisations, in which fifty-six names of associations of varying sizes were named. This overview showed that the Turkish minority, of which roughly a quarter are Kurds, was socially poorly integrated and only very few of the second and third generations proved to go on to university and acquire higher social functions. A business class has, however, emerged in the meantime: in 1997, a kind of portrait gallery of the top ten business people of Turkish origin in Germany, written by two television journalists, went straight to the top of the bestseller list in Turkey.

The Turks have still not penetrated the core of German civil society, however. They exhibit the traits of people living in the diaspora and, partly for that reason, are drawn to adopting extreme political and religious viewpoints. By banning the Kurdish PKK as a political party, the German government backed the Turkish government. This is relevant because it also colours the German police's vision of today's problem of drug trafficking and organised crime. In their eyes, this is virtually exclusively a Kurdish affair, with the revenue flowing into the PKK terrorist organisation. Extortion by Kurds for the purposes of this organisation is also a major problem in Germany. German parents and teachers are even warned of Kurdish children disappearing to camps in concealed places in Germany, where they will be trained as terrorists. The children generally go voluntarily and are instructed in sport, culture and ideological education. A minority of them then go on to Syria or Turkey for guerrilla training.

The German cooperation with the Turkish police can be seen as comparatively good. That also applies to a large-scale, highly labour-intensive scientific project by the BKA (the German police's scientific department) called Anadolu, which describes the 'families' of the eight major heroin smuggling bosses operating in Germany. These are all Kurdish families originating from the poorest parts of Turkey. They are all extremely large, consisting of dozens and even hundreds of people. As a result of their mutual origin from the same tribes, villages and families, they can protect themselves from the outside world and implement a duty of silence. This type of discovery produces a different interpretation from that in the Netherlands, for example, where the political activities of the PKK are not prohibited and where organised crime factions have been observed with connections with ultra-right politics. In the meantime, the PKK protests against this portrayal of the facts. In its struggle to gain recognition by the German government and to show to the outside world that he had nothing to do with drug trafficking, the leader of the PKK, Abdullah Öcalan, even offered to overpower the major drug bosses and hand them over to Germany in exchange for political recognition.

*

The Belgian government also appears to be preoccupied with the question of whether or not the PKK, when committing crime, should be approached as a criminal organisation. It has been established that Belgium houses the headquarters of the PKK in Europe. In its penal policy, Belgium gains both the approval of the Turkish government and the disapproval of the Turkish minority in Belgium; the Turkish government is always enthusiastic when Kurdish political activities are tackled.

In September 1996, a television channel broadcasting Kurdish propaganda throughout Western Europe was dismantled. This was Med-TV and the police operation in which Belgium and Turkey cooperated was given the code name Sputnik. The Belgian police raided the station because it had reason to believe it was being financed partly with money deposited in a Luxembourg bank account, which reputedly came from both extortion and trafficking in arms, drugs and people. When arrests were made at various addresses, Kurds were apprehended and the Turkish government was delighted; after all, the Kurdish emigrants were all under the influence of PKK propaganda, weren't they? The German government supported this commendation. In Germany, the Turks and Kurds have been unjustifiably forced to experience the import of a Turkish political conflict to Western Europe. All those arrested in Belgium were later released.

Shortly afterwards, in November 1996, in the middle of the woods in Zurendaal, in Belgian Limburg, a PKK 'ideological training camp' was cleared out. Of the thirty-six Kurdish young men who were arrested, but immediately released, most turned out to come from Germany and were being trained in the camp for the armed struggle against Turkey. Some of them had already been reported missing by their parents. They had proved susceptible to PKK propaganda, run away from school and reported to the camp without telling their parents. No arms were found in the camp in the Zurendaal woods, but it was just a stone's throw from the firing range of the Belgian factory manufacturing FN brand arms. The leader of the police team executing the operation said that from the hand-written 'last letters' from the young men to their parents, it was clear that they were prepared for no less than suicide operations. The inhabitants of the rural community were flabbergasted. 'Fancy the PKK being in such a peaceful community as ours!' said the mayor. 'It's unbelievable.' The Kurdish community, incidentally, claimed that it was nothing more than a 'folk art meeting', but that convinced nobody.

Serious criticism had earlier been levelled at the Belgian police, or more specifically the Belgian gendarmerie, by the Turkish and Kurdish communities in the country for having used 'unconventional' investigative methods. On 1 July 1996, the Flemish journalist Walter de Bock revealed in the daily newspaper *Morgen* that, in 1994, the gendarmerie had screened the entire population originating from Turkey to determine who among them should be considered potential criminals. Following this report, the Upper House Commission for Justice invited Minister of Justice De Clerck to answer the following questions: 'On what legal grounds had the population register been used as an investigative register for criminal offices?', 'Had this not seriously violated the right of privacy?' and 'Should the gendarmerie's methods be seen as a form of racism and discrimination?' The most awkward question for the minister was how it was possible that he, as the national magistrate who should grant permission for such sensitive action, had not been aware of it in time.

The head of the gendarmerie leading all investigations into Turkish criminal factions in Belgium, Captain Juan Corriat, had given the investigation the name Rebelle in honour of the great reformer of the Turkish state, Atatürk, who, according to Corriat, had carried the nickname of 'rebel'.* Corriat is the spider in the web in all 'Turkish affairs' in the country and told us in 1997 that he was involved in one way or another in as many as a hundred and twenty criminal cases in this sphere every year. The approach he had chosen of using population registers appears to be theoretically well grounded. In all police investigation into organised gangs, such as those of drug smugglers, in his view the police are far too dependent on unreliable informers from the underworld itself. The police receive the most wonderful tip-offs that, in retrospect, turn out to have been nothing more than a diversion, while the big business was being carried out elsewhere. Other tips serve no purpose other than to put a competitor under suspicion and eliminate him. There is also the additional ethical problem of whether you should pay criminals for grassing. 'I wanted to develop a system of information that would not rely on dubious characters,' said Corriat. 'I wanted to tap an independent, objective information source.'

Ninety percent of all confiscated drugs in Belgium are 'brown', which means that Turkish criminal organisations control the market entirely. It is also known that Turkish crime mobs are engaged in illegal arms dealing – the serial numbers are removed from firearms by giving them a 'metal bath' – extortion, laundering money and human trafficking. A chain of Turkish bakers in Ghent was a distressing example of human trafficking. They transported children locked up in containers on a truck from Turkey to Belgium, where they were put to work in appalling conditions.

---

* This nickname is unknown to us.

The police in other Northern European countries have long been in possession of crime profiles like those he compiled in his Rebelle investigation, is Corriat's opinion. What's more, in those countries there is plenty of scientific documentation of empirical investigation into the social structure of ethnic population groups. There is hardly any of that kind of documentation in Belgium. 'What I actually wanted to do with my Rebelle investigation was nothing other than lay the foundation for such knowledge,' said Corriat. 'If police people want to investigate such a specific group, they should be aware of a number of basic facts. These are what my method generates. I do, indeed, use the population register, but also other databases, to get hold of simple demographic data. I'm not interested in all personal data, by any means. Apart from which, after producing our statistics, we destroyed the basic material.' The investigation has shown Corriat where most of the Turks in Belgium live and work and from which parts of Turkey the various communities come. 'A relatively large proportion of Turks living in Brussels come from Diyarbakir and, in Limburg, a lot of the Turks come from Gaziantep. We know that a relatively large number of smugglers come from these two places. Such information is important. And the fact that truck drivers with contraband on board often come from Kilis is something those involved in investigations should know.'

The criticism of Corriat's method is chiefly that it brands certain categories as 'potentially criminal'. Corriat goes even further than that by also screening these 'risk groups' in other databases and finally finding out for which members of these groups there is concrete criminal data already available. This operation generates the targets eligible for criminal investigation. Corriat told us that this has made it possible to identify twelve criminal Turkish family factions in Belgium. Where drug trafficking is concerned, the Turkish families in Belgium, too, restrict themselves to wholesaling. They leave the sale to individual customers to Italian dealers, who are better integrated in the country and more able to assess the risks.

Whether the police are allowed to use such general registers as the population register is also disputed in police circles, but Corriat sticks to his guns. 'Based on our knowledge, police people have made the effort to learn the Turkish language. Gendarmerie officers have established contact with key figures in the Turkish community,' he says. 'We are gaining the trust of these people, for instance with a specially designed video on the effects of heroin; what it would do to their children, for example.' But all these positive effects were wiped out by the riot that followed the revelation of his strategy in the newspaper. Prominent members of the Turkish and Kurdish communities responded indignantly and the issue drew international attention. Corriat was furious: he is convinced the information was leaked to the newspaper by a rival police force prompted by jealousy, as they had been granted fewer authorities in investigating Turkish organised crime and had there received less attention.

*

At the end of October 1996, the British Home Office minister, Tom Sackville, returned from an official visit to Ankara. At London's Heathrow airport, he responded to reporters' questions that eighty percent of the heroin intercepted by the British customs came from Turkey. He had already said exactly the same thing to the Turkish press in Ankara, for whom it was no surprise. Announcing something like that in public and to the world press, however, was considered an affront. The Turkish minister of home affairs was insulted and responded by saying he had access to better figures than Sackville. Turkey had just discovered new smuggling routes to the north, via Russia, and to the south, via Syria, he said, which would make the percentage coming via Turkey far lower. The Turkish ambassador and spokespeople from the Turkish Cypriot communities in England also registered their protest. The fact that it was a minister who had expressed these accusations did, of course, have more impact, but the Turkish objections were identical to their response to the statement by the Frankfurt judge two months earlier concerning the involvement of Mrs Çiller in organised crime and those to the revelations before the Parliamentary Commission on Investigative Methods in September 1995 in the Netherlands.

For the Turkish police, a remark like Sackville's is very irritating. The head of the drugs squad said, 'What we have said to England is: Let's take a look at our country's borders. Turkey borders on problematic countries such as Russia, Armenia, Iran, Iraq and Syria. We also have enormous terrorist problems with the PKK. We are fighting a hard battle in this situation. But England? Surely it can check its own borders? If it's true that heroin is being sent from Turkey, then why aren't they intercepting it at their own border? They say that, as a developed country, they are fighting the battle against drugs professionally – so why aren't they capable of intercepting more drugs?' On the other hand, for the British it is annoying that so many drugs still get into the country supplied by Turkish and Kurdish dealers, all the more so since the British government donated $5 million to the Turkish government to help in its battle against drug trafficking. But in May 1997, Derek Plumby, the British Ministry of Foreign Affairs' coordinator of international drug affairs, arrived to patch up the relationships and, in particular, restore the police cooperation.

For the Turkish and Kurdish drug traffickers, the United Kingdom is an appealing market because the drug prices are so high. As in all European countries, dealers have realised that they can use the infrastructure of an established Turkish Cypriot migrant group: cafés, kebab takeaways and drinking and gambling joints.

England's immigration history is slightly different from that in the rest of Europe, as there was no migrant workers system. A total of 250-300,000 people with a Turkish background now live in North and Northeast London and in scattered 'communities' (the British always think about their immigrants in communities) formed in the 1960s and 1970s through immigration from or via Cyprus. The Turkish Cypriot immigrants have a name for being good at business; many are successful restaurant owners, for example. Until the minister announced it so plainly, the British public therefore didn't immediately think of Turks or Cypriots in connection with the import of heroin. It was known that the Chinese had imported small quantities, but that was primarily for their own communities; the state of affairs in that respect was similar to the opium dens of Amsterdam in the 1960s. The British market was conquered by the Pakistanis, whose community in Great Britain was larger and longer established, and also chiefly by the Dutch, who transported the drugs over the Channel in trucks and cars.

The public, however, is only aware of the visible level of the street dealers: white and black British and Chinese. The Turks and Cypriots in drug trafficking, however, are the wholesalers, as they are elsewhere in Europe. A big drug boss in England, David Telli, was sentenced to twenty years in prison in 1995, later reduced to eighteen on appeal, after British customs found £10 million worth of heroin in a horsebox arriving by ferry. Telli is a British citizen with an anglicised name; he was originally called David Telliaĝaoĝlu. He was portrayed in the media as an example of a modern, professional trader who, instead of sending his profits to

Turkey, invested them via Scottish and Northern Cypriot banks. The way the British police see it is that there is a generation of Turkish Cypriot businessmen who became rich through drug trafficking and are now investing in legitimate companies: cafés, bars, wholesaling companies. The Bank of England began an offensive against the numerous Turkish and Cypriot banks in England used for laundering drug money. The first bank to be closed, in October 1996, was the Cyprus Credit Bank, owned by the Boyaci family, which is related to Rauf Denktaş, then president of the (unrecognised) Turkish Cypriot Republic. The Susurluk incident in 1996 also aroused British police and customs' interest in Turkish drug smugglers.

A number of murders and attacks on Kurdish business people have attracted a great deal of attention in England. There was one famous case in 1995: the Kurd Nafiz Bostanci, a political refugee who helped found the Halkevi Kurdish and Turkish Community Centre in Stoke Newington, North London, had appeared on British television to complain about human rights abuses in Turkey. He was subsequently threatened so often that he had had a special steel door fitted to his shop. One evening, he was closing up outside the shop. Stooping to pick up the keys he had just dropped, he heard shots. The bullets whizzed over his head, sparing Bostanci's life. The affair was widely reported on in the English press, as the Turkish secret service (MIT) was purported to be behind the attack.

Scotland Yard's special branch is responsible for the political side of these affairs, chiefly the PKK and Dev-Sol. As in other countries, the police have set up an operation to tackle the extortion problem, but Turks and Kurds hardly ever lodge complaints. Right-wing criminal factions are also acknowledged as enemies. Specialists in the British police are unable to detect much in the way of idealism in the activities of the *ülkücü,* which literally means idealists. According to a Turkish expert in the British police, they are 'criminals doing nothing other than lining their own pockets'.

According to the National Crime Squad, since the second half of the 1990s ninety percent of the heroin trafficking has been carried out through the clan of the Baybaşin family, from Lice in southeast Turkey (see Chapter 7). After clan boss Huseyin Baybaşin started a life sentence in a Dutch prison, the leadership seems to have been transferred to his brother Abdullah, who operated from North London. From his wheelchair – he was shot and crippled in an Amsterdam bar in the 1990s – he ran a sizeable gang, sixteen members of which were sentenced in 2006 to up to fifteen years for blackmail, arson, firearms offences and conspiring to supply heroin. What makes Abdullah's story interesting is the question of how he managed to gain legal status in England after having entered the country from the Netherlands in 1995 with false papers and after having been arrested for the first time in 1998. According to information received by the *Guardian*, Baybaşin had done a deal with MI5 or one of the other secret services and reciprocated by keeping a close eye on PKK activists in the Kurdish community. In 2006, though, Abdullah was arrested, nevertheless, and sentenced to twenty-two years in prison.

The Turkish Police and International Cooperation

Turkey treats drug trafficking as a crime against humanity and each phase of the production process up to and including sale to the consumer and laundering the proceeds is, in principle, a punishable offence. There is no distinction made between hard and soft drugs. The maximum punishment was recently increased from six to twenty years in prison and the cases are heard in special courts for state security. One main reason for taking drug trafficking so seriously is that the government believes the revenue provides the basis for terrorist activities against the Turkish state, or, more specifically, by the PKK and, since 2001, naturally, also international terrorism.

Turkey has two police forces: the national police, the Emniyet Genel Müdürlüğü, who operate in urban areas, and the gendarmerie, which patrols rural areas. The gendarmerie is largely founded on a military structure and comes under not only the Ministry of Home Affairs but also the military chief of staff. The national police are part of the Ministry of Internal Affairs; they include the 'smuggling and organised crime' department. Then there are the Turkish coastguards, charged with the task of investigating smuggling by sea. The policy of the drugs section of the smuggling department of the police in Ankara was explained to us by two successive heads of the department. The point of departure for their analysis was that Turkey is essentially confronted with the same problems as all European countries through which the Balkan route runs and that only international cooperation between police forces on an equal basis is effective. One also felt the critics applied double standards to the way Turkey approaches the issue. A number of Turkish officials have since started a diplomatic offensive within the international police world to explain their policy.

Since the regulation of the early 1970s, no more illegal opium comes from Turkey. Where cannabis cultivation is concerned, this too is only permitted in eighteen districts, for medical use and under strict supervision of the Ministry of Agriculture, and no breaches have been detected in the restriction of these activities. Turkey functions as a transit country for illegal heroin and cannabis. The production of illegal heroin takes place in countries to the east of Turkey, its consumption in the countries to the west. As in the rest of Europe, the Turkish police are doing their best to combat smuggling. Judging by the number of kilos of heroin confiscated, they are succeeding: In the top year of 1995, this number was higher than in all other countries along the Balkan route put together. Instead of criticising Turkey, police forces in Europe should be grateful for the fact that Turkey actually acts as a shield, feel the Turkish police. Colleagues in those other countries, on the other hand, feel that the chance of intercepting large shipments is also greater because Turkey only has to observe one or two main suspects while, after Istanbul, the whole thing fans out westwards into smaller transport arteries with a lot of smaller quantities per transport.

In any event, the Turkish police confiscate thousands of kilos a year and the repeated accusations that eighty to ninety percent of all heroin confiscated in Western Europe comes from Turkey therefore causes bad feelings: Why then don't the bodies controlling the borders of those countries stop more transports? Furthermore, Turkey can't be blamed now branches of the Balkan route have been discovered that don't run through Turkey at all: those from Afghanistan northwards via the Black Sea and through the former Soviet Union to Poland and the route via Syria, Lebanon, Southern Cyprus, Greece and onwards.

Western Europeans always claim that the drugs are brought into their country from Turkey, but the reverse is equally true. To manufacture heroin you need not only opium but also acetic anhydride and this substance is transported from west to east. It is relatively easy to buy acetic acid and claim it is being used in the textile or paint industry. It then goes through customs with the aid of forged papers or it is first transported through so many countries before reaching Turkey that it is no longer possible to trace the vendor. To tackle this problem, Germany and other countries producing this acid should be as sensitive to events concerning the sale and transport of the substance as they are with opium. There is no investigation into the background of companies ordering the acid. Interviewed in 1997, the head of the smuggling department,

Çalişkan, huffily brought up the fact that when he approached his foreign colleagues on the matter, the counter-argument was always that there is no point in checking chemical companies because the customer then switches to countries such as Russia or China, where you can buy such substances more easily.

Another problem is that cocaine and chemical drugs such as ecstasy and Captagon, a Dutch medicine known as a typical drug for pimps, come into Turkey from Europe. The Netherlands, in particular, is famous as a supplier of ecstasy, a lot of which is also currently confiscated at the border between Bulgaria and Turkey. This drug is partly destined for the Turkish market, but it is also transported from there to Arabic countries, for example; here again, Turkey is in the awkward position of being geographically at the centre of the international traffic.

Since the 1980s, Turkey has shown itself prepared to cooperate internationally with other police forces. It started with Italy and these days is proceeding well with the Netherlands and Germany. They are also now cooperating fully with the United States, as we will see further on from the major operation with the *Kismetim-1* in the Mediterranean. Bilateral conventions have been concluded with a growing number of countries and there are police liaison officers stationed on both sides to concretise the cooperation.

Admittedly, Turkish politicians have been rather slow in formulating regulations for the financial side of the problem, but they are now cooperating in introducing legislation against laundering money obtained through drug trafficking. The confiscation of such illegally obtained profits was made possible by law in 1996. This law also stipulates that Turkey can use the investigative method of controlled supply, which the police in other countries had pressed so hard for. Since the mid-1990s, the Turkish police have also been enthusiastically cooperating in an international project aimed at dismantling prominent Kurdish and Turkish drugs families, the members of which appear in all kinds of countries. Since it became legally permissible in 1998, the enthusiasm of the Turkish police has gone so far that they insist on applying the controversial investigative method of controlled supply – following the trucks containing the drugs along the Balkan route without intervening, with the intention of catching the bosses on delivery at the end – whereas people in Europe have become wary of using the method. With each police investigation, all the Balkan countries have to be convinced and then the countries in Western

Europe. When trucks from Turkey are stopped in Edirne at the border with Bulgaria, the smugglers switch to the route via Greece. In that event, the case is handled by the American Drugs Enforcement Administration in Athens.

The fact that various governments and police forces in Europe appear to underestimate the enormous problem of PKK terrorism prompts criticism from the Turkish side. European governments see the PKK as a political problem, but in Turkey the PKK is considered to be nothing other than a terrorist organisation. The Netherlands, in particular, has got itself into Turkey's bad books by allowing the Kurdish parliament in exile to gather on Dutch soil. The former head of the drugs squad, Yilmaz, asked us to quote him literally: 'We as police officers are fully aware that drugs and terrorism are interdependent. In our opinion, we are the victims of terrorism and we feel Europe – and the Netherlands in particular – are not favourably disposed towards the Turkish state. What are we supposed to do if the Netherlands feels it should tolerate terrorist factions such as the PKK? There are a hundred and fifty thousand police officers in the whole of Turkey. I assure you that, if asked, a hundred and forty thousand of them would say that the transport of drugs should then be allowed unhindered into the Netherlands and other European countries!'

Çalişkan feels that European countries do not deal properly with the Turkish smugglers they arrest. The smuggler Hüseyin Baybaşin was arrested in the Netherlands and the judicial authorities refuse to extradite him. 'Everything that man says in the Netherlands, even to the press, is assumed to be true,' he complained. 'That man is an international smuggler, for goodness sake; he's been in prison in Turkey and then for another six years in England. They believe that man and nobody listens to us. What kind of nonsense is that? Baybaşin shows a photograph of a dinner he happened to be at, for example, with a governor and a security official and says: "I worked with those people." The media swallow that hook, line and sinker and everybody, even a judge in Europe, believes him. He says: "I'm a Kurd, so I'll be murdered immediately if I go back to Turkey." People believe him. But something like that isn't possible. The man will simply be tried and have to serve his sentence.'

In Baybaşin's own account, which is dealt with in Chapter 7, we will see that drug traffickers are, without doubt, supporting the Kurdish independence movement. The police, like all Turkish civil servants, are convinced the PKK itself is also directly involved in drug trafficking. The difficulty is that, to date, this has never yet been incontrovertibly proved and some other countries refuse to believe the Turkish government's categorical statement that the PKK deals in drugs without supporting evidence. That galls them.

In mid-March 1997, Turkish governmental officials triumphantly announced that a recent report by the American Ministry of Foreign Affairs on drug control confirmed the Turkish government's theory concerning the PKK as a criminal organisation. This was the *International Narcotics Control Strategy Report* of March 1997. Page 418 of the report states, 'According to Turkish sources, smuggling narcotics through Turkey to Western Europe has become a major revenue source for the Kurdish Workers' Party (PKK), a terrorist organization. European law enforcement officials in six countries conducted raids on PKK-linked Kurdish drug distribution networks.' As it also states, however, that the information comes from Turkish sources, the report can't be seen as independent evidence. This looks suspiciously like what is referred to in police circles as a U-construction: you plant information somewhere and then get it back from the same body or another body. The investigation of the drug network in six countries, as referred to in the report, suggests six independent sources. It does not establish the fact that the PKK itself is dealing in drugs but confirms that there are connections between drug trafficking organisations and the PKK, which is something slightly different.

Since the end of the 1990s, the international community has been urging Turkey to take serious steps against human smuggling organisations. Istanbul has become a centre for international human smuggling and it is clear that, gradually, this is starting to generate more money than drug trafficking. Countless conferences are organised for the police and courses held, but these don't help much. The scale of the problem – a million people are trying to enter Fort Europe or travel to the New World – and the high costs entailed in the repatriation of illegal migrants make it impossible for Turkey to intervene effectively.

*

The liaison officers from various European countries and the United States DEA working in Istanbul and Ankara, together with their Turkish counterparts, find themselves at the point where various national cultures, political insights and police structures come together to serve one objective: frustrating drug trafficking. When they shared their experience and insight with the present authors, we felt like students at a course in inter-cultural management. One of the barriers that has to be removed is the difference in management style. In one system officers do their best to work together in an orderly fashion in the context of an impersonal bureaucracy; in another, they achieve efficient cooperation based on personal relationships. From the outside, the relationships appear extraor-dinarily formal to the Europeans and Americans, but anyone who wants to get anything done in Turkey does so by building up and carefully main-taining a personal network of contacts. Agreements are complied with not because they are set down like that, but because the relationship has to be maintained.

International cooperation is based on the principle of scratch my back and I'll scratch yours. It is not easy to build a relationship of trust with a police force where the officers are continually being replaced by others. The staffing of the police mechanism relies on political patronage and with every change of power, even when a chief inspector leaves, the top of the entire department is replaced. Another stumbling block is the absence of registration of all kinds of data that is quite usual in the west, but does not exist in Turkey. It is not so, however, that you can't find it at all. A bank account, a telephone number or a name can easily be found in Turkey; not by going to the Chamber of Commerce or the electoral regis-ter, but by finding someone who knows someone else who knows the district, the street, the bank or the family of the person in question. Anthropologists call this form of contact 'friends of friends'. For European police officers stationed in Turkey it is frustrating to find that they are bound by formal rules while, once they are in Turkey, their Turkish colleagues in a certain investigation – interpreters, for example – can easily find out all kinds of information via their network.

Then there is the problem caused by the varying interests and priorities of the police in different countries. Western European police forces are eager to see Turkey taking serious action against human smuggling, but the problem of international refugees is becoming too great for Turkey to deal with. They notice that a lot of investigations into this quickly grind to a halt and no gangs are being rounded up. An English investigator showed his immense frustration. He provided a device for tracing people. 'This device is so sensitive, that we can hear a mouse's heartbeat from outside a steel shipping container,' he said. Months of work were to no avail, however. Turkey, in turn, would like countries such as the Netherlands to be more active in tracing ecstasy being transported via Istanbul to the Middle East. The Turkish police feel they are intercepting vast numbers of kilos of pills at a time. For the Dutch police, however, these quantities are too small to bother about. Much larger shipments travel to the US and Canada.

A serious problem is caused by European distrust of the integrity of the Turkish police. Information on suspects in Europe from the sphere of the PKK is often not supplied, for fear that their family in Turkey will face repercussions. Additionally, thanks to the reports by Amnesty International it is known that the Turkish police torture suspects and the judicial authorities in Western Europe are not keen to see their cases fall apart based on information that turns out to have been obtained under physical duress during interrogation.

All this causes extraordinarily awkward problems. On the European side, there is the tendency to avoid sensitive issues of this type by with-holding information. Confidentiality is, in any event, a standard part of police culture all over the world, but the Turkish police, who want to do their work properly and without reserve, are extra sensitive to this. The Turks show that they feel their personal honour is being tarnished, which is understandable. The Europeans say, however, that in their experience there are leaks from the Turkish police to the underworld.

The fact that such issues can lead to unpleasant confrontations is something the first liaison officer from the Netherlands experienced personally. For a proposed visit by a high-ranking Dutch civil servant, the policeman was given a report indicating which part of the ministry they were going to visit was corrupt and what they had to watch out for. The secretary who was supposed to send the documents had unfortunately sent the envelope to the Turkish embassy in the Netherlands instead of the Dutch embassy in Turkey. The Turks were furious and the Dutch liaison officer was from then on persona non grata in Turkey.

Some European police forces are also dead scared of 'losing their case' because their Turkish colleagues leak information to the press. An Amsterdam detective was hopping mad when, a week before the arrest of the main suspect A. in the Exodus case in Amsterdam West (see Chapter 8), he read details of the crime in the Çinar restaurant in the Turkish press that could only have come from his reports. There are innumerable contacts between the police in Turkey and the press and crime reporters hang around continually in a lot of police stations. In this case, it was even worse, as the gang in question was portrayed in the Turkish newspaper as being involved in the PKK, while they were actually from the other end of the political spectrum, the Grey Wolves.

For some police in Europe, the reason for no longer cooperating with colleagues in Turkey is due to the difference in the way they handle Kurdish and Turkish drug organisations. When the case concerns Kurds and if there are connections with the PKK, then the information flows in: 'The fax just never stops going,' says a team leader from the Amsterdam police who knows the Turkish criminal community in Amsterdam and the surrounding area like no-one else. But if information is requested concerning the connections between Turkish traffickers and the Grey Wolves, which is clearly the case in Amsterdam, then nothing arrives. The team leader doesn't like the idea of being used for the political purposes of the Turkish police. Most police in Europe who have been involved for some time in this area share this type of experience.

Probably the most flagrant case of conning was in 1988. The head of the Turkish drugs squad, Attila Aytek, sent a cordial invitation to the police in the various European countries, including Greece, Italy, Switzerland, Germany and the Netherlands, where certain criminal families were operating who were reputed to have mutual connections in a large network that the Turkish police in Ankara were now going to reveal in their full scope. The initiator had named the operation after himself, Attila.

The Dutch delegate Cees de Bruijne remembers a grand reception, with an unforgettable trip to Cappadocia and an exclusive guided tour of the drug squad chief's large weapon collection. The delegates were given an overview of criminal families – chiefly with Armenian names – whom they had never come across in their investigations. The names of two known traffickers were also on the overview: Ismail Oflu and Mehmet Baybaşin, the latter the uncle of the more infamous Hüseyin, but they were both currently in prison, which made their involvement impossible to verify. In the course of the visit, it became increasingly clear that the Turkish government was doing its best to convince those European police forces interested in fighting drug trafficking to participate in the battle against the political movement that, at that time, was still considered the great enemy of the Turkish state: the Armenian ASALA. De Bruijne told how they did their best to trace the Armenian contact they were given in

Ankara in Rotterdam, but that, as they had expected, led to absolutely
nothing. This first Interpol conference on Turkey was an unfortunate start
to the international police cooperation, which currently is proceeding
better.

5

The Susurluk
Incident

The Crash

It happened on the evening of Sunday, 3 November 1996. Late-night television viewers in Turkey saw their programme interrupted by a line of text appearing under the picture. Three people had been killed and a fourth injured in a traffic accident near the town of Susurluk, in western Turkey. Ever since the advent of commercial television, people in Turkey had grown accustomed to this kind of shock news. Every night, there were sensational interruptions to boost viewer ratings. In retrospect, most of them were fairly insignificant, particularly traffic accidents; after all the Turkish traffic claimed the lives of so many victims every day.

A lot of viewers tried switching over to find something more cheerful, but there, too, the programme had been interrupted. More information came in. The people who had died in this accident were a police chief, Huseyin Kocadaĝ, a man by the name of Mehmet Ozbay, and a Mrs Yonca Yucel. The injured man was Sedat Bucak, a member of Parliament for the province of Urfa in the southeast of the country and known as the commander of an army of village guards set up to protect the region from the PKK. A couple of pistols, several machine guns and a set of silencers were found in the wreckage of the car. Weapons were something Bucak was normally associated with.

Half an hour later, a new line of information appeared on the screen. 'Mehmet Ozbay' was actually Abdullah Çatli. In the 1970s, Çatli had been vice-chairman of the Grey Wolves. He had been wanted by the Turkish authorities since 1978 on suspicion of a number of murders, one of them involving seven students. He was also wanted by Interpol, as he had been arrested by the French and Swiss police as a heroin dealer but escaped from a Swiss prison in 1990.

Soon, the full story came out. A luxury Mercedes carrying four people and travelling at 200 kilometres an hour on the 'NATO' road, a road initially intended as the landing strip for an airport, had gone straight into the back of a rickety truck emerging from a petrol station. There was more information on the driver and his passengers. Police chief Kocadag, the director of the Police Academy in Istanbul, had been one of the major founders of the police's special units, set up in 1985 under the responsibility of the directorate general of police to combat the PKK alongside the army and the village militia. It was generally assumed that their members were recruited from MHP circles, the ultra-right wing political party that protected the *ülkücü*. These units were expanded in 1993 and gained their current form under Tansu Çiller, who was then Prime Minister. The woman in the car was Gonca Us, the winner of a minor beauty competition and girlfriend of the fugitive Çatli. It was an extraordinary combination of people.

Just about everyone in Turkey was both shocked and intrigued. New reports kept coming in on the course of the events and the entire country began speculating as to the actual circumstances. It was quickly established that the MP Bucak, the criminal Çatli and his girlfriend Gonca Us had taken the car from Istanbul to the coastal town of Izmir. They were driving a Mercedes 600, equipped with twelve cylinders. A team of bodyguards was following them in a similarly expensive Mercedes. Bucak had asked his good friend, police chief Kocadağ, to go to Izmir with them and he had arrived that evening by plane. They had spent the night in a hotel in Izmir. The next day, the four of them had gone to the tourist area of Kuşadasi to the south of Izmir, where they stayed in the Onura Hotel, which shortly before had been in the news when the boss of the its casino, Ömer Lütfu Topal, was murdered on July 28. No culprit was found. Two days later, on Sunday evening, the party left for Istanbul.

What created such a stir was that Çatli proved to be carrying a police identity card and had an arms licence issued by the police. On November 5, the *Hürriyet* headline read, 'The state is aware of corrupt relations.' The Turkish Secret Service (MIT) proved to have already been aware of the relations Çatli maintained with Bucak and Kocadağ. The service also knew that Çatli carried identification in a fictitious name. This criminal could not be arrested due to falsified papers issued by the government. These included a service, or 'green', passport. In his initial response to the events, the Minister of Internal Affairs said that Bucak and Kocadağ had been on their way to Istanbul to arrest Çatli there. Nobody believed that, however, and

Milliyet outlined the situation the same day under the headline, 'Major rot,' bringing the skeletons out of Çatli's cupboard. According to the paper, Catli had played a key role as a Grey Wolf and agent provocateur in the coup of 12 September 1980; he had organised the escape of Mehmet Ali Agca, the man suspected of the murder of the editor-in-chief of a major daily paper and a later assault on the Pope. Çatli had played a role in a whole series of political assassinations and attacks, including the apparent assassination of Tarik Ümit, who worked for MIT and maintained shady relations with the underworld. Çatli also allegedly played a role in the attempted coup in Azerbaijan against president Aliev, in favour of the nationalistic ex-president Elçibey.

Following this report, the fateful car accident took another political turn. Whereas the little town of Susurluk may have been known before 3 November 1996 for the exceptional quality of its buttermilk, its name now evokes connotations of sinister connections between the state and the underworld. After the crash, references were made on television and in the newspapers to the recently published report by the Turkish Secret Service which had not always been taken entirely seriously until then, but the contents of which now rang true. According to the weekly *Aydinlik* of September 22, the report stated:

A criminal organisation has been set up within the police force in such a way as to give the impression that the people involved are combating the PKK and Dev-Sol. The group consists largely of former ülkücü and specialises in crimes such as intimidation, robbery, extortion, drug smuggling and homicide. The group is under the direct command of the General Chief of Police, Mehmet Agar, and the day-to-day management is in the hands of the advisor to the general police department, Korkut Eken. The members of this group have been provided with 'police' identity papers and 'green passports'. They give the impression of being active in combating terrorists but are, in reality, smuggling drugs to Germany, the Netherlands, Belgium, Hungary and Azerbaijan. The police officers working for the police's special unit, Ayhan Akça, Ziya and Semih, collaborate with this group and provide it with protection. The major names in this group are:

1. Abdullah Çatli, born in 1956, vice-chairman of the Ülkü Ocaklari (literally Idealists Association) in 1978, suspected of the murder of seven members of the Turkish Labour Party, assisting in the escape of Mehmet Ali Aĝca; wanted since 1982 for murder, wanted since 1984 for trafficking in heroin and arms; organiser of the attack on the Pope, sentenced to death. He is in possession of identity papers in the name of Mehmet Özmen (or Özbey). He has police identity papers and a green passport.

2. Haluk Kirci, born in 1958, ex-ülkücü, wanted for murder. In 1988 he was sentenced to death.

3. Sami Hoşnav (Arnavut Sami) has contacts with Dev-Sol; smuggles cocaine, to Spain, the Netherlands and Colombia, in particular. He is co-owner of the casino in the Sheraton hotel and acts as the financier for the entire group.

4. Sedat Peker, involved in ülkücü activities in 1983 in Germany and in 1992 in Istanbul.

5. Other members of this group include Ali Yasak (Direj Ali), a number of members of the Bucak clan from Urfa, various known figures from the underworld and police officers at various levels.

The underworld figure Tarik Ümit collaborated with the police and was provided with a special passport and a car by police chief Aĝar. Ümit also supplied green passports to drug smugglers, such as Nurettin Güven and Yaşar Öz. At the time of writing, he is missing, suspected murdered.

Finally: the group is part of a network of people engaged in drug trafficking, from which they earn enormous sums of money, and murders that take place under the protection of the state. If this group is not stopped, it cannot be ruled out that they will also carry out political assassinations.

All kinds of details in the Secret Service report turned out out to be true after the Susurluk incident: Çatli's identity papers in the name of Mehmet Özbay, his green passport, his gun licence, the relationship with Bucak. These details did not go unnoticed by the press, which therefore closely followed the aftermath of the case. First came the funerals. Abdullah Çatli, an internationally wanted heavy, was buried in his hometown of Nevşehir in the presence of 5,000 *ülkücü*. Numerous major figures were sighted in the crowd, such as Muhsin Yazicioğlu, chairman of the Great Union Party, who had risen in the 1970s to general chairman of the *ülkücü*, and Ali Yasak (Direj Ali), a big underworld man whose name was mentioned several times in the Secret Service report. There were also a lot of former MHP members of parliament present. Çatli's coffin was draped in the Turkish flag and lowered into the grave to the accompaniment of Turkish folk songs and the chanting of religious cries: 'Allah is great.'

The coffin containing police chief Kocadağ made a minor tour of Istanbul and Ankara before burial and in both cities senior police officials were received by the family. Gonca Us was buried in Izmir by her family.

Then there was the question of precisely what had happened. Vice-premier Tansu Çiller made it clear that she was concerned, but declared that no one need doubt that the affair would be thoroughly investigated. The investigation into the accident proceeded. The weapons found in the Mercedes were sent to a laboratory for examination, but that provided no new insight. No explanation was found for the silencers. Other things were found in the car in addition to the weapons: 'brown stuff, possibly drugs.'* The leader of the opposition at that moment, Mesut Yilmaz, was afraid that evidence would be lost. The only survivor, Bucak, was plagued by 'memory loss'. Escorted by Direj Ali, Bucak left the hospital in the middle of the night and both of their bodyguards prevented journalists from talking to them or taking photographs. He was taken straight to his home in Ankara. Just before, Bucak had nevertheless managed to throw a doner kebab party for his clan in the garden of the hospital in Istanbul and a minister visiting him commented that Bucak was a 'national hero' and that, on closer examination, his memory was fortunately functioning perfectly well.

The press and politicians kept pressing for more information. Newspaper columnists, in particular, lived up to their typically Turkish

---

* It was not until August 1997 that it was discovered that the weapons belonged to the 'special operations' section of the directorate general for security – see *Turkish Daily News*, 26 August 1997.

reputation of always wanting to know more. Professor Mahir Kaynak,* a former member of the secret service often consulted by the media on events of this kind, stated, 'This chance occurrence proves the claims I have been making for years. There are two wings in the state. One of them is visible; this group is of the opinion that the Kurdish problem cannot be solved via the model of the constitutional state, which is why they have set up this second, illegal organisation.' The political opposition, the Motherland Party (ANAP) and the Republican People's Party (CHP), wanted to pose questions in Parliament, but the government would not comment. Agar, still general chief of police at the time of the events described in the Secret Service report and Minister of the Interior in 1996, was discredited the most but continued to act as if the whole matter was insignificant. To this day the most important body of the Turkish state, the National Security Council, which includes the chiefs of staff of all the army units, the President, the Prime Minister and several ministers and studies all major state issues, has never had the Susurluk issue on its agenda. The topic of drugs was discussed once, but the discussion concerned the measures the government should take to combat use among young people.

And what about Çatli's gun licence? The inspectors from the Ministry of Internal Affairs published a report that showed it had been issued by no less than Minister Ağar himself. Çatli had obtained seven different sets of identity papers, including three passports, from the Turkish consulate in London. When the identity papers fell into the hands of the press, *Sabah* devoted its entire front page to them. Next to the picture of Çatli was the name Mehmet Özbay: he supposedly worked for the general police department as an expert and was authorised to carry a gun. Beneath that was the signature of Minister Ağar himself in his previous position: general chief of police. Ağar stated that he remembered nothing of this. In a subsequent working visit to the provinces, he spoke only to those officials he had invited himself. But he let it be known that it would not be

---

* Mahir Kaynak was an MIT agent and, at the same time, a lecturer at the University of Ankara. He was well informed about leftist circles in the 1970s and involved in preparing a left-wing coup. After the army ultimatum, these groups were brought to justice and, in the trial of the Madanoglu group, Kaynak had to blow his own cover. He later became professor at Gazi University in Ankara.

wise to make too much of a fuss about the Susurluk incident, as that would 'only play into the hands of those committing or commissioning acts of terrorism' in Turkey. Agar had no intention of accepting any political consequences, as 'We never did anything to make us lose face.'

With no end to the awkward questions, however, something had to be done. The attitude of Premier Erbakan and his religious Welfare Party was characterised by aloofness. The other political parties had always wanted to keep them outside the political centre, so now they had to solve the problems created during the premiership of his predecessors, such as Mrs Çiller, themselves, without his assistance. This attitude gave Erbakan a wonderful tool for blackmailing his coalition partner, Mrs Çiller; there had already been rumours of her having her own gang and about her True Path Party and he could always threaten real in-depth investigation. He simply announced, 'Don't worry. We are doing what has to be done for Susurluk.' As far as he was concerned, that was the end of the discussion. Çiller had no choice but to take concrete steps and, to her great regret, she made a sacrifice and asked Mehmet Agar to step down. But she, Premier Erbakan and his own party leader expressed their thanks to him. The comment of the sacked minister himself was revealing. He told the editor-in-chief of *Hürriyet* that he was afraid nobody would ever want to take risks for the state after these events. He saw working within organised crime for the state as a patriotic act. Mrs Çiller herself recalled in public that people such as Çatli, Çakici and other ülkücü had been heroes in the state's struggle against the Armenian ASALA activists in the 1980s. Without citing the names of Çatli and other Grey Wolves, she declared, 'Anyone who fires a bullet or receives one in his body for this nation, for this country, is a respectable person. These are honourable people.'

A second affair the press and politicians were loath to let drop was the officially unsolved murder of the 'king of the gambling joints', Ömer Lütfü Topal. If there were, indeed, conspiracies such as that in Susurluk, then the suggestion in the Secret Service report that the state was behind them could also be true. Who had committed Topal's murder and why? Ömer Lütfü Topal was shot dead with a Kalashnikov on 28 July 1996 on his way home in Istanbul. As there were already speculations concerning police officers in special teams working on their own account, three suspect policemen were arrested in Istanbul and interrogated for thirty-six hours. According to the Turkish media, that interrogation was recorded on videotape. That tape supposedly contained all these officers' confessions to Topal's murder, but other murders were also apparently mentioned, the culprits of which were unknown. No fewer than ninety-one murder cases were involved. The officers reputedly said, 'If we are suspects, then so are others, such as Minister Ağar and President Demirel!' An order came from Ankara's general chief of police to transfer the three suspects to Ankara. The chief of the police special unit concerned, Ibrahim Şahin, went personally to Istanbul to fetch them. In Ankara, the three suspects were immediately released. MP Bucak then enlisted all three as his bodyguards.

What was the motive for the murder? The team of officers allegedly wanted to extort the sum of $17 million from Topal. Topal thought it was too much and offered ten. As they were unable to reach an agreement, he was eliminated. There was also speculation, however, that the extortionists themselves had increased the amount. In the spring of 1997, we asked the prominent ANAP MP (now minister) Eyüp Aşik what he thought happened. According to his information, Topal had to pay $10 million not once, but twice. The transaction apparently took place through the Iş-Bank in the town of Van. 'After the payment, Topal told his friends, "I've saved myself. I paid, so they won't do anything to me."' That proved to be a miscalculation.

Both Bucak, who had employed the suspected police officers as bodyguards, and the officers themselves used the freedom of the TV channel HBB to tell live how important the special units and Bucak himself were for Turkey. One of the officers – arrested, incidentally, on suspicion of involvement in ninety-one murders – gazed sentimentally into the camera. The Istanbul police had arrested him on the very day of his son's circumcision! Straight afterwards, pictures of the party were shown and the disappointed face of the son who was 'looking for' his father.

Based on the fingerprints on the Kalashnikovs, the Istanbul police came to the conclusion that Abdullah Çatli, who died in Susurluk, had been involved in Topal's murder. Prompted by a conversation with the then opposition leader, Yilmaz, President Demirel sent a letter to Premier Erbakan, quoting Yilmaz's claim that there was a group of a hundred to a hundred and twenty men involved in 'drugs, gambling, extortion and murder' and that these murderers were in the employ of the state.

The Aftermath

On 22 December 1996, President Süleyman Demirel invited all the leaders of the political parties represented in Parliament to a meeting to discuss the Susurluk accident. They met for five and a half hours and drew up a seventy-three-page report. Necmettin Erbakan, the new Prime Minister, set the tone by remarking, 'The situation is more serious than we think and the public knows. There are military men, police officers, politicians and mafia people involved. Events have taken place that are unknown to the public. We now know the names of fifty-eight people involved in these shady affairs and have been able to locate forty-seven of them. Ten of these forty-seven people have been murdered or are, in any event, no longer alive. Some of the more important of these fifty-eight names are: Mehmet Agar, Sedat Bucak, Korkut Eken, Huseyin Baybaşin, Ali Yasak, Abdullah Çatli (deceased), Haluk Kirci, Tarik Umit (disappeared) and O. Lutfu Topal (murdered).' At the same meeting Mrs Çiller, the vice-premier, responded to an earlier statement by her political opponent, Ecevit, who had declared, 'I first discovered this illegal organisation in 1974 when I was Prime Minister. During my second term as Prime Minister I asked the military Chief of Staff to disband the organisation. But it did not stop. Later, Çiller used this very same organisation for her own dirty business.' Vice-Premier Çiller responded by saying, 'I was a secondary school pupil when Mr Ecevit, opposition leader in Parliament at the time, revealed the existence of a counter-guerrilla organisation, a kind a "state gang". Similar claims are now being made. Mr Ecevit later served twice as Prime Minister. I investigated what Ecevit did about this. Nothing.'*

At the time of the Susurluk incident Mesut Yilmaz was leader of the opposition. Time and again he declared that, once he was prime minister,

---

* This information on her age cannot be correct. In this period of the 1970s she must at least have finished her university studies.

the 'mystery' of Susurluk would be solved within twenty days. But when he did, indeed, become prime minister, he demonstrated his impotence. On 7 December 1997, he granted a local television station in Bursa an interview, in which he said, 'We can't do better than to obtain twenty to twenty-five percent of the truth. Civil servants fail to supply us with evidence, or the documents are forged.' Not long afterwards, on 4 January 1998, he added on the state television channel TRT-1, 'I am doing my utmost to solve the Susurluk affair. But you have to understand how things are. Even a prime minister is unable to control everything and obtain information on everything. Whatever I find out, I will make public, unless it concerns state secrets. Every state has its secrets and Turkey is no exception.'

The people of Turkey were appalled by these revelations. Starting on 1 February 1997, millions of people all over the country turned off all their lights every evening at nine for one minute to protest against the widespread corruption and abuse of power in political and official circles. The gesture was supported by artists, journalists, trade unionists, politicians and businessmen alike. Two skyscrapers at the Sabanci Centre in Istanbul, owned by one of the country's biggest businessmen, were plunged into darkness for one minute every evening from February 1 onwards. Many radio and television broadcasting stations informed the audience at a certain moment that it was time to turn the lights off, 'one minute without light to lead the country out of the darkness for good'. People went out onto the streets to protest further. After a few days, the initiators stopped their protest, but the message was clear.

A sociological study was set up at the 9 September University in Izmir. More than 34,000 people in sixty-one towns in Turkey were asked questions about Susurluk. Eighty-nine percent of respondents found that Turkey took no serious measures against the mafia. Fifty-five percent felt that the state politicians and the mafia had mutual relationships and eight-four percent thought the people responsible for Susurluk would not ultimately be punished. Nothing that came to light in Susurluk has had any direct legal consequences and the revelation of the links between the government and the underworld gives little hope, in itself, of things changing. The death sentence was demanded for the commander of the special unit, Ibrahim Şahin, and three of his men for Topal's murder, but shortly afterwards they were released. Former minister Ağar remained out of range until his immunity was suspended in December 1997 by a permanent parliamentary commission and, later, by parliament. 'I have not committed any crime,' he declared. 'We are simply engaged in great works. We fear only Allah and no-one else. We are the Sultan in the heart of the nation.* Nothing else matters.' It was the same with Bucak. 'I chose the side of the state,' was his comment. None of this led to the arrest of these politicians. There are, nonetheless, exceptions. The driver of the truck that caused the accident was ordered by the judge in Susurluk to pay 6.4 million Turkish lira for dangerous driving and to pay compensation of 100 million lira to the widow of police chief Kocadağ.

In January 1997, Parliament appointed a nine-man commission to investigate the crash, leaving no stone unturned. Mehmet Elkatmis, a religious Muslim, was appointed chairman and his political leader Erbakan said militantly, 'If we come across a gang, we will wipe it out.' The committee took just over three months to examine more than 100,000 relevant documents and accounts of interviews with fifty-seven people during the hearings. We interviewed the chairman of the commission just before it published its final 300-page report and another 2,500 pages of transcriptions of hearings. On the basis of this interview and the newspaper accounts of what Elkatmis said, we know that the commission was unable to go anything like as far as it intended at the start, or as far as Erbakan's statements suggested. The committee would have liked to be able to find out much more about the role of the gendarmerie's secret organisation JITEM. The chairman told us, however, voicing the official government standpoint, that the PKK was ultimately the villain, as it was involved in drug trafficking.

During the hearings, the sole survivor of the accident, Sedat Bucak, was questioned. His story now differed from the one he had earlier told on the HBB channel. According to him, the weapons in the Mercedes belonged to Çatli, whom he knew as Özbay. And his guards, who were suspected of Topal's murder, had committed the deed on the instructions of the head of the special team. 'Yes, it's possible that the murderer has stayed in my house,' said Bucak. The next day there was a full-page photograph of Ibrahim Şahin, head of the special police team who had denied he knew Çatli during the hearings, together with Çatli at the circumcision party of the sons of a number of members of the special

---

* A saying which roughly means 'the people see us as heroes'.

team who were suspected of various crimes. Şahin and Çatli were acting as *kirve*. When all the blame appeared to have been shifted onto the shoulders of the late Çatli, his wife appeared in public. She said, 'My husband worked for the state. Twenty-two days after the coup on 12 September 1980, the military leaders sent him abroad for training. Then the state helped him escape from the Swiss prison where he was serving a sentence for drug smuggling.'

One of the commission's most sensational findings was that the annual turnover of the drug trade was £25 billion, which was more than the total Turkish state budget of £24 billion! This figure might look more precise than it actually is, but it does give an indication of the dimensions of drug trafficking. One of the problems the commission came up against was that financial information on individual people could not be examined, due to the bank secrecy obligation. Commission member Saglar regretted that this prevented the commission from gaining insight into how the profits from drug trafficking were distributed.

Another drawback for the commission was that the former head of the National Security Service at the time, Teoman Koman, and the head of the gendarmerie, refused to appear before it. According to *Radikal,* the commission did not receive any substantial information. The files it requested, which were deposited with the state security courts in Ankara and Istanbul or held by the Ministry of Internal Affairs, the general police department, the MIT and the gendarmerie (including the secret service JITEM), remained incomplete, as no 'state secrets' could be released.* Mrs Çiller was initially invited, but the commission later found it unnecessary for her to appear after all. Mehmet Ağar did appear, but made a

---

* One notorious affair requiring clarification was the plane crash on 17 February 1993 that killed General Eşref Bitlis, head of the gendarmerie. His plane crashed a few minutes after taking off for Diyarbakir. The following day, the military chief of staff called it an accident and a later report said the wings of the plane had been frozen. This was contested by the pilot's family, who asked a court for clarification from the airline. According to technical experts, there was nothing wrong with the plane and the incident therefore had the appearance of an act of sabotage. Doğu Perinçek, chairman of the Labour Party, declared before the parliamentary enquiry commission that Cem Ersever, the founder of JITEM, was responsible. He and Bitlis apparently had different views of how the Kurdish issue should be resolved. The same Ersever was later involved in drug trafficking and shot dead in an internal conflict by Çatli.

meaningless statement. In the meantime, the Public Prosecutions Department initiated proceedings against him for leading a gang and, as long as the case was sub judice, he said, he was keeping his mouth shut. He had, however, already announced in the press that he would talk one day: 'Ultimately, it will come to a showdown between traitors and non-traitors. We are fully aware of who the traitors are in Turkey. I was employed by the state. I did everything for the state. Nobody can prove otherwise. I didn't do anything for myself. All the senior state officials should get together and then everyone should go ahead and say who did what. I can tell the president everything.'

The commission felt obstructed by the lack of a safe crown witness arrangement. If there had been one, more inside information would probably have been supplied. Within the commission, which became divided during the investigation, the representatives of the ruling coalition parties formed a united front. Members of the opposition parties wrote alternative reports, jointly or individually. Yilmaz voiced the opposition's concern during the hearing:

Chairman Elkatmiş: 'You told the president that there were some hundred to two hundred people involved in crime. The prime minister has named fifty-eight names. What are your concrete findings?'

Yilmaz: 'From the information I have, it appears that roughly eighty people from the special team and another thirty to forty people from the underworld are involved in this matter.'

Chairman: 'Can you name names?'

Yilmaz: 'They are almost the same names as the prime minister already named: Mehmet Ağar, Sedat Bucak, Korkut Eken, Abdullah Çatli, Tarik Ümit, Yaşar Öz, Baybaşi, Ibrahim Şahin. A third of these people are dead. Behçet Cantürk, Tarik Ümit and Savaş Buldan are already dead, for example.'

Chairman: 'Are there any politicians involved other than Ağar and Bucak?'

Yilmaz: 'Mrs Çiller's husband... It is possible that people did business for the benefit of the state in the past, to act against terrorism. But there was no question as yet of individually pursuing profit in that period. It was like that up until the end of 1993.'

Chairman: 'Was the group the same?'

Yilmaz: 'Yes, it was. But in my opinion those people started to work for their own profit from 1994 onwards. So the end of 1993 is an important period. After that, the state, the serious side of the state, lost control of it all… The state and the mafia have become one.'

Chairman: 'Since when is that the case, in your opinion?'

Yilmaz: 'There were already initial signs in the first MIT report. But from 1993 onwards…'

Chairman: 'That report also named Mehmet Ağar and Ünal Erkan (when they were still civil servants). Ağar was a senior police chief under your party's government. Later, when you formed a coalition with Çiller, they were both ministers in your last cabinet. Ağar was even minister of justice. Why, as premier, did you not tell Çiller that they had been named?'

One of the commission members who was dissatisfied was Fikri Sağlar, who had a seat in the commission on behalf of the CHP. He submitted his objections to the commission in writing. Yilmaz had said that things had gone 'well' until the beginning of 1994. In other words, action was acceptable, even if it was executed without democratic control, as long as it was in the interest of the state. From 1994 onwards, they had become uncontrolled gangs, working for themselves. Sağlar, on the other hand, stated that the problem had manifested itself even before the 1980s: in a democracy, it was illegal to create bodies that carried out illicit action, in any event. All in all, there is plenty of reason for further investigation.

Organised crime in Turkey is linked to the national state in a unique way. Susurluk is generally acknowledged in Turkey as proof of the existence of ties linking the state and the underworld. It is hard for Europeans or Americans to understand how a state gang like the one exposed after Susurluk can still essentially be tolerated. All the parties involved have since been acquitted and cleared of criminal charges. Agar was elected to Parliament again and Bucak was released because, as the court stated in June 2003, 'his clan has a long history and, in the revolts of the Kurds in 1925, for example, his clan chose the side of the state'. According to Fikri Saglar, a member of the commission and of the Republican People's Party, not much has changed since then; we have not been able to establish the whole truth, due to political and bureaucratic repression and the fact that witnesses have failed to appear or given incomplete evidence. The report simply cannot be complete.

According to the popular politician D. Fikri Saglar and his co-writer Emin Ozgonul, the scandal that involved the notorious former Grey Wolf and mafia boss Alaattin Çakici gave an initial indication that links had not been severed. Çakici was arrested in 1999 in France for allegedly having threatened the potential buyers of a Turkish bank on the telephone. They were told not to purchase the bank, as there were other candidates. This criminal, who was wanted by Interpol, turned out to have contacts in the Turkish cabinet. After his extradition, Çakici did spend some time in prison, but it was not long before this *ülkücü* was released. On the day of his final arrest, 3 May 2004, Çakici escaped to Italy on a visa provided by the Italian consulate. He was going to do business for the Besiktas football club. The question still remains, though, as to whether the state is actually involved in human trafficking. It has become more difficult to neutralise state intervention. As long as a campaign was being waged against the Kurdish PKK, the state could afford to take plenty of chances. Funding was needed and the state was in danger. The people who played an active role did not feel guilty because they were serving sacred state aims.

In 2007, at the time of writing, the people from the Susurluk incident were again active in politics. The sole survivor of the car crash, Bucak, was running for the Turkish parliament for the party of the former minister responsible, Agar. At the same time, he was standing as a candidate for the Democratic Party, headed by Agar Ibrahim Şahin, and Çatli's brother's extreme right party, MHP.

*

In the 1990s, it could be said that events transpired in secret and that the Deep State agents worked discreetly. Susurluk changed all of that. Since then, many similar incidents have come to light and revelations are almost everyday occurences. Two recent cases serve to illustrate the point.

Semdinli is a town in the eastern province of Hakkari, which lies in the triangle of Iran, Iraq and Turkey. In the afternoon of 9 November 2005, a bomb was thrown at a left-wing Kurdish bookshop. One man was killed and a number injured. The obvious culprits, who ran away, were stopped by people in the street and their car was seized. In the car, they found weapons and bombs, hand-written route descriptions for certain addresses and a list of people from the political opposition living in Semdinli. Two of the men were carrying identity papers that showed they worked for the Turkish military. A third suspect was a former PKK militant who was now working for the Turkish government. This incident gained national publicity. The Minister of Internal Affairs stated that he would investigate the affair thoroughly and the Minister of Justice stated through his spokesperson that they would get to the bottom of it.

After the three suspects had been arrested, the head of the Turkish army, General Buyukanit, made a statement, saying that he knew one of the three well from operations in this field and that he considered him to be a 'good soldier'. The public prosecutor rapidly came to the conclusion that the investigation should be extended, as there was evidently an entire organisation behind the incident, stretching as high as General Buyukanit himself. This did not happen, however, because to carry out criminal investigations into members of the military in Turkey you need the consent of the military authorities, and that was not granted. The Turkish army vehemently denied any soldiers were involved in the Semdinli incident, sending lawyers to defend the bomb throwers who had been arrested.

What happened to those involved is unknown, but the public prosecutor was suspended and even explicity prohibited from practising as a lawyer any longer. The similarities in the way this case and the Susurluk case were dealt with are clear. The difference lies perhaps only in the fact that the Semdinli suspects, popular in right-wing nationalistic circles, did not put themselves forward as candidates for the next Turkish parliamentary elections. The public prosecutor is now unemployed and General Buyukanit has been promoted to chief of staff of the entire Turkish army.

A second recent case involved the so-called sauna gang. After repeated complaints from customers of saunas in Ankara, in 2006 the police decided to carry out a large-scale operation. According to the complainants, the saunas were being used as brothels and the sexual practices of prominent customers, including members of parliament, were being filmed in secret for later use in blackmailing. The complaints proved to be valid and a mountain of material was seized, plus firearms and explosives, from a gang that controlled the saunas. In one sauna, extremely confidential governmental documents were found amongst the confiscated material. These included a 'constitution in a red binding'. This was something over which there had already been much speculation: a description of secret rules concerning the state system intended only for the eyes of the most senior government officials – essentially, the military. Journalists asked Demirel whether *he* had seen this document when he was president. The fact that Demirel replied with modest pride that he had, indeed, been privileged enough to read the constitution in the red binding was a clear illustration of the real balance of power in Turkey. In November 2006, Demirel said the following, according to widely available reports: 'It is fundamental principle that there is one state. However, in our country there are two. There is one deep state and one other state,' he elaborated. 'The State that should be real is the spare one, the one that should be spare is the real one.'

The scenario of the criminal investigation into this incident is by now quite familiar. Members of the cabinet and army officers openly declared that they would make everything public and that nothing 'would remain concealed'. 'We will do our utmost,' said the spokesman for the cabinet and the chief of staff General Ozkok. The case was heard by a military court and the counsel for the prosecution immediately demanded a session in camera, due to the sensitivity of the material. There could be no question of public reporting. The judges agreed and nothing more was heard. In this case, one of the suspects, eager to use his popularity to further his political career, did come forward. Ibrahim Tatlises is the best-loved Turkish singer and a successful businessman. Allah willing, this Kurdish artiste sought to take his place in the nationalist Young Party, at least as long as this new faction attained the elective threshold of ten percent at the 2007 elections. It did not.

How can we comprehend this pattern of organised crime and state crime? A brief excursion into the history of the Turkish state will help.

6

The Deep State

The Turkish Political System

The Susurluk event is generally considered in Turkey to be evidence of the existence of cooperative links between parts of the state and the underworld. The virtually unanimous opinion is that this was not an isolated incident but an event that fits into a bigger pattern. The size and scope of this pattern is perhaps the single most intriguing – and misunderstood – aspect of the rise of the Turkish *mafia*.

Susurluk is synonymous with the failure of democratic control. Turkey officially has the bodies and rules and regulations of a democracy but, in reality, it is only a limited form of democracy, a political system with 'the state' as the centre of power – though in Turkey the state is not a collective term for the political parties and the government. In theory, the state includes the entire institutional power mechanism. In practice, it is embodied by the National Security Council, founded in 1960 by the army officers responsible for the first military coup that year. In Turkey, Parliament, the political associations, some of the press and everything we envision as part of a modern democracy only function within the space allowed by the National Security Council. Only against this background can the rise of Turkish mafia politics be put in the proper perspective.

The Republic of Turkey that was proclaimed on 29 October 1923 in Ankara is not the result of a social and economic revolution from the bottom up; it is the product of a social and cultural reform enforced from the top down, which came into being within an authoritarian political structure. It was a grand effort to modernise the country in one fell swoop and there is no doubt that this reform jump-started modern economic development, equal rights for women and the secularisation of the country. Kemalism, the ideological foundation for the reforms and named after Mustafa Kemal Pasha Atatürk, was derived from fascism in general and the doctrines of Benito Mussolini in particular. Kemalism still constitutes the ideological basis for the state and, as such, it is kept outside the political discussion. This ideology is strongly nationalistic and centres on striving to create unity among the various peoples and cultures that remained in Turkey after the Ottoman Empire. The Turks and their culture served as the basis for the unity the country aspired to. Kemalism is populist in the sense that class, religious and ethnic differences are overlooked and organisations based upon them are not permitted to exist. It is statist to the extent that economic reforms are led by the state from above. Kemalism advocates a secular state, which does not necessarily mean church and state are separate, as is usually the case in modern societies; it simply means that religion is subordinate to the state. The government pays all the expenses, the salaries of the imams and the cost of constructing the mosques for the one approved school of Islam, the Sunnite school. The Islamic system of law and custom has been officially abolished and replaced with civil law. The state controls religion via the Directorate of Religious Affairs. Since the 1980s, this has also been the body the state uses to influence Turkish communities in Europe.

According to the political scientist Professor Doğu Ergil, this kind of politics can be interpreted as a forced attempt at forming a nation state within a territory that was the product of a military conquest and not the representation of the wish of a group of people wanting to belong together from a sense of historical solidarity. The primacy lies therefore neither with the state nor the nation, but with the political creation and not with the authority of the people. This state interpretation is directly opposed to pluralism, in which group rights are recognised and democracy is made concrete by designing rules for mutual relationships. It obstructs the emergence of a modern state citizenship, where people themselves and the associations they set up to be able to actively participate in the modernisation process can develop.

The authoritarian Turkish model is a unifying one. Based on equality as the point of departure, its aim is to turn all the people in the country into Turks. One of the ways this unity is being created is by constantly citing new enemies who threaten the integrity of the nation. Internal enemies include Armenians, Kurds, communists and Muslim fundamentalists and external enemies, potentially, are all the countries in the world, as 'the only friends Turks have are other Turks'. The term 'enemies' can be interpreted as the United States in the period of boycott due to heroin production, the Soviet Union due to communism, the Netherlands because it allows the establishment of a Kurdish parliament in exile, or Germany blocking Turkey's entrance into the European Union. The 'perfidity' of these external enemies is reflected in this strictly nationalistic interpretation in, for example, the fact that it finds allies and supporters within Turkey itself. These 'attacks'on the Turkish state justify powerfully repressive conduct against those who threaten this unity.

The Kemalist one-party state continued until 1945. The following year saw the first general elections in Turkey's history. This is not the place to describe the intricate political history of post-war Turkey but attention does need to be devoted to the prominent role of the military, who defend that Kemalist heritage by continually designating the limits to which politics is permitted to go. This they do by means of assembling, making a show of power from time to time, by producing memoranda, setting ultimata and, above all – three times so far – staging coups. In the Cold War era – Turkey entered NATO in 1952 and, bordering as it does on the Soviet Union, is an extremely important partner – they continually succeeded in gaining support from the United States. In political views within Europe, the military or the National Security Council is often allotted a progressive role; they watch over politics by eliminating irresponsible politicians and then returning to their barracks to give democracy another chance. This portrayal is incorrect or one-sided. What is being guarded is the Kemalist ideology, and that is not entirely democratic.

The first military coup took place on 27 May 1960 and brought an end to the Menderes government, which had been confronted with a great deal of political opposition, some of it originating from the Prime Minister's own Democratic Party, and had increasingly responded in an authoritarian fashion. The Kemalist system was for the first time essentially challenged by left-wing parties and movements in the 1960s when, under the influence of student movements in Germany, the United States and France, the country witnessed a lively intellectual debate. Small radical groups broke away in 1970 to engage in a battle with the state in the form of propaganda, terrorism and an urban guerrilla campaign.

The response was the political mobilisation of ultra-right-wing movements. One of the strongmen of the 1960 coup was Alparslan Turkes, an officer in the Turkish army. In 1965 he converted an existing political party into an outright fascist group with a manifesto that was surprisingly nationalistic and reactionary for the post-World War II period – the MHP or Nationalist Action Party. A paramilitary organisation of idealists (*ülkücü*) called Grey Wolves was set up in these same circles and they were to serve as storm-troopers against left-wing groups. For the military leaders, the political divisiveness resulting from economic difficulties in the late 1960s and growing anti-Americanism among leftist intellectuals was ample reason to submit an ultimatum to the government. It came on 12 March 1971 with the order to reform the country's politics in keeping with the spirit of Atatürk. Martial law was declared and was to last for two and a half years. The left-wing movement was purged and many of its militants went underground, as there was no protection for them under the various right-wing regimes of the National Front, of which the MHP was part. The security service and police force had ties with the MHP and, consequently, more or less gave the Grey Wolves free rein.

In the 1970s, the Grey Wolves began a veritable reign of terror. They shot and killed many people who had nothing to do with the violent side of the left-wing opposition: students, teachers, trade union leaders, booksellers and politicians. It was an extremely unequal battle, as the ultra-right had the support of the state. The MHP used deliberate provocation to stimulate clashes between various segments of the population and reinforced the hatred of minorities. The 1970s were plagued by severe economic setbacks and, as a result of the destabilisation, the decade culminated in a chaos that pushed the country to the verge of civil war. The battle between left and right cost twenty-seven lives in 1974, thirty-seven in 1975, a hundred and eight in 1976, three hundred and nineteen in 1977, almost nine hundred in 1978 and more than 1,000 in 1979.*

There are various theories about the fighting. Prominent Turkey expert Feroz Ahmad does not exclude the possibility that the chaos was deliberately created by the military leaders to serve as an excuse for a new coup. Years later, an editor for the daily newspaper *Hürriyet* wrote that, in those years the same gun could be used in the morning for a right-wing operation and then in the afternoon for left-wing action.

Throughout this entire period, the underworld was smuggling arms into the country for both right- and left-wing organisations and heroin was being smuggled abroad to pay for these purchases, as was later revealed

---

* The 1977 figure includes thirty-nine victims of 'unknown snipers' who opened fire during a May 1 meeting in Taksim Square in Istanbul and the 1978 figure includes more than a hundred Turkish and Kurdish Alevites in Kahramanmaraş, who, according to Zürcher, were killed and burned by Grey Wolves.

by investigative reporter Uğur Mumcu. To give an impression of the size of the trade and the profits the smugglers must have been making, the following illegal arms were confiscated between 1980 and 1984: 638,000 revolvers, 4,000 submachine guns, 48,000 rifles, 7,000 machine guns, twenty-six rocket launchers and one mortar.

On 12 September 1980 came another military coup. Chief of Staff Kenan Evren dissolved the political parties and forbade a number of prominent political leaders, who had demonstrated that they were incompetent to run the country any longer, from participating actively in politics: Demirel and Ecevit, amongst others. A new constitution was established. A referendum was held, in which the population expressed the wish to see various political freedoms from before 1961 revoked. Thousands of people were sentenced to long periods of imprisonment for left-wing activities, in military mass trials. Some were even sentenced to death. Under Evren's leadership, the junta did its best to present itself as the enforcer of law and order and, in an effort to do so systematically, referred to suspects who had played a role in the growing violence as terrorists. People from the extreme right-wing also disappeared into prison, even if not for long. A number of them felt misunderstood in their patriotism, leading in turn to the formation of private violent gangs, including the cheque mafia.

In 1983, the military handed the now-limited political arena back to the politicians. The party spectrum that emerged subsequently can only partly be understood in the light of political considerations. There is a party of 'Islamists' – whose critics charge that they have a hidden agenda to turn religion into the state ideology – under the leadership of Necmettin Erbakan, called the Welfare Party, and there are two social-democratic parties: the Republican People's Party and the Democratic Left Party. The other major parties are to the right of the political spectrum and should actually be seen as a host of personal followers of past prominent political leaders. The Motherland Party was in government in the 1980s, with Turgut Özal as its leader. He died in 1993. It was then led by Mesut Yilmaz. The True Path Party was run by Tansu Çiller. The Motherland Party later merged with True Path under the name Democratic Party. Its failure in the 2007 elections led to its collapse.

These are all parties who claim to preserve the legacy of Atatürk; they form left, centre and right within the philosophy of Kemalism. It is ironic that the only small party in parliament from which any 'original' sounds are to be heard – calls for more democracy and serious action against torture practices, for example – is the real legacy of Atatürk himself: the Republican People's Party.

*

The major problem of the 1980s was the Kurdish issue, once again a typical product of the enemy theories the Kemalist state invented for itself. The Turks had always more or less looked down on the Kurds as a backward people and, until well into the 1960s, the state successfully implemented an assimilation policy. But by the end of the decade, Kurds in the cities began to connect with the left-wing movement and there was a Kurdish awakening, based in part on awareness that southeast Turkey had been deliberately kept underdeveloped. In the course of the 1970s, this Kurdish consciousness increased as part of the battle between right and left. Immediately after the 1980 coup, the Kurds were subjected to measures designed to suppress their emancipation movement. A number of these measures now make a bizarre impression and, essentially, can only be comprehended in the framework of the ideology described above. Even in private conversation, it was prohibited for Kurds to speak their own language, as it might 'weaken their national feelings'. The PKK, the most radical Kurdish movement, was the only one to survive the repression. All Kurdish opposition that rejected violence as an instrument was effectively oppressed.

In 1978, the Kurdish leader Abdullah Öcalan managed to escape to Syria. The complete Kurdish population was behind him and today his movement, the PKK, still has the mass support of all Kurds. It is a totalitarian movement with a virtually religious culture of leadership and violence. Öcalan initially operated on the basis of an almost quaint revolutionary model that seemed to be rooted in the romantic period of the Third World revolution of the 1960s. He deliberately addressed the poorest and least educated youngsters in villages and cities and stimulated their revolutionary potential by advising them not to go to school. The movement was inspired by the Palestine Liberation Organisation, and launched its own guerrilla war in 1984, the Kurdish intifada.

That started to change, however, in the late 1980s. The party became more open and attempted to shake off its violent image, up to the moment when, in 1993, Öcalan announced a unilateral ceasefire, stating that he was prepared talk to President Özal. The president died, however, before that could happen and when Çiller and Yilmaz were willing to give the détente another chance, this was advised against by 'the state'. The military responded with what can hardly be termed as anything other than civil war – which has since cost an estimated 37,000 lives – and by establishing a corps of village militia, charged with the task of protecting the villages in the southeast against the PKK, alongside the special police units and the army. Sedat Bucak, of Susurluk notoriety, was one of the heads of this corps. A total of 62,000 village guards are employed by the Turkish government; volunteers make that number up to more than 90,000. Under the command of local tribal leaders, they more or less go their own way as far as the area of Northern Iraq is concerned, without much supervision of what they get up to; officially, 3,500 guards have been indicted for serious offences such as murder, kidnapping and smuggling drugs and arms. On 14 September 1997, Minister Salih Yildirim calculated how much the struggle against the PKK in the southeast of the country had cost the state so far: 27,000 human lives (including 10,000 members of the security troops) and eighty-four billion US dollars. Very likely, the same kind of sum could be made for the opposing party in the conflict.

Abdullah Öcalan was arrested on 15 February 1999 at the Greek Embassy in Kenya, where he had sought refuge. He is now serving a life sentence on the high-security island of Imrali. The Turkish public was enthusiastic about this arrest and Premier Ecevit's Demokratik Sol Parti (DSP) won the elections in 1999. Ecevit formed a coalition with the ultra-right MHP. In this period of government, serious attempts were made to break the ties with organised crime. The Motherland Party and the True Path Party had already granted themselves amnesty for all mafia scandals. The MHP had endeavoured to rid itself of its criminal image. 'The current leader of the MHP, Bahceli, genuinely wants to break the connection between his party and the illegal and semi-illegal organisations, such as the counter-guerilla,' explained Tanil Bora, a well-known right-wing Turkish intellectual. 'Up until now, the Turkish government has used MHP officers for various dirty operations. The key player was Çatli, the man from Susurluk. Well, Bahceli wants things to be different now. But we have to realise that the extreme right is not only represented by the MHP or the Grey Wolves; you will find ultra-right views in all Turkish political parties. The AK party, which is currently in power, also has a nationalistic wing and that even goes for the Social

Democratic CHP.' The right-wing powers in the Turkish state mechanism are extremely well organised, like the Special War/Anti-terrorist Department. They work independently of one another, but have mutual contact. Various famous godfathers have been imprisoned: Musullulu from the Pizza Connection, Uruglu the 'heroin king' and Oflu Ismail, and it's quite likely that a few other *babas* who were less publicly known have been quietly eliminated. A series of new scandals, however, showed that the problems were not solved by any means.

In the 2002 elections, Ecevit received no more than one percent of the votes. He was now eclipsed by the party headed by the Islamic-inspired popular mayor of Istanbul, Recep Erdogan. From this moment on, Turkey's politics were dominated by the contrast between the moderate Islamic programme of Erdogan's AK party and the secular, Kemalist state with the army as watchdog. First, the Kemalists had dismissed the Islamist Erbakan, who had been premier at the time of the Susurluk scandal, and now they had got the far more powerful Erdogan in return. To everyone's surprise, Erdogan directed his politics at Europe. The first country he visited as leader of the government was Germany. His standpoint was clear from the start: Turkey wanted to and would become a member of the European Union. All kinds of changes were being made to the structure of Turkish law, with the intention of becoming acceptable to Europe. Most of these changes remained no more than paper promises. In practice, better rights for religious and ethnic minorities did not materialise. After all, according to Kemalism, there are no minorities who ought to be grateful for being Turkish citizens and the Turkish Republic remains undividable. Europe, on the other hand, appreciated the courageous step in their direction and Turkey was recently accepted as a candidate member. Once Turkey has obediently done its homework, things should turn out all right.

The 'modern' Turks, typified by men without a beard or moustache and women with bleached hair, and the 'healthy' forces – the military – are not afraid of change. But Erdogan has to take his Islamic followers into account and is dragging his feet. That is causing irritation in the EU and the hope that any real changes will be implemented in Turkey is fading. Those European countries who have had objections on principle to accepting Turkey, for reasons of a religious, geographical and historical nature, are seeing their views confirmed.

In Turkey itself, the issue at the time of writing had actually become a forgotten topic. The political issue of whether the new president should be elected by referendum took priority. President A. Necdet Sezer profiles himself in office as a guardian of Atatürk's legacy. Sometimes things are a little over the top. He continually invites his prime minister and minister of foreign affairs to receptions without their wives. After all, those wives wear headscarves and that is intolerable in Atatürk's palace!

In the meantime, no solution at all has been found for the problems of the previous era. The Kurdish issue has again been a prominent item on the agenda since the Kurds have been able to form a relatively independent state in northern Iraq. In 2003, after a self-proclaimed truce, the new PKK leaders announced that the armed struggle was to be resumed. And, in view of the new scandals we keep seeing emerging, it is clear that the problems posed by the links betwen the Deep State and the mafia are still entirely unsolved.

The State and Organised Crime

It is no longer easy to separate crime and politics in Turkey. Representatives of the Turkish state claim that the PKK funds its activities by engaging in heroin trafficking and extortion, which is why they ask foreign police forces to help them combat this form of crime. Representatives of the PKK say, in turn, that it is the Turkish state that is active in drug trafficking and puts its own bands of assassins on their trail, therefore working towards the downfall of the constitutional state itself.

What we are dealing with here are essentially political viewpoints, but each of the parties in the conflict defines the other's conduct as criminal. In themselves, these disputes are outside the scope of criminology and of this book. It should be noted, though, that the both the PKK and the Turkish government, or in any event parts of them, are involved in drug trafficking, extortion and murder, whether by organising the trafficking themselves or by profiting indirectly from it via extortion or donations from traffickers. By engaging in these activities, they enter the field of organised crime; they all co-operate in their own way with classic Turkish and Kurdish mafia groups. So what exactly is the relationship between politics and crime?

Because illegal acts are involved, criminals will always initially attempt to follow a strategy of avoidance and remain as far outside the government's field of vision as possible. The most primitive form of smuggling is an example: smugglers devise ingenious routes and install storage places in unexpected parts of vehicles to avoid being noticed. This kind of tactic is insufficient, however, as part of the activity takes place more or less in public, and a lot of people are involved. The customers in the grey and black markets are aware of what is going on; transporters, lawyers, estate agents and other professionals provide the logistical and financial links with the legitimate world and it is impossible to keep the illegal activities concealed from everyone in the vicinity or in the company itself where the activities take place. A more active strategy is therefore required and this forms the next variant for keeping the controlling bodies at a distance or ensuring they turn a blind eye. Individual government officials in the police, customs and the secret service can be bribed or blackmailed. When organised crime gains power – and that happens when a lot of money is being earned – instead of individual policemen, they endeavour to bribe the entire staff of the local police station or the customs post. Once that stage has been reached, then it would be odd if the police didn't want to use their superior power to organise the corruption itself. And so a kind of symbiosis is created between the police on one side and the underworld on the other.

In Turkey, the evidence is overwhelming that parts of the government started organising operations themselves. The next stage in the proceedings can entail the state as a whole going into business with, or directing, organised crime. The replies of the former opposition leader, Yilmaz, to the Susurluk Enquiry Commission and the minority report by commission member Sağlar concern this most sensitive of topics: has the stage been reached where the state as a whole is involved and, if so, since when? And subsequently: have the state bodies managed to keep a rein on the affair, or have the organised crime gangs gone their own way?

*

From the moment when the military proclaimed martial law in the big cities in 1971, three phenomena became evident, which, on further investigation, appear to fit into a longer tradition. The first is that the military ostensibly eliminated the cooperative links between the police and the underworld in various parts of the country. The army put itself in charge of the police force and Istanbul's General Faik Türün enlisted the aid of the Secret Service (MIT) to break the power of the *babas* locally. A group of MIT agents came from Ankara to work with the Istanbul police. Members of notorious families, such as the Uğurlu, Ipek, Mirza and Cantaş clans, were arrested for arms smuggling. They were released after brief sentences. In the interrogation of these smugglers, the MIT agents learned that a senior police official had close ties with criminals who were smuggling arms into the country from Bulgaria; this was a former head of the Political Intelligence Service (now the Antiterrorism department), Şükrü Balci. At that time, in the early 1970s, that was sensational. Even more sensational was that this faux pas did not prevent Balci from afterwards being promoted to deputy director of the police in Istanbul. The same Şükrü Balci later even made it to director of the Istanbul police, in practice the second in command after the general chief of police. We will come across this state of affairs – the involvement of a policeman in organised crime not damaging his career but, on the contrary, advancing his prospects – more often and it creates the impression that those involved did not act off their own bat but were operating on government instructions. At the end of the decade, in November 1980, the head of the Secret Service's counter-espionage department included in his memoirs a letter he had written earlier to another senior official at MIT: 'Smuggling has become a major factor in the expansion of anarchy and terror, as the organisations involved need arms. According to our information, drugs are going out of the country and arms are coming in. But smuggling is a "tainted" issue and, as we knew a number of military officers and civil sevants in the customs department to be involved, the MIT was unable to carry out sufficient investigation.'

The second relevant phenomenon since 1971 is the prominent role alloted to the *ülkücü*, or Grey Wolves. The *ülkücü* infiltrated numerous governmental institutions and their terrorist action against the left-wing was actually tolerated. One of the most infamous incidents took place in 1978. Fights between right and left were the order of the day at that time and some districts and even whole towns were under the control of the right or left in this battle. Bahçelievler was a district of Ankara important to the ultra-right MHP. Apart from the party's head office, this was also the district where Chairman Türkeş's house was located. According to confessions of the former *ülkücü* Ali Yurtaslan, Türkeş wanted to bring this district under the complete control of the Grey Wolves. After investigation, it turned out that seven students who were members and sympathisers of the Turkish Labour Party were living in a flat in the area. In the night of 9 March 1978, all seven were shot dead. In 1980, one of the suspects, Haluk Kirci, said in evidence to a military court in Ankara, 'I don't regret having shot those students.' His statement indicated that the attack had been set up by the national vice-chairman of *ülkücü*, Abdullah Çatli, who later died in the Susurluk incident. Çatli was already suspected of various other murders. The Grey Wolves training institutes provided plenty of potential for people who did not shun violence and who could be deployed in sometimes protected positions in criminal activities. In the

1980s, they also produced people for the police special units who were fighting the PKK in the southeast.

The third post-1971 phenomenon that fits into a broader context is the murders and other activities, such as sabotage, that remained 'without culprits'. In the 1970s, attacks were carried out on public places, such as the arson in the Culture Palace in Istanbul and the sabotage on board the ships *Marmara* and *Eminönü*. Left-wing circles were combed to find the alleged perpetrators, to no avail. In speculating who was actually behind this, the possibility was suggested that a secret organisation run by the state and the army could have played a role. The underworld boss Baybaşin later claimed he was involved in that action and that it was provocation organised by right-wing politicians.

The secret organisation being hinted at would later be defined by various names: the counterguerrilla, the army's special war department and, finally, Gladio. This was a name that had come to the fore in the late 1980s in Italy as a secret, illicit NATO organisation. Prime Minister Andreotti had made every effort to give evasive answers to questions asked in the Italian parliament, but it gradually became clear, also because the same discussion followed in other countries, that a secret network had been set up in all the NATO countries, on the initiative of the United States and financed by the CIA, with the intention of leading the resistance in the event of a communist invasion and occupation. In Turkey, its history began in 1952. Turkey became a member of NATO on April 4 that year, and in September, Seferberlik Tetkik Kurulu, later to be called Gladio, was set up. Various sources indicate that this was all done on the instructions of the United States, which is confirmed in a publication by the former head of the department in question. In 1994 followed confirmation by the chief of staff of the Turkish army, who said that the organisation would only be deployed against foreign enemies and not internal enemies. 'The Turkish army does, indeed, have a special department, called the Special War Department, which will take action against the enemy in the event of war,' reiterated another former commander of this department to a journalist. What he was insinuating was possible sabotage.

There was open speculation of the existence of this department following the attack on Çiğli airport in Izmir in 1977, during which Premier Ecevit was shot at, but, by chance, not hit. An accident, was the court judgement. Later, when Ecevit, then leader of the opposition, wanted to hold an election speech in Istanbul's Taksim Square, he received a confidential letter from Premier Demirel the day before, telling him that he would be shot at from the luxury hotels in the vicinity if he appeared. Ecevit announced that he had received this message and went ahead the next day to Taksim Square. No shots were fired. Gladio is reputed to have been behind both cases.

There was further mention of such a body from a public prosecutor in Ankara, Doğan Öz. After an extensive investigation, he had discovered that a single organisation had been behind certain murders. In 1978, he wrote a report on the subject to the then premier of Turkey, Ecevit: 'There is such an organisation. It includes people from security forces, such as the army, the police and the secret service. During the first and second National Front governments, in particular, they largely adapted the state mechanisms to their own purposes. Their ultimate goal is to introduce a fascist system in Turkey, with all the associated organs.' Doğan Öz was gunned down in front of his home on 24 March 1978. There were witnesses and Ibrahim Çiftçi, the later MHP candidate chairman, was arrested as the main suspect. After the coup in 1980, the military court sentenced him to death, but the military Supreme Court overturned the judgement after lengthy proceedings. A second suspect escaped to Bulgaria with the assistance of Oflu Ismail.

On 1 February 1979, Turkey was stunned by the murder of the editor-in-chief of the daily newspaper *Milliyet*, Ipekçi. This event and its consequences had all of Turkey in its grip for months and, later, it was seen as the catalyst in the coup of 12 September 1980. In searching for the murderers, the names of criminals came to the fore who would later achieve world fame. Based on a tip from someone who then did not survive long, incidentally, Mehmet Ali Ağca was arrested. In his initial statement he admitted, 'Yes, I shot and killed Abdi Ipekçi. I was alone and I fired four or five times.' But a total of thirteen spent cartridges were found in the vicinity of the car in which Ipekçi was killed, which meant there had to be other culprits. Apart from which, witnesses stated that they saw two people running away.

Ağca turned out to be affiliated with the extreme right Ülkü Ocaklari. He had obtained his gun from other extreme right people working with the MHP. The names he named were Mehmet Şener, Yavuz Çaylan and Oral Çelik. Later, Ağca denied that he had killed Ipekçi, stating that he would shortly name the real murderer. According to the investigative reporter Mumcu, that announcement was the reason why Ağca, who faced a death sentence, was allowed to flee. Oral Çelik and Abdullah Çatli collected him from the prison with the aid of a number of army officers.

In November 1979, the Turkish government was busy preparing for the visit by Pope John Paul II. On November 26, three days after Ağca's prison escape, the newspaper *Milliyet* received a phone call informing them that a letter from Ağca had been deposited in a rubbish bin near the paper's office. The handwriting proved to match Ağca's, which prompted the editorial department to inform the Istanbul police. The letter was rather intriguing, particularly in the light of later developments: 'Fearing that Turkey is attempting to realise a new political, military and economic power with its Islamic brother countries in the Middle East, in this highly sensitive period the western imperialists are sending John Paul who, behind his religious mask, is a commander of the cross, with all speed to Turkey. If this senseless and poorly timed visit is not cancelled, then I will not hesitate to shoot the Pope. This is the only reason I escaped from prison. Revenge will certainly be taken for the attack on Mecca by the United States and Israel.'

Ağca was the man who was to carry out the murder attempt on Pope John Paul on 13 May 1981.

The Attack on the Pope

Specialists in organised crime in Turkey are unanimous in their opinion that the attack on Pope John Paul II in 1981 is of real significance in fathoming the process and development of the history of the mafia, but this attack has not, until now, been cleared up. We may know who pulled the trigger, but what exactly was the culprit's motive and who had put out the contract? Italian examining magistrates have been seeking the answer to these questions for over a quarter of a century.

On the morning of May 13, the Pope arrived in St Peter's Square in the back of his car and was waving to the public when, from the midst of the elated crowd, a series of shots was fired. The Pope was hit in the stomach, his right hand and his left index finger. Two American tourists were also hit, but not fatally. A Dutch coach driver saw it happen and stated later that, in addition to the marksman, he had the impression that there had been two more men in the crowd who were associated with him. Police who investigated the case had the same impression, but when he was arrested, the gunman, Mehmet Ali Ağca, did not make any usable statement. He recounted his version of the attack, 'At one point he was right next to me, but when I got ready to shoot him, all of a sudden he was further away again. I didn't think he would get near enough again and I'd missed my chance for today, but suddenly, there was the Pope, right in front of me. That's when I shot.'

Numerous theories have been developed for the background and circumstances of this attack. The Americans thought the KGB was behind it, but the Russians and the Bulgarians were convinced it was the work of the American CIA. Journalist Uğur Mumcu reconstructed the gunman Ağca's movements. The circle in which Ağca moved is now known to us. The following names have already come up several times before in this book: the arms and heroin smugglers Bekir Çelenk, Abuzer Uğurlu and Oflu Ismail Hacisuleymenoĝlu, all three underworld figures who maintained close contacts with politicians, the police and the military. From the circle of the Grey Wolves, two men also mentioned earlier, played a role: Abdullah Çatli, the internationally wanted murderer who was later killed in the Susurluk accident, and Oral Çelik, wanted in Turkey on suspicion of a series of diverse crimes and on the run in Europe. Mehmet Ali Ağca came from this circle himself. He was convicted, jailed and eventually released from the Ancona prison in Rome on 12 January 2006. He became world famous when the Pope had a conciliatory talk with him and the photographs have been published innumerable times.

In the period preceding the attack, the Vitoshya Hotel in Bulgaria was popular with the Turkish underworld; the baba conference in 1980 chaired by Oflu had taken place there. Ağca went straight to this hotel in 1979 after escaping from a military prison in Turkey, where he was serving a sentence for the murder of the journalist Abdi Ipekçi. One of the other Turkish guests at that moment was the *baba* Bekir Çelenk. When questioned by the Italian police, Ağca said it was no coincidence that they were both there at the same time. He had also spoken, he said, to the European *üklücü* leader Çelebi there and to Çatli. According to Mumcu, it was Abdullah Çatli who had organised Ağca's contacts with the smuggling world. After Sofia, Ağca went first to Tunisia, then to Palermo and from there by ship to Rome, Milan and finally to Switzerland. Everywhere he went on this trip, Ağca spoke to people from the *üklücü* movement. After Switzerland he went to Germany, Milan, Majorca, back to Tunisia and again to Italy. Mumcu points out that the route Ağca followed is precisely the same as that which the drug smugglers used in those days. Ağca, Çatli and Çelik were making plans to combat communism in Afghanistan and fight for Islam. The last place Ağca was sighted, between 25 April and 9 May 1981, was Majorca. On May 9, Ağca returned to Rome, where he bought a gun through one of his friends from an Austrian with a Nazi past. There the trail goes cold, and where Ağca was until he appeared four days later in St Peter's Square is unknown. The movements of Çatli and Çelik, possibly the other men involved in the murder attempt in St Peter's Square, in the days leading up to the attack are also known. They, too, travelled throughout Europe.

On 22 February 1982, Çatli was arrested in Switzerland with another *üklücü,* who was a co-suspect in the murder of the Turkish editor in chief of *Milliyet,* for having a false passport. He was immediately released. After that, we can only pick up the trail of the two in the course of that year. In June 1982, along with another *üklücü*, the currently highly prominent underworld figure Çakici, Çatli and Çelik were instructed to take action against Armenian activists in Beirut and France, together with ten other hardened *üklücü*. They did, indeed, liquidate a group of between ten and twenty Armenians. The costs of these operations were paid from one of the president's special funds.

The two names arise again in a Swiss police operation, named Corn Cob, in 1984. The report on the case gives good insight into the way the *üklücü* organised themselves abroad. On June 4 of that year, the Swiss police had intercepted part of a shipment of four kilos of heroin in Kaiseraugst. The shipment was hidden in the spare tyre of a vehicle travelling from Italy to Switzerland. 'The heroin traffic discovered up until now is only the tip of the iceberg,' wrote the Swiss police to Interpol. 'Our inquiries also show that this group of heroin traffickers is from extreme right-wing and Islamic circles in Turkey. In addition to the Turks, an Italian is also involved in the group. The main culprits were the terrorists Abdullah Çatli – alias Hasan, Oral Çelik – alias Atilla, and an *üklücü* arrested earlier with Çatli. They have been in Switzerland since 1981. We don't know who is behind this group in Europe and Turkey.' And about their organisation, 'They affiliated themselves (through mosques, for example) with already well-organised right-wing "Associations for Turkish culture". Çatli and Çelik were treated as heroes within these associations. They quickly found people prepared to take risks and sacrifice themselves.' The group maintained contacts with Yugoslavia, Italy, France, the Federal Republic of Germany, Austria, Liechtenstein and Switzerland. Çatli and Çelik travelled unhindered throughout Europe.

The two were also sighted in the underworld in Amsterdam, where they were in contact with the organisations of Bekir Çelenk and Oflu Ismail. By 1985, Çelik was known in the underworld as Atilla and continually rowed with political opponents. At the end of 1985, Çatli was arrested by French police in possession of four hundred grams of heroin, which earned him a seven-year prison sentence. In 1988, before he had served his sentence, he was extradited to Switzerland to be tried for drug smuggling. There, on 21 March 1990, he escaped from prison. Çelik was picked up in the Netherlands in possession of a small quantity of drugs and three firearms. He was on his way to or back from Çatli's wife in Paris. He was deported to France, as he had a French residence permit. After his release, Çelik was again sighted in 1986 and 1987 attending meetings in the Netherlands. In 2000, Mehmet Ali Ağca was extradited to

Turkey, where he had to serve a sentence for a bank robbery in the 1970s and the murder of the journalist Ipekci. On 12 January 2006, Ağca was granted an early release by a Turkish court. He was picked up from the prison by a businessmen in a swanky car, which took him straight to the Bosporus for a glass of tea. Eight days later, he was rearrested and imprisoned because the court had made a calculation error in his sentence, but also because there had been protests against his release.

State Gangs

Nineteen eighty-seven was the golden era of Premier Özal's liberalisation politics. The people could buy goods of all brands in the shops, at least if they could afford them. American hamburger chains attempted to gain a niche in the market for their product next to the Turkish *lahmacun*, a kind of pizza. An Istanbul journalist from the nationalist and largest Turkish daily newspaper, *Hürriyet*, was allowed into the MIT building in Ankara to be informed of some gold smuggler or other who had become incredibly rich in a strikingly short time. The MIT staff were not in a hurry. That evening, they went for a good Turkish meal together with the journalist, washed down with raki. The next day, the journalist realised where Özal's wind of liberalisation politics was leading. For lunch, he was given a hamburger on a plate with white napkins, a combination that was to be printed over the following period as a kind of logo next to articles on a 'highly confidential' report. He was also given a report, dated 10 November 1987, to read and was allowed four hours to make notes. This document described relationships between the underworld and the Istanbul police, a couple of prominent generals and top civil servants. The editorial department of the newspaper decided not to publish after all. The weekly magazine *Nokta* also declined. The left-wing weekly *2000'e Doğru* did publish the information, 7 February 1988.

The report showed that one of the developments already observed in the 1970s had continued; connections with the underworld do not constitute any obstacle for the further career of high-ranking governmental officials, which suggested more than incidental involvement or individual corruption. Below is a brief summary of the report. It named numerous civil servants, but here we only reproduce the most well-known names. Next to them, where possible, we have listed the position that person currently occupies. It is an impressive list.

- Turkish political parties (both left-wing and right-wing: SHP [now CHP], ANAP, DYP) maintained relationships with the underworld.
- A general and former member of the general staff, who was known to have a weakness for women, had relations with a drugs and arms smuggler and his son had a company together with Dündar Kiliç. In 1981, an underworld figure known as 'the king of the *gazinos*' had delivered the famous Turkish singer, Emel Sayin, to the general in the Sheraton Hotel. [This general was a serious candidate for the presidentship. Premier Özal, who himself had aspirations of becoming president, was suspected of being the one who revealed this MIT report to reduce the general's chances.]
- The governor of Istanbul, Nevzat Ayaz, who was responsible during his term of office for issuing licences for cafés and *gazinos*, publicly awarded one of the underworld figures he had come into contact with and who was the subject of an investigation at the time a certificate to make everyone believe the man was 'clean' [he was later elected to parliament and made it to Minister of Defence].
- In 1981 and 1982, the head of the MIT in Istanbul had close connections with Dündar Kiliç and his lawyer. He organised storage space for smugglers in the port. When questioned, it turned out that Kiliç, together with the said head of the MIT, the governor and the highest police chief of Istanbul, had extorted large amounts of money from non-Muslim minorities [the case was immediately hushed up and has done nothing to prevent the MIT officer from becoming an advisor to premiers Demirel and Çiller].
- According to the MIT report, the city had never been so 'free' as under the supervision of the Istanbul chief of police, and Mehmet Aĝar and a retired head of homicide were primarily responsible for that [this chief of police later became governor of the 'region in state of exception', in other words Southeast Turkey. He was later elected as a member of parliament for the True Path Party and, even later, was briefly a minister in the Yilmaz and Çiller coalition cabinet].
- In his function as deputy chief of police of Istanbul, Mehmet Aĝar put in a good word with high-ranking governmental officials in Ankara for a number of underworld figures. He made sure these figures, including Turan Çevik, Fevzi Öz and Necdet Ulucan, were able to establish contacts with highly placed civil servants and

ministers and so legalise their activities. Ağar continually maintained close connections with drug traffickers and passed on secret information. From his time as head of the second department (homicide), he built up good contacts with the underworld. He owned eighteen houses in Istanbul. One of them, in which he organised secret meetings with his director, for example, was paid for by *baba* Behçet Cantürk. He supplied high-ranking police officers from Ankara with women, had them photographed together and then used the pictures for blackmail [this same Ağar was successively director of police, governor, general director of police and Minister of Justice. He was dismissed from this last position due to the aftermath of the accident in Susurluk].

- A fraudulent banker enjoyed the protection of senior police officers in Istanbul. When the case leaked out, those involved took the initiative to write a 'constructive' article on the case together with a journalist from *Hürriyet*. A policeman who criticised it was transferred to Eastern Turkey. [Note: some journalists still write articles with the 'assistance' of the officials involved.]

- Yahya Demirel was also named in the MIT report. He maintained relationships within the party with gangsters such as Enis Karaduman. [His uncle was later to become president of Turkey.]

The publication of the report prompted massive discussion in Turkey. Initially, all the bodies involved denied its existence. A spokesman for the cabinet announced in a written statement that no such MIT report existed and therefore no Turkish official had ever received a copy. It later came out that the report did exist, albeit in draft form. The head of the secret service had instructed Mehmet Eymur, head of the service's anti-smuggling department, to write it. It was later proved that President General Evren and Premier Özal of Turkey, who had denied its existence, had examined the report at an early stage. The affair had no consequences other than a few officials, including the writers of the report, being transferred or dismissed from the secret service.

*

At the end of 1992, there was a great commotion concerning the large number of 'murders with unknown culprits'. It was particularly striking that, in that year, officially more than nine hundred people had been murdered, without it being clear who the murderers were, or even worse: without it being clear whether the police and the judicial authorities had actually initiated investigations. On 9 February 1993, the Turkish parliament finally took the plunge and compiled a commission to investigate the issue. In 1995, the commission published its conclusions.

The murders commited in Eastern and Southeast Turkey were politically motivated, but the commission also named two cases that showed clearly, for the first time, that criminal gangs were being equipped and instructed by the government. The first was the fatal bomb attack on the journalist and writer Uğur Mumcu, who had conducted a great deal of research on his own initiative into Turkish criminal organisations and the relationships between these and the government and the *üklücü*. It was initiallly assumed that the culprits would be found among Islamic fundamentalists or the PKK, as Mumcu's last research and rather critical articles had been aimed primarily at those groups. The commission came to the conclusion that the Turkish judicial authorities had not instituted any serious criminal investigation into this case. They had even deliberately made 'errors' so that aspects of the investigation would have to be halted. When the commission demanded particular details from the police on behalf of the Turkish parliament, they were withheld, on the grounds of a letter from the public prosecutor of the national security court. The police took an important witness the commission wanted to hear to the Turkish official TV station before allowing him to appear before the commission. This was clearly obstruction and the last sentence in the commission's report on Mumcu's murder was therefore, 'Almost every opportunity has been taken to ensure the case remains unsolved.' Those personnel from the police and the judicial authorities who had obstructed the report were named in full. The indications were enough for Mumcu's family to look primarily to the Susurluk circle.

The second significant finding concerned the activities of the gendarmerie's espionage department. Legally, the department didn't even exist, but some personnel had given details of the department, mentioning it by name: JITEM. According to these witnesses, the JITEM people had themselves been engaged in smuggling arms and drugs in Eastern and Southeastern Turkey. The fact that officers in the army were also accused of trafficking in drugs in this affair was immediate cause for the parliament to put an embargo on the commission's report. Some said the commission had gone too far in its conclusions. Further investigation was halted and the party chairman, Mrs Çiller, degraded the chairman of the commission to a non-electable place in the party. He is now no longer in parliament.

These leaked findings, from which we also quote here, led the newspaper *Cumhurriyet* to write about the 'state within the state'. This idea was further reinforced by the announcement in September 1995 by the deputy prime minister of Turkey and general chairman of the Republican People's Party, Deniz Baykal that, according to his figures, no less than forty-eight percent of the chiefs of police in seventy-seven regions of Turkey could be considered fundamentalists or extreme right *üklücü*. Of those directors, thirty-six percent apparently maintained connections with the mafia. According to Baykal, only those candidates who could produce a sufficiently 'nationalist' reference were admitted to the police schools, particularly to train for the special units.

In 1996, a delegation from the same People's Party went to Eastern and Southeastern Turkey and came back with the announcement that there were military officers dealing in drugs there, extorting money from people and guilty of other shady business. More and more came to the surface, sometimes by chance like Susurluk, sometimes due to mutual conflicts. The head of the delegation, Ercan Karakaş, concluded in 1996, 'Those illegal activities were initially attributed to the PKK. But it now appears that the state also has a hand in them: "gangsters in uniform". Our investigation in the town of Hakkari, for example, has shown that members of the security troops had had PKK receipts printed to camouflage their activities.' According to Karakaş, this was 'a network of secret sabotage groups, which were supposed to commit sabotage in the event of a Soviet invasion, but which in practice up until now appear to have been guilty of irregularities varying from drug dealing to killing Kurdish civilians.' Following these and other allegations, the military chief of staff lodged a complaint with the Public Prosecutions Department concerning the reports of such parliamentary delegations, which, in his opinion, consisted of nothing other than 'separatist propaganda'.

The bad news kept coming. High-ranking police and army officers were involved in a gang from the town of Kocaeli, near Istanbul, and in the gang of the Söylemez brothers – which included eleven police, four soldiers and a doctor. The arrest of the Söylemez brothers degenerated into a fight, in which they proved to be in possession of heavy armaments.

Another discovery was a major gang in Yuksekova, in the area where Turkey, Iran and Iraq meet. The People's Party responded to increasing complaints from the town by sending a delegation there, and in September 1996, it published a report showing that a gang was operating throughout the region including people from military circles who had turned their back on their earlier PKK affiliation and had now formed a special team of village militia. Where drug smuggling was concerned the report stated that 'Hakkari, Van and Yuksekova are intersections in drug trafficking world. The aforementioned gang plays a major role in the route from Afghanistan, through Pakistan and Iran to Turkey. Until 1993, the PKK controlled this trade route entirely. Since then, however, the position was taken over by the state. Armoured cars and other official vehicles are being used for transporting drugs. No-one has been arrested for drug trafficking in the area for years.' The gang was also engaged in blackmail, extortion and murder. While doing so, they pretended to be PKK supporters. The chief public prosecutor of the national security court in Diyarbakir called the discovery of the Yuksekova gang more important than what had come to light in Susurluk. It resulted in an indictment that stated that raw morphine was being transported from Iran and Iraq to Yuksekova and then converted into heroin on the town mayor's farm. Officers from the army, the police special team and the village militia were involved in the smuggling itself. The heroin was then transported in official cars or by military helicopters to the west of Turkey.

Unfortunately, proceedings concerning the issue commenced in the three towns individually. The evidence was not combined and the statements remained incomplete, so it was impossible to obtain a full picture. The case is still being heard.

*

The Turkish government has been setting up and financing units to carry out special assignments since the beginning of the 20th century. These units are outside any democratic control and the most important politicians, sometimes even the prime minister, are not told of their activities. Part of these forces were recruited from the underworld. Their financing is external and remains confidential – and that makes them difficult to control. The amazing criminal coalition brought to light in Susurluk did not surprise a lot of Turkish politicians in itself, perhaps, but the way such gangs are evidently free to go their own way and work for themselves in such an uncontrolled manner probably did.

To see how deep are the roots of the phenomenon of the 'state gang', it is necessary, finally, to go back further into Turkish history. The late 18th century Ottoman ruler Sultan Selim III would go down in history as a progressive politician and romantic poet. Among his less-known deeds is the establishment of an 'illegal committee' in 1792, which was to make decisions on all important matters. The establishment of the secret service still had to wait almost another hundred years and the 'committee' was nothing other than a secret, personal force charged with the task of protecting the sultan, on whom several attacks were made in the turbulent days of the war against Russia and Austria. The committee operated so much in secret that even the second in command in the empire, the Grand Vizier, knew nothing of it. At least one historian has called it an 'illegal' secret organisation, which operated outside the official forces, the police and the army.

This established a tradition and all the sultans who came after Selim set up their own protective organisations. At the beginning of the 20th century the tradition was broken insofar as such organisations were no longer answerable directly to the sultan, but were controlled by the army and, more specifically, certain high-ranking officials. This became the new tradition, and when Turkey became a republic in 1923, the President, who himself came from the army, was the actual commander of this secret unit.

On the eve of World War I, under Enver Pasha, the group of officers that had united at the beginning of the 20th century in the last government of the Ottoman Empire, the Committee for Unity and Progress, organised the Teşkilat-i Mahsusa group, which more or less means 'special unit'. This reported directly to the War Ministry. According to an American historian who conducted doctoral research into this organisation in 1963, not just prominent officers but also intellectuals such as doctors, engineers and journalists were members of it. The rest of the group consisted of people from various ethnic minorities who might have had a shady past, but were considered reliable: they were of 'dubious origin, but there was no reason to doubt their loyalty'. Erturk, one of the former heads of Teşkilat-i Mahsusa, who later published his memoirs, cited innumerable examples of criminals who were part of the organisation. In 1913, heavy criminals were even granted a special amnesty if they went to the front with the Teşkilat-i Mahsusa.

The former commander presents these people as 'patriots' who stood up for a holy objective, for the fatherland. They were deployed during the Balkan war to defend the Ottoman Empire against external enemies including Libya, which was then occupied by Italy, and to retain the Suez Canal. But they also fought against internal enemies who threatened to endanger the 'unity of the Ottoman Empire'. The Teşkilat-i Mahsusa played a role in the genocide of the Armenians in 1915 and 1916 and in aggression against religious minorities in the preceding years. Such a large organisation required external financial support and that was provided by Germany. The special unit was set up for the Ministry of War partly with a secret budget of German money and gold. The fact that prominent Turkish politicians were also involved in this organisation at the time is shown by, for example, the membership of Kemal Pasha, the first president of Turkey, and that of the third president, Celal Bayar.

At the end of World War I, there was a debate in the Ottoman Empire parliament about Teşkilat-i Mahsusa, which by this time had become notorious. It was disbanded, but its leader, Erturk, went on to found the Organisation for the International Islamic Uprising, which met for the first time in Berlin. However, it was suppressed, and the movement was forced to continue in secret under Kara Vasif and Kara Kemal. As both had the first name 'Kara', which means 'black' in Turkish, the new movement was named Karakol, or Black Arm. This movement initially protected primarily the former members of the secret organisation, but was also involved in the fight at that time for the independence of Anatolia.

Mustafa Kemal was able to keep this faction well under control. In 1921, he also established a new secret group, National Defence. The former head of the Teşkilat-i Mahsusa, Erturk, was instructed to organise the group. It was later to evolve into the national police force. In 1920, Mustafa Kemal also set up his own espionage, which consisted exclusively of members of the military. In 1927, this was given a new name, Milli Amele Hizmeti, the – uncontrolled – predecessor of the current Secret Service.

During Ecevit's government in the 1970s, the army chief of staff requested extra money from the prime minister for a special military division. This turned out to be the Special War Department. 'Until then, I had never heard of the existence of such an organisation, either as prime minister or chairman of a political party,' Ecevit said later. Ultimately, this department proved to have been accommodated by an American aid organisation from the 1950s onwards. The costs were paid by the Americans.

Precise details of these groups are not yet known, but it is clear that there is an entire history of special units and secret organisations and gangs working for the state. The special troops, the secret units or, rather, the contra-guerrillas, in which the criminal element is widely represented and which was considered necessary to guard the Ottoman or Turkish state from enemies from without and within, therefore have a long, unique tradition. The gangs known now and the Susurluk incident are typical of this tradition. The former prime minister and minister of foreign affairs, Tansu Çiller, once even declared that the Turkish state couldn't manage without the protective force of such gangs and that their members were national heroes.

7

Hüseyin Baybaşin

Growing up

On 27 December 1995, the Dutch police stopped a car coming from Belgium. In it sat one of the greatest *babas* of Turkey, now – by his own account – a Kurdish businessman. Hüseyin Baybaşin was a wanted man. The chief public prosecutor for the national security court in Istanbul had requested his extradition on 9 March 1995 and, shortly afterwards, Interpol had issued a warrant for his arrest at the request of the Republic of Turkey. His description had been circulated internationally. Baybaşin already had an eventful history in the global underworld. Not long before his arrest he had revealed in a number of extensive interviews with the media how the Turkish state had long been involved at the highest level in drug smuggling and the murder of political opponents.

Baybaşin, who was not wanted in the Netherlands itself, was remanded in custody in Breda and then detained until the minister of justice decided whether or not to extradite him to Turkey. The court decided extradition was possible and on 17 December 1996 the Supreme Court upheld the decision, but advised the minister not to go ahead, as the person involved had already been tortured before in Turkey and that would happen again, 'as a Kurdish businessman suspected of financing the PKK, he would even have to fear for his life'.

Baybaşin was allowed to leave custody and reside at an unknown location in the Netherlands. This generated a political dispute with Turkey, which was strongly of the opinion that the Netherlands should immediately extradite Baybaşin. That was exacerbated by the fact that Baybaşin sought publicity and repeatedly levelled accusations at prominent Turkish politicians. The Turkish ambassador to the Netherlands announced that these allegations 'have been plucked out of the air' and considered it unacceptable for the media to publish such statements from the lips of a notorious drug trafficker without questioning them. The Dutch minister of justice wanted to carry out the extradition, but in interlocutory proceedings it was finally decided that Baybaşin could stay in the Netherlands.

Shortly after Baybaşin was detained, we contacted him through his lawyer in Turkey and were granted permission to talk to him in prison in Breda. His story amazed us from the point of view of the behaviour of the Turkish state gangs, the involvement of high-ranking people and the activities of Turkish consulates abroad (the Susurluk incident had not yet happened, but after it, Premier Erbakan provided the president with a list of the top figures involved from the underworld, and Baybaşin was near the top of the list). At the end of the first visit, we were given a pile of newspapers and magazines in which he was featured prominently, often on the cover, as homework for any further discussion with him. As we were not sure how long he would be in prison, we tried to speak to him as often as possible in a short time. In total, we had twenty two-hour meetings.

Virtually all the conversations were in Turkish with the odd word of Kurdish. Baybaşin is stocky and extremely strong. He talks animatedly, with plenty of hand gestures, has good manners and, like so many under-world bosses, is socially skilled and charming. He is clearly not used to being contradicted often and, combined with his enormous wealth – he once considered setting up his own Kurdistan airline, for which he said he wanted to buy nine planes 'with nothing on the clock' – he will undoubt-edly have been able to 'help' a lot of people.

He courteously begins each answer with the term of address 'scholar' and then, when he wishes to say no more on a particular subject, starts with 'my brother'. It is difficult to keep him to the chronology of his story and he skips from one subject to another. In his world, other things – such as with whom did I conclude which deals? – are more important than chronological order. It can't be as simple to maintain such an extraordinarily extensive network of social relationships as he would have people think.

How reliable is the information he gives us? His story is, by its nature, a subjective account of what Baybaşin has experienced, in the form that favours him most. That also applies to the politicised form in which he sometimes phrases things. His account nonetheless corre-sponds strikingly with what is known about the development of organised crime in Turkey. What follows is the story as Baybaşin told it.

*

Hüseyin Baybaşin was born on 25 June 1956 in the village of Lice in the Kurdish Southeast of Turkey, a hundred and fifty kilometres from the Syrian border and more than three hundred kilometres from the Iraqi and Iranian borders, in the smuggling province of Diyabakir. While this is one of the least developed parts of Turkey, where people still live in more or less feudal conditions, Lice itself enjoys a certain intellectual, socialist-Kurdish fame. Baybaşin came from a family of landowners and his uncle on his father's side, who had inherited this position from his father, was the ağa. Such a clan chief has a mediatory function. 'If there was an argument or a crime had been committed, then people met at my grandad's house,' said Baybaşin. 'It was a kind of court. Only if my grandfather was unable to solve it alone did he also call in an imam.' The family had become rich from trading in the dried sap of raw opium, which they bought in Afyon in Western Anatolia and exchanged in Iran for gold and cash. The family is extremely large. Many of the men have impressive criminal records and are well known to police forces in other countries.

Baybaşin always strives to make plain that the underworld would never survive without the government, even though, of course, it was the government that should be fighting smuggling. He talks of his uncle as one of the people who 'were supported'. Gentlemen such as he constituted a governmental link with the state, which was represented in the village by the police and the lower-ranking army officers. The symbiosis with the state was also reflected in the many connections his uncle had with senior state officials.

The major event that overshadowed Baybaşin's youth was the murder of the village chief and the local commander of the gendarmerie. He is deliberately vague on the details, but it may have been a clash to do with smuggling. In any event, his uncle was involved. The government restored its authority with a hard hand: Baybaşin's nineteen-year-old brother was killed and his uncle wounded. 'They obviously didn't realise who they had killed, because our family was powerful and was every-where, even in Iran and Syria, and it wasn't the kind of family you looked for trouble with.' Once the government had acted, both parties returned to the earlier *modus vivendi*. 'My uncle had been in prison for a while, but he'd had it good there and came home every day. He finally settled the affair with the police.' This meant that the collective suspicion on the family was lifted.

Where does a *baba*'s criminal career begin? 'I think I probably would have been left-wing if I'd happened to get involved with people with left-wing ideas. Or a thief, if I'd happened to go around with a bunch of thieves. Not that I would have stolen myself, because my upbringing taught me that stealing was not allowed. In our circles thieves are humiliated. We tried to help each other if someone was in difficulties. If someone needed something, then we made a collection, but stealing was dishonourable. Even later, in prison, I blushed with shame and anger when I heard about someone having stolen. It was in prison that I saw a thief for the first time in my life.'

His first offence was robbery. 'I've never gambled myself, my mother cured me of that straight away. Once, when I was a boy, I was tossing a coin and when she saw that, she held my foot in the fire. I've still got the scar and I've never gambled since. But I didn't mind doing other things. The kids in Lice tossed coins on feast days. When they played, I took everything off them, whether it was heads or tails. I put that money in my pocket and bought fruit with it. When I got home, my mother asked where I'd got it from and I said I'd got it at the cemetery [where people gave children fruit on feast days], but they'd seen through me, because they never gave away as much as I'd got. Other children had told my father in the café, too. He came home while I was eating dinner and hit me really hard: "How could you start gambling and then taking other people's money from them?"'

After robbery came smuggling. 'I started dealing secretly, selling roses and paprikas to rich people. I hadn't told my father anything, but he saw me when I had to move three donkeys loaded with paprikas to the side of the road in the dark when the bus from Diyarbakir passed. When he got home he hit my mother; why hadn't she told him? I said I'd only done it because I wanted some money and didn't want to ask him for it. After that, I becames a street trader in my spare time after school. I bought stuff in the town and went with a friend from village to village, where we exchanged the things for butter, leather and so forth, and then we sold them again in town. My father said nothing more, but he thought it was awful. If you really think about it, it was smuggling because we didn't pay any tax. We also went by horse to Syria to fetch stuff, like clothes. It wasn't legal, because you're not allowed to import anything from Syria, but well… we didn't have any passports anyway, we didn't even know what they were.'

*

Baybaşin left home around seventeen to move to the big city of Istanbul because of conflicts with his father. Hüseyin was becoming increasingly uncontrollable and his father knew no other remedy but hitting. 'He hit me so much! I was dead scared of him. When he called me I started trembling. One time he shouted that he was going to murder me. That was the last straw for me. I wasn't putting up with it. There was a weapon in the house... After that, he never hit me again.'

Once in Istanbul, Baybaşin quickly found his way into the cigarette smuggling scene. 'The cigarettes and whisky in Istanbul were entirely under the control of the underworld bosses. Of course they couldn't work without help from the state.' By this, he meant individual corrupt police officers or groups of officers, not the government itself. 'There were babas who controlled individual districts. In the east of Istanbul, for example, you had Zihni Ipek and Bagteli Doğan, who controlled all the ships in Maltepe. And Koç ağa, who was murdered later. He was one of the really big boys and had had a disagreement with Abuzer Uğurlu. The people from Kilis there, they were big smugglers, too.

'I was still in the distribution part of smuggling at that time, but you learned exactly what went on. We knew which car was whose, who controlled which district and how much room the police gave him. Dündar Kiliç was just starting to make a name for himself, as was Kürt Idris, who was involved in gambling, and Oflu Osman, who controlled the entertainment. Those were the names you heard. It is striking how many of those top figures have had their characters formed by family feuds; all those I named came to the city after being directly involved in a vendetta as a young man. In the beginning we were too small to ask gambling joints and companies for protection money. There were others who did that and we didn't get a look in. Those who were higher up than us collected the money. Our circle did, however, become more powerful than others involved in smuggling, because we used military vehicles for transport; there was a military base we used near Yalova. The advantage was that such transports weren't checked.

'We formed a group and everyone started to get scared of me, because I was unusual. "Spider", they called me, because I was involved in everything. People would ask me for help and – the funny thing is – I wasn't afraid of anything. Very often it was fighting. I always visibly carried a weapon, the police could see it and everyone on the street: a gun.'

That was when his cooperation with the police began. 'Wherever we went, people knew us. If the café was "ours" we were automatically treated with respect, but if they didn't know us, we turned the place upside down. If anyone gave us a belittling look, then we demolished the place. Once I'd used a gun for a year, then I threw it away, or we sent it to Diyarbakir, because they didn't do any ballistic investigations for Istanbul there.'

The headquarters for contact between the police and the underworld was the famous Marmaracafé. 'I did what I was told. We set fire to a car, for example, but we never thought about who the car belonged to or why we were doing it. We just carried out the two policemen's orders and thought about the money it would earn us. The military were in power, but they couldn't touch us. We were the ones who set fire to the culture palace and a ferry, for example. We didn't know why we were doing it; we only heard that later.*

'We thought about the respect we would earn from our success. When I went to certain police stations, they couldn't touch us. I was also different because, from quite a young age, I'd started giving food to the poor on certain days. The newspaper *Tercüman* even wrote at that time – I was twenty – that I had opened a restaurant for the poor. That was a gross exaggeration. But it was a family tradition in the area I came from. We always had guests eating at our house. In Istanbul, I took between five and twenty people to a restaurant.'

In 1975, Baybaşin returned to Lice when he was called up for national service. His expensive clothes and unusually large watch made a big impression there. He gave out cartons of Marlboro and 'everyone was looking more at the cigarettes than at me'. His family wasn't sure what to do with this troublemaker. 'My father and uncle had already been to Istanbul a couple of times looking for me and my uncle had said to an acquaintance that he would kill me for what I was doing. I replied to that

---

* This refers to the arson in the culture palace on 27 November 1970 and, a couple of days later, the burning of the Eminönü and Marmara ferries. The media treated these incidents as communist attacks and this prompted the arrest of left-wing intellectuals. On 12 March 1971, the military presented an ultimatum due to the anarchy that was ruling the country. Nowadays, most critical authors treat the attacks as having been committed by the contra-guerrilla movement.

acquaintance that it was more likely that I would murder him and my father. In my mind my father hadn't been able to hit me for a long time. Back in Lice, my father asked me what I was doing and I said I dealt in cigarettes. My father kept telling me I had to stop that trading, I had to go into the army now and I had to get married. But life in Istanbul was far more appealing.'

On 6 September 1975, an earthquake of Richter magnitude 6.8 occurred near Lice. Two thousand and eighty-five people were killed and 3,339 were injured in the disaster. Thousands of homes in almost two hundred villages were either destroyed or badly damaged, while landslides virtually demolised Lice. 'At that moment, I was in the mosque, because I prayed five times a day, I didn't drink, I was a true Muslim. Loads of members of my family died and, in the days that followed, I saw how completely helpless the population was. I wanted to help straight away, I gave away all the money I had with me and immediately emptied my bank account. Then I went back to Istanbul to get more money, because my thoughts were still with the victims.'

The way Baybaşin lived was asking for continual clashes with the police and, from the age of eighteen or nineteen, he was in and out of prison. The first time is a watershed in every criminal career and it was then that Baybaşin was introduced to the prison mafia. 'Fighting wasn't ususally necessary in the Bayrampaşa prison, because there were people who you listened to. You also listened to what the officer from the judicial authorities said. The warders and the board did what we wanted and some people could even go outside now and again. If you had money, you could arrange anything with the warders. I didn't smoke or drink myself, but it was allowed.

'If they thought you weren't behaving well, then they could transfer you. When I got into that position, they sent me to the prison in Edirne, one of the four most heavily guarded regional prisons in Turkey. I'd already built up a certain reputation there and my name was mentioned in the newspapers in all kinds of events taking place within the prison walls during that period. Even if I had nothing to do with it, like a fight one night when five people were killed. They were so scared of me that, if I didn't like a fellow prisoner, they took him away because they were worried he might die overnight. But I was involved in certain events. Sometimes the board didn't like one group; then they got them to fight with another one. Then they came to me with this story that the other guys were bad and I was powerful and they'd uncovered a conspiracy against me. Then you started fighting. Everyone in prison has *şiş* (skewers used for kebabs). We used those skewers when we fought. At one point, a couple of child rapists were brought into the prison. They were housed in a special department, where everybody had to wear army uniform, so we wouldn't know which ones they were. But it wasn't that hard. It only took three days to find out. We broke down the doors and first murdered two grasses and then the ones who had abused the children. There were five dead in total. After that event, we were locked up in unit five.

'It was in that department that I met Abdullah Palaz. In the prison, people who were destructive were called devils. Abdullah was a real devil. Everyone was scared of him, he was crazy and he'd already been there twenty years. When you went to sleep at night, he could bump you off just like that, without any reason. He'd killed his wife and children, too. And he could have murdered me. Of course my friends would have got him back, but that's not much use to you then, is it?'

In 1995 , a prominent doctor, Turhan Temuçin, published a monograph on Palaz, a serial killer known as the 'Angel of Death', which describes the events Baybaşin recounted exactly. The only thing that mattered to Palaz was recognition: according to Temuçin, he was a man who demanded respect because he adhered to the code of honour. The doctor's assessment is disconcerting. No psychiatric examination established any disorder in Abdullah – except that he couldn't stop murdering. He had killed at least forty-eight people.

'After the prison, I went straight back to Lice to rest. There, I saw that every shop and every café had become part of a political faction.' Turkey in the 1970s was riven by violent politics. On the grounds of the Kemalistic principle, it was not permitted to establish political parties 'based on class interests' – in other words communism – according to articles 141 and 142 of the penal law. Instead, factions organised themselves as the 'sympathisers' of certain magazines and everyone knew where, for example, the Maoist 'faction' met. 'When I went into a café, people thought it was strange that I didn't know which faction I belonged to, they thought I ought to listen to what certain leaders had to say,' said Baybaşin. 'But as far as I could see, those people were just out to benefit personally. That's where I first heard of the PKK, too. They had attacked a Kurdish family. I was furious about it; how can you allow Kurds to be victims when you want to found a Kurdistan?

'It became clear to me then that my uncle was far more powerful as head of the tribe than I was in Istanbul. He had relationships with security people and never went out without being surrounded by five or six armed men. No-one wanted to make him angry and anything he said went. If anyone raised any objections against him, then they were killed – that's how powerful my uncle was. He was brave and determined, but he cooperated with the state, too.

'My uncle called me to him and told me that the life I was living held no future. He told me I was upsetting my mother because I kept ending up in prison and he felt we should start working together in his fabric business. So I did, and things went well, because the turnover rose by twenty per cent and my uncle shared the profits with me. I drove around in a car and sold the stuff. They'd never expected me to work so hard! But I didn't enjoy it, because Diyarbakir was so unsafe that you couldn't expand. It was a time of mounting tension, there were an awful lot of arms around and not a day went by, literally, without a shooting. Cafés were held up, too. The local authorities couldn't stop it. That's why, despite my uncle's fury, I soon picked up with my old friends in Istanbul again.'

He acquired a share in a nightclub and again saw a chance to build up his career under the watchful eye of corrupt authorities. 'I only had to show my face now and again at the club and it was a gathering place. If there was a fight somewhere else, we made sure that it stopped. The smuggler Zihni Ipek came to the club and with him came senior police officers, including Nejat Küçüktaşkiner, who was then a member of the MIT Secret Service [and later Baybaşin's lawyer]. People played cards in the club, business people came and we were able to live well on the bale [the amount that had to be paid to be able to gamble]. Apart from that, I also received my share of all business deals concluded there and I earned so much that after only being back in Istanbul for three months I was already able to buy a house.'

The American term protection racket means that business people are forced by the underworld to pay money on a regular basis, otherwise their place will be 'turned upside down', as Baybaşin expressed it. But if the initiative comes from the businessman, if he is prepared of his own free will to pay for private protection in the real expectation that he will receive it, then what should you call that? In the gambling 'market', which is controlled by the underworld, this is still less innocent than simply taking on bouncers. Baybaşin distinguishes between the *haraç* –

the extortion sum, or *pizzo* in Italian – and the *pay*, which literally means portion or share. In the latter case, he is really providing the customer with a service. He makes use or his personal authority, for example, if a certain illegal economic transaction is to be concluded.

'I was first introduced to drugs in the Bayrampaşa prison. There was no heroin or cocaine in the circles I moved in in Istanbul. There hadn't been any drugs in Lice when I was a kid, either, there were no laboratories there. But everything was fully organised in prison. Both the warders and the public prosecutor were well aware of what was being brought in wrapped in aluminium foil.'

Edirne, where Baybaşin was later in prison, is on the main road to Europe on the Bulgarian border. It was there, in 1977, that Baybaşin first heard about heroin smuggling to Germany. The first time he had anything to do with it himself he was, by his own account, framed by his friends. 'When I came back from Lice in 1976 they found drugs at my house, at least that's what they said. They got me to sign some papers at the police station, without telling me what was in them. Then they sent us to prison. I was furious, but I was used to it; usually they let me go after a couple of hours or two days, but not this time; they even shaved my head. Three days later, someone from Kars took me to his cell. He had posters of a [grey] wolf [identifying himself as an ultra-nationalist] on the wall. The prisoner asked me if I needed any money: if I needed anything, I could ask them now.

'Up to that point I'd managed to keep the fact that I was in prison from my family. But when they found out, they sent our lawyer from Lice and he asked me if I was mad, signing a statement like that. I would definitely get twenty years, he said. I'd obviously been framed, because the file quoted a street and house number that didn't even exist. Later, we found out that they hadn't found any drugs at my house at all. I got off with a total of two years. They took me with a group of forty-eight people to the military prison in Edirne, where I had to spend four months and eleven days in solitary confinement.'

After that, they considered that the 'disciplining' had been completed. Evidently, a deal had been concluded: Baybaşin would keep his mouth shut and would have to do odd jobs for the police other than just running the protection racket the police had organised. And that's what happened. Baybaşin became one of the provocateurs who were used to destabilise politics in the 1970s. 'At the funeral of a law student who had been beaten to death in 1975 at the police station, a couple of right-wing demonstrators were expected to be beaten up. We had to protect them. Out in front of the funeral parlour, the people were shouting: "Death to the fascists!" and we joined in, because we had been told to do whatever the crowd did. We also had to beat up an editor from the newspaper *Milliyet*. We had to say the man was an infiltrated spy – he was a foreigner – which would give the people we were protecting the opportunity to beat him to death. The next day, we read in the paper that the man hadn't been a spy, but an editor for the newspaper. They said that left-wing factions had killed the man, but that wasn't true. Unless you've been through it yourself, it might be hard to believe, but we did things like that. When I was in prison, I knew a special event was going to take place in Taksim Square, where a lot of people would lose their lives.'

Here Baybaşin is referring to the attack by sharpshooters during the May Day demonstration in 1977, when thirty-nine people were killed. 'We had a very limited vision in those days: what were all those people doing in Taksim Square? They all had to be killed.' Baybaşin considered the Grey Wolves who had infiltrated the state institutions to be very well organised. 'There were a couple with power and the rest were puppets who were simply used. They couldn't get out: then they would be killed.'

Drug Trafficker

At that same time, Baybaşin became a drug wholesaler. 'I was sitting chatting to old friends and we were talking about what was actually most profitable. Everyone agreed that it was drugs. Tonnes of heroin came in by boat from Beirut in Lebanon, which were transported on by ship to Europe. Our group went to find out who it was and where it was. Another uncle of mine from Lice was in drug trafficking himself. When I was still selling fabric for my other uncle, he'd already said to me that all that uncle did was pray five times a day and there was another way I could earn far more money.

'I also got involved in that world through a certain Mahmut from Malatya, who had been brought to me because he came from the same area. Mahmut knew Europe really well. They called him Mahmut the Anarchist and he became one of the active people in our group. There was a man in my group who organised the route out of the country. He was also involved in selling land the fleeing Greeks had left behind.* He arranged for the drugs to be concealed in coaches. He looked for places in the coach where nobody would ever search. Later, someone slightly older, who had excellent connections with people in the army, took over from him. He put us in contact with the Greeks and we did their purchasing and sales. Two Greek brothers had a fish export company and they took the stuff by boat to Greece and from there on to other European countries. In 1981, we set up a travel agency, with twenty-eight coaches going to the Netherlands, Germany, Belgium and, later, England, too.'

The travel agency was a legal firm, which he used as a front. The money earned from smuggling was taken back to Turkey in the coaches, but they were never used for transporting the drugs themselves.

'These drugs were from Afghanistan. They talk about an annual production in Afghanistan of two hundred tonnes of heroin and another

---

* Tens of thousands of Greeks fled Turkey during decades of persecution.

hundred thousand tonnes of hash, but I'm sure it's more; I've investigated heroin production myself. Marijuana isn't so interesting, because it's everywhere these days; people in Europe can grow it in their own gardens. But heroin is different. In the first few years after 1980, the period of Russian rule, things were bad in Afghanistan. There wasn't much heroin being produced then, but after the Russians withdrew, everyone could do as they pleased. First, the stuff was brought into the Kurdistan region of Turkey via Iran. At the border, the transport was taken over by the Turkish army. It used to go over the montains, but now they do it differently. There are airlines controlled by the Turkish state, like Turkish Airlines used to be, whose planes they use especially for this purpose. Navy vessels are also used for the European region, but that's another story.

'Between 1989 and 1991, large amounts used to go from Afghanistan via Azerbaijan, but that stopped when the Soviet Union collapsed. With the arrival of Haydar Aliyev's government in Azerbaijan, which was less favourably disposed towards the regime in Turkey, things stagnated. Since then, the heroin has been taken via the operating port in the town of Mazar-i-şerif to the border with Uzbekistan and Turkmenistan, through the area controlled by the military leader Dostum, who cooperates with Turkey. From there, the stuff is flown to Turkey or Russia. Turkey sends this Dostum great planes full of the resources he needs. Or the heroin goes by car via the border area with Armenia and Iran. There, they have so-called army camps, which are actually laboratories.'

The reverse route is equally important. 'To make one tonne of drugs you need twenty tonnes of other substances, water, calcium and so forth. If you work that out for the total production, then we're talking about thousands and thousands of tonnes of resources. In Turkey, big planes were used to take all that to Afghanistan.'

Baybaşin became extraordinarily rich, which he made no secret of. 'If I went to a gazino, my people drove behind me in a string of cars. At the gazino they asked which musician I wanted to hear. If the managers wanted to make a change to the programme, that was discussed with me first. Women who were out to make a career for themselves came up to me, smiling in the hope that they'd be allowed to sing. I hated that kind of behaviour. I told them straight away to stop it.' Baybaşin wants to make it clear that he was above such unsubtle temptation. 'If I went out to dinner with a singer, she behaved either as if I was her possession or as if she could spend the night with me. But sometimes I told them to shove off. Well, that's all part of it. But for me, a woman's beauty was never the most important thing; her popularity as a singer determined whether I went out with her. The only thing she wanted was to be seen in public with someone of my reputation. At that time, the press had no permission to write about me. If someone did it anyway, it cost him his head. People from the state also made sure nothing was published.

'Mahmut the Anarchist sometimes said to me that I didn't understand what we were doing and now I can see he was quite right. In actual fact, everything was controlled by people from the government. The ones who came regularly to my club were sometimes described in the press as the police mafia, the Laz mafia, the ülkücü mafia or the Kurdish mafia. But they weren't really, those were higher up; it was governmental officials who organised things. Police came, people from the secret service, and I hung around with people like Mehmet Ağar and Kemal Yazici. Those were the people who wanted to keep the illegal affairs in one hand, to increase the profit. That's what they told us and we accepted it. But there was the other side; once you were in, you could never get out again.

'Everyone had a specific function. Nejat Küçüktaşiner, a member of the secret service, and later my lawyer, was one of them. When I met Mustafa Erik, who also comes from Lice and owned hotels in Van, he told us about the drugs business; they were being traded at the highest level. Erik was close friends with [later president] Süleyman Demirel. Another friend of Demirel's I knew well was Kemal Yildirim, the owner of the Royal Hotels, but he's never been in drug trafficking. He was involved in the sale of land that had belonged to Armenians. After the coup on 12 September 1980, it was easier for us to manoeuvre. That winter, we went to Van in police cars and when we were transporting the stuff we did it with military vehicles. Usually a hundred and fifty to two hundred kilos at a time.'

In 1982, Baybaşin travelled in Europe for the first time, to set up the smuggling network. The days when only police officers and people from the secret service formed the corruption chain were over. According to Baybaşin, the government itself was involved at that point, too. For him, the most important representative of the Turkish state was Şükrü Balci, the chief of police in Istanbul.

'Şükrü Balci came to talk to us himself. Our money came from the Netherlands and Germany via the Işbank, but it was not recorded. We went to our man at the bank and he gave it to us. The same thing happened at the Pamuk Bank. I didn't even realise myself that it was also the state itself organising it, but in some cases we were told that the money was intended for the development of the state. Half the money from every transaction went to the state. To us, it was a kind of tax, in exchange for which we received protection in all aspects. If the money was confiscated or we were arrested, then our contacts with the government came to fetch us and said that we worked for the state. They even protected us in Europe. When I made a second trip to Europe that year, I saw for myself how all the consulates were involved in the trafficking. There is a member of staff at each consulate for that purpose. That person is supposed to set up cultural centres and Turkish schools, for example. So we gave them money for that. The Turkish Culture Association, for example, was entirely financed with money from drug trafficking. Practically no contribution came from Turkey itself. These officials organised meetings and produced posters in all the capital cities for promoting Turkey.'

*

The basis for Baybaşin's current left-wing and pro-Kurdish attitude lies, so he says, in his first prison experiences, and was primarily formed during and after the earthquake in southeast Turkey in 1975. The circumstances in the prison were not, in themselves, favourable for developing a political conscience.

'We weren't allowed to read any books or newspapers and we weren't interested in doing so, either. When the news came on the television then, we all shouted that they should turn it off or find a film. I didn't know anything about politics. I mixed with everyone, without bothering about whether they were left- or right-wing. Once, in Edirne, a prisoner told the minister of justice, who was visiting, that there was extortion going on in the prison. This man had left-wing ideas and I could feel he was in danger. I took him in with me so they wouldn't do anything to him, but three days after I was released, I heard that he'd been murdered after all. They said it was the right-wingers who'd done it. That didn't mean so much to me at the time. But after the earthquake I woke up. Every day we saw and heard on the television and radio that the government was offering plenty of aid, but we hadn't noticed anything. There was a shortage of tents, blankets and food. You couldn't bury the dead and it stank of corpses everywhere. There wasn't enough help at all. The disagreements between the people that dominated the region evaporated at that moment. Cantürk's [the other big *baba* in Lice] younger brother and I organised a march from Lice to Diyarbakir, to demonstrate that the government was actually doing nothing.'

It started to dawn on Baybaşin what it meant to be a Kurd. 'After the earthquake, I felt like a Kurd, too. My friends were angry about it. After all, we were all Turks, they said. But I said I wasn't Turkish, because when it came down to it, the Turkish government had left us to our fate. But after the 1980s, I really learned to see through politics and started to understand the concept of Kurds and Grey Wolves.'

In 1981 or 1982, during General Evren's government and before the 1983 elections, Baybaşin also fought the political battle in the Gulizar *gazino*. 'I'd asked Faruk Tuncer, who could sing in Kurdish too, to sing a song, but he said it wasn't allowed in Kurdish [after the coup of 1980 it was forbidden to speak Kurdish even on the street]. After him came a female singer and then I couldn't control myself any longer; I screamed at her to piss off. Then Faruk was called back and I made him sing for me in Kurdish. There was a soldier sitting next to me and he, too, was acutely aware that if anyone had contradicted me at that moment I would have shot them all dead. One time, I emptied my entire gun in the Bulvar gazino at midnight in fury. I wanted a Kurdish singer, but the owner came and said that they hadn't been able to find anyone who spoke Kurdish. Some soldiers tried to take me away. They said I'd shot at them, but that wasn't true; I'd only shot at their car. And HB [Hüseyin Baybaşin] could do as he pleased, couldn't he? The next day, my friends from the state locked me up; they said they were going to kill me. They said I'd better watch out and not go around shouting that I was a Kurd. At moments like that, you realise that it's not you who's powerful, but the whole group you're in.'

Baybaşin came from the birthplace of the PKK and the struggle couldn't fail to appeal to him. Even though his old friends from the state tried convincing him to turn against the PKK, he still developed into the left-wing type of Kurdish *baba*, like Behçet Cantürk, who was a good friend of his. In 1984, a British court sentenced Baybaşin to twelve years in prison for a serious drugs offence. He claimed someone had 'planted' a small amount of morphine in his house: 'You don't think I'd ever let myself get caught with drugs, do you?' he asked us, in good English. He served four and a half years, after which he was released in exchange for an English prisoner in Turkey, returning to his home country in 1989. Politically, he now had to decide his standpoint.

'I don't sympathise with everything the PKK does,' he said. That is quite understandable, as he knows the PKK set fire to the brick kilns he was having built in the mountains because he didn't want to give them any money. Baybaşin was livid and humiliated the leaders of the PKK. They offered their apologies and said that the arson had been a personal initiative. 'But I do sympathise with the battle as far as fighting to stand up for the Kurdish people is concerned. We must have a Kurdism to guide us. I have to be able to exercise the right to express myself as a Kurd. Just as a Turk in Germany has the right to be a Turk. As long as that right doesn't exist, there will be a faction such as the PKK; if there was no PKK another resistance movement would appear on the scene. Those people give their lives for my people. I was really furious when they caused me damage, and I told them off about it, but I will never see them as enemies. I've announced these views publicly, even to people in high positions. But I've never accepted a position in the PKK.'

Just as Cantürk did, Baybaşin supported the struggle financially. 'That's the issue the police forces in Europe understand so little of: does the PKK extort money from Kurdish drug traffickers or not? How does that work? A Kurd comes to me asking for help, in setting up a newspaper, for example. I make a contribution, but it doesn't go directly to the PKK. I support an "institution" which describes the Kurdish problem in an honest, objective manner. And I ask friends to donate a contribution, too. When something like that has been asked of me by people I respected and who clearly explained their objective, I've often given that help. My contribution was generally quite large. If people qualify that as "helping the PKK" then that's their problem. I, myself, just feel I'm contributing to developing Kurdish identity and solving the Kurdish issue.' This system proved not without risks, and Baybaşin was only able to do things like that with people he knew well and trusted. In Istanbul, for example, was an association that organised Kurdish meetings. In retrospect, however, everyone realised that the state had only permitted it as a sneaky way of finding out who was supporting Kurdish separatism.

From the moment Baybaşin backed the Kurdish cause, he came into conflict with his former friends. First, these friends did everything possible to get him to work for them by infiltrating the Kurdish movement.

Baybaşin had spent five years in prison in England under the false name of Nejdet Yilmaz. There, he was visited by the Turkish authorities, who were aware of who he really was. They proposed to the British exchanging a British convict in Turkey for Nejdet Yilmaz – and they did. Once he was in Turkey, Baybaşin was not released but kept in prison. As he was supposed to be sick, he was allowed to stay in the prison clinic, where he was visited by the deputy director of the Istanbul police drugs squad. In the meantime, he had begun legal proceedings to change his name back to Hüseyin Baybaşin. 'The police man, who said his name was Bayram Akbal, told me, "I'm the head of the narcotics department. There's been a mistake. You should never have been sentenced. You're our friend and our friends know you well. They all admire and respect you." Once he had delivered his message, he said he wanted me not to be so rebellious in prison any longer and he would come back later. I replied that the prisoners actually got on very well with each other and the only thing that bothered us was the behaviour of people like him. Soothingly, he said we would talk about that the next time.

'That second time, I had to go to see him in an office in the clinic. Then he said, "You did some bad things in England, but now you've changed. You've even improved. There are a lot of young people in your family and they're all brave and courageous. Everyone will listen to you." To my utter amazement, he then said he wanted a hundred and fifty thousand German marks from me personally; as a token of friendship. If I was looking for work, he said, they could help me find a job straight away. Of course what he meant was I would be smuggling heroin. "It doesn't matter how much you want," he said, "we can supply as much as necessary. As long as you know people who want to buy it, if you check out the market for us. Just say the word and we can work together. But if I'm going to arrange all this, then of course you have to pay me that money personally." I was incredibly angry. "Are you out of your head? I've been inside for five years and you're demanding money from me?" I grabbed him by the collar and picked him up chair and all. He was really shocked. Everyone was watching: the doctors, the warders, the army officers. Bayram Akbal had put his name and signature in the visitors' book; it was no secret who was visiting me. Bayram's parting words were, "I'll teach you. You won't have a chance to survive this. Be sensible." He talked like that.'

The next day, the police seemed even to have got the Turkish media to convince him to resume his trade, as a report on this exchange of words was featured in the *Tercüman* of 7 March 1989, under the heading, 'Drug baba Hüseyin Baybaşin arrested during fight.' After that, another drug boss and fellow prisoner, Enis Karaduman, called him to his room in the prison clinic 'to watch television. In the programme, they showed the so-called interception of my heroin in a restaurant and at a farm. Four days before I was due to leave prison, another head of the drugs squad came to see me and my lawyer. He said, "Bayram sends his greetings. He wants to know your answer: friend or foe?" I asked what that meant. The chief then told me that in Silvan [in eastern Turkey, near Diyarbakir] my brother, my cousin and thirteen members of personnel of the hotel I owned there had been arrested. He said they'd picked them up for drug trafficking. "If you make friends with us, then we promise we'll release all those people immediately. But if you say no, you'll come across them mutilated here in the prison."

'I got mad and started yelling, but even my lawyer said I'd better listen to this Mustafa. Enis Karaduman, my fellow prisoner, who had even been to the military academy and who had heard a lot about me in that capacity, started putting pressure on me by saying it would be better for me to reach an agreement with these people. "They're the state and, in Turkey, they call the shots. It's better for you not to resist any longer. It's ridiculous to have any sense of pride any more in Turkey." I replied to Enis that I understood very well what he was saying and that I respected his view, but I really couldn't do it. "A couple of jackals claiming they represent the state? That's not what I call the rule of law. Never in my life will I cooperate with them again. I just can't. I'm not going to go along with them, no matter how much you want me to." When Enis saw I really meant it, he dropped it. Then we called the drugs officer in and I told him I definitely wasn't working with them.'

From that moment on, it was war between Baybaşin and the Turkish state and both parties described the nature of the conflict as a vendetta. The day Baybaşin was released, he was taken straight from the prison to the drugs department on suspicion of smuggling eighty kilos of heroin. He was interrogated at the station from 11 to 23 March 1989. He received twenty-eight injuries, including three broken ribs. After that, he lodged a complaint of torture and abuse against Bayram Akbal and two of his colleagues. After a two-year court battle, the court acquitted the suspects, a judgement upheld by the Turkish Supreme Court.

Baybaşin was continually harassed by the state. He was arrested again and held for four days for allegedly having kidnapped the owner of a Turkish bank for a ransom of two billion lira. 'They connected my little fingers and toes to the electricity. They'd pulled a kind of sack over my head and they kept tipping water over my hair to increase the effect of the electric shocks. Each shock was incredibly painful. I still have difficulty pressing buttons; it's left me with a phobia. There's a television set in my room in the cell now and I switch it on and off with the handle of a toothbrush. I know nothing can happen, but it's still there in my head. They hung weights on my feet. That made my ribs stick out and they stuck things in them. The flesh between my ribs was badly damaged and my eardrums were burst.

'After those four days, there was a press conference. There were roughly twenty journalists. I had to stand with my back against the wall and wasn't allowed to speak. That wasn't hard, because I couldn't even open my mouth; they'd beaten me up badly. If I hadn't been able to lean against that wall, I would have collapsed. My legs wouldn't support me. It was the policeman Doğan Karakaplan, the bastard, who spoke. He told them I'd kidnapped a man, what kind of gangster I was, how dangerous and what a nuisance to the Turkish state. But how would I have been a nuisance? I'd only been back a month from spending five years in prison in England. When I heard him say "this filthy Kurd" to the journalists, something snapped. I ripped my T-shirt open to show the press all my injuries. I walked over to Karakaplan and told him I would kill him and that it was he who had kidnapped the bank manager for the ransom. I said I was so rich there was no way I'd do something like that for a mere two billion lira. I can't remember everything I said exactly, because after that I passed out. But it was in the papers like that the next day.

'In the meantime, they beat me black and blue and, due to my injuries, the doctor said I shouldn't actually talk. Everything hurt. I hadn't been allowed to say anything during all the torturing, because they didn't ask me anything. If they'd asked me if I'd murdered Allah, I might well have admitted it at that point. I would have signed or confessed to anything if they'd forced me. But they didn't ask me anything while they were torturing me, and they went on until I collapsed. Without intervention from Kadir Aksu, the minister from Diyarbakir, they would have beaten me to death. My family had approached him.

'Before going back to the prison, I was taken to the Public Prosecutions Department. I couldn't walk, but the public prosecutors supported me. Muhammer Gence, a member of the secret service, came to the court, too. It was he who they said had carried out the kidnapping with me. Of course that was rubbish and, luckily, he made a disculpatory statement for me: I hadn't had anything to do with it. The judge looked at me and asked me if I would stand. "Why has all this happened?" he asked. I got mad and said, "Why are you asking me?" The man froze and I said, "I've been tortured and you ask me how it happened? I've still got injuries." At that point I took off my shirt, so the newspaper photographers could take pictures of them. Thirty-eight days after being tortured, I was still covered from head to toe in bruises. It turned out that nothing in my file corresponded with the facts. I was supposed to have carried out fifty armed robberies in the very period I was in prison in England, between 1984 and 1988, and in Bayrampaşa. No weapon had actually been found in any of the incidents, but that's what was in the file.'

The police had forged a conspiracy against him, that much was clear. In any event, this time the judge acquitted him.

They thought up all kinds of ruses to get their hands on Baybaşin and even equipped hit squads to liquidate him. His account seems to come straight out of a crime thriller, but it is the truth. 'They tried everything to get near me and to convince me to work with them after all. They employed famous artistes. I don't blame them, they were just doing their job. They told me honestly that they had been instructed to ask me certain questions and then our conversation was recorded. This was not a success. Then they used women to try and approach me. They had to pretend to be in love with me. I had loads of calls from such women, who said, for example, "I can't go on living if I can't see you." They did all the things people in love do in films; it was despicable. But I developed a certain sense for women who were trying to set me up.

'What my enemies didn't know was that I was tapping their telephone conversations, too. I had taps at the security service in Istanbul, in hotels and at tennis clubs, which were a gathering place for security service officials. It's reasonably easy to tap telephone conversations in the region with a device and, if you need the telephone company to intervene, that's no problem. It's just a question of money. You have to pay a certain amount and then there are engineers who'll do it for you and bring you copies of the taped conversations. That way, I found out how they were tapping my calls.

'One incident confirmed my suspicions that they were trying to kill me. If my car hadn't been armoured, then I would have been shot to pieces. I was driving a Mercedes 200, at least that's what it said on the back of the car, but it had been tuned up to the power of a 300. They couldn't understand how I could get away so quickly when they chased me. And they didn't know I'd had the car bullet-proofed. That summer evening, in 1991 in Istanbul, a meeting was organised by an association of people from Diyarbakir. I'd organised everything and paid the majority of the costs. I'd accepted a seat on the board that evening. What we were trying to do was get high-ranked people and civil servants in our area together to look after our interests and change something in the situation in the country. Nothing happened that evening that really disturbed the peace and I was totally unprepared for what was to come. We had artistes singing in Kurdish; there were some complaints, because that was forbidden. One of our chairmen, who was a retired bank manager, asked, "What on earth is going on here? Why are they singing in Kurdish?" I said that, as a member of the board, I was responsible for security and if he had any complaints he should make them to the member of the board who was announcing the artistes. He said the artistes wouldn't listen and they would only stop if I said they weren't allowed to sing in Kurdish. But why should I do that? It was a Diyarbakir evening and there they speak Kurdish. I thought what was happening was great. But it was plain to see from his red face that he didn't like it. The Minister of Foreign Affairs, who also came from Diyarbakir, was there, too, and it didn't bother him. Or the people from the security service.

'I was brimming with self confidence because I was carrying a weapon and driving an armoured car. When the evening came to an end at around three or four in the morning, I went out to my car. Then I noticed I was being followed. Who could that be? Apart from the police there was nobody who would dare open fire on me. At first, I was going to go to my own hotel in Aksaray, but when I saw a car behind me, I changed my mind. I was alone and I had to make a snap decision. Instead of the road to my hotel, I drove in the direction of the Vatan Caddesi. I noticed they were still following me. I got my gun ready to fire, loaded it and stuck it with the barrel down the back of the seat to my right. Like that, I could grab it and shoot at any time. I was in third gear and made it look as if I was about to accelerate, but then I suddenly changed back from third to first without braking. I moved over to the side of the road and, because they didn't see my brake lights come on, they had to overtake me. I looked and saw panicky faces and arms. Then they tried the same manoeuvre on me, so I had to overtake them and then they started shooting. Smack, smack, smack, against the bulletproof glass of my windows. We raced past the amusement park in that street and then it was my turn. I steered the car to make it look as if I was going to change to the left lane. They looked at me as they passed, but I'd opened the right window arm using the automatic control and grabbed my gun from the seat. I wasn't going to give them a chance. As soon as the front of their car had reached my open window, I started shooting and went on until I saw the backlights of their car. All the windows smashed to pieces.

'We both came to a stop on the pavement. I don't know how many bullets I fired. I checked my reverse mirror to see if the other cars were still far enough away. No headlights nearby. Quick as a flash, I crossed over to their car and went on shooting until there were no more bullets left in my gun. Then I jumped back in my car and drove off towards the Bosporus. That brings you up again at the Kasim Paşa roundabout. Then I noticed there was still a car following me. I cut it off and jumped out of the car with my gun in my hand. I started firing, but I was so completely off my head that I'd forgotten I had no more bullets in my weapon. Looking back, I think I must have imagined that second chase. In any event, I smashed their windscreen with the butt of my gun and beat up the two people inside. I went back to my own car and drove to a car park in Etiler, where I called a friend. I was covered in blood, it turned out, but I hadn't even noticed. He took me with him and we picked up the car later. The next day, I understood from various people in high positions that they were, indeed, police officers in the first car, but I've got no idea who was in the second car.

'The only other time anything like that happened to me was when I was attacked in my own home. I was amazed. I'd never expected things to go so far that they come for me at home and, to be honest, I'd never expected them to be able to find my house. I never directly used the telephone in my house; I always called from a second phone in the car. Then I called a number to which the two other numbers were connected. If I wanted to call my business number in Istanbul, then I first called the number in Ankara. The person there then called the number in Istanbul. Then the call was transferred. So Ankara didn't know I was calling from Istanbul. I also sometimes used my car phone to say I was calling from Germany and would be staying there a few days on business. Another time I'd just be calling from my bedroom. You have all kinds of secret language: if I called my boys and told them to say hello to Ali for me, that meant they had to bring the car round to the front.

'That day, the car came round to the front and I got in next to the driver. Then I saw a slightly dirty white car parked in the cul-de-sac in between all the neighbours' chic, highly polished cars. There were three men in it. Idiots. The police always go around in threes. We made as if to drive straight into the street, but on the corner in from of the house, we pretended the engine had cut out. I told the guy sitting next to me to just stay were he was. I unexpectedly jumped out of the car, immediately shot their front tyre to shreds and yelled, "If anyone dares get out of the car I'll shoot him dead." The man opened the window and said, "What do you want from us, brother?" I replied, "What do you mean, brother? Listen to me, you filthy bastards, if you get out of the car I'll shoot you to pieces." They didn't dare do anything. When we drove off to the left, I saw them with their walkie-talkie, it was patently obvious they were from the police.'

*

On 7 October 1991, the freighter *Kismetim-i* left the harbour of Izmir with a cargo of car tyres, iron, resin and washing powder, on its way from Piraeus, near Athens. Once out of the port, the ship turned towards the Suez Canal and, after the cargo had been unloaded in Akaba and Dubai, it put into the Pakistani port town of Karachi, on October 24. It was an old ship and had a certain reputation, as it had been used previously for ficti- tious exports in a subsidy fraud. According to the official version later given by the Americans, Baybaşin then went personally to Pakistan to arrange a heroin cargo. It took a long time and the ship sailed up and down to Dubai a couple of times with fertiliser, as it would be noticeable if it were to lie idle so long in port. Captain Tayfun Erkan supposedly loaded the heroin at 7 A.M. on 10 February 1992 in open water, near the island of Astola. The merchandise apparently arrived by boat in the form of a hundred bags with a total content of 3,100 kilos. The crew hid the heroin in the rear ballast tank. When they arrived in Dubai after two days' sailing, a sailor was picked up for having transported ten kilos of heroin on his own initiative. The ship was held under arrest until his trial and, in the meantime, the rest of the crew went home to Turkey.

Once the ship was released after the sailor's trial, Baybaşin apparently flew in a new crew by plane. On 26 November 1992, the ship set course for Turkey and, after a tip-off, the Istanbul police prepared to intercept the huge shipment still hidden in the tank. On the way to Turkish territorial waters, three naval ships were waiting for the *Kismetim-i* and when the crew saw what was happening, they decided to scuttle the ship, along with its expensive cargo, off the coast of Cyprus. On December 25, Baybaşin's business partner, the Kurd Şeyhmus Daş, was killed in an armed attack. Baybaşin was suspected of being responsible and a warrant for his arrest was issued. Baybaşin hit back by going to the press and accusing the Turkish state and its gangs in the newspapers of large-scale heroin trafficking.

He recounted the story in detail. 'After I was released from prison, I found out that I was absolutely no match for the Turkish state and its bands of robbers with my drug trafficking. Drugs were being imported from Pakistan and India hidden in bales of cotton. You can't keep something like that secret; at one point hundreds of people knew this was happening. At that time, the odd car or truck would get stopped with drugs in Turkey, but now they wanted to intercept a ship-full of drugs. I'd learned from my contacts that the Americans had a finger in the pie and that they had given this instruction. The Turkish state was willing and saw a chance to revenge itself against me and the ship, *Kismetim-i*. That was foolish; after all, the ship was contaminated, as it had been used for fictitious export. If the ship entered Turkey's territorial waters, for that reason alone it would be immediately seized.'

The ship was used only for cargo trade between Pakistan, Dubai and Africa and Baybaşin only heard afterwards that something had gone wrong with the sailor and his ten kilos. 'That ship was searched from top to bottom in Dubai. You know, that is the only country in the Gulf area that is actually run by the state where the Americans supervise. If there had been more drugs, they would definitely have found them. After that sailor was convicted, the ship was used to set me up.' It had belonged to the shipowner Ayanoğlu, who had died on New Year's Eve 1991 in an armed attack in an amusement hall, after which ownership transferred to his daughter Gülçin Derya, who was married to one of the sons of the murdered Şeyhmus Daş. According to Baybaşin, Ayanoğlu was himself involved in the conspiracy and was cooperating with the Turkish state. Ayanoğlu's daughter is convinced, however, that Baybaşin murdered her father.

'Why would we send a ship full of drugs to Turkey that was certain to be arrested?' said Baybaşin. 'I would at least have changed the name of the ship. They say I murdered the shipowner, but the Turkish gang is wrong: Ayanoĝlu had already been dead a year when all this happened. No, that ship had simply been written off a long time before and could be scuttled without costing anything much. Then they could say to America, "We arrested a ship with a load of drugs on board belonging to the big drug boss Baybaşin, but the crew scuttled the ship." That way they get a lot of money from America for having intercepted the stuff. It's also a question of prestige in the eyes of the world; the Turkish police have had a great success in their fight against drugs. But they hadn't reckoned on the possibility of me fighting back. I went to the press to bring things out in the open. It is completely implausible for three NAVO ships to have met the ship outside territorial waters and sailed around it for thirty-eight hours without doing anything. The idiots. They could at least have gone to look on the ship by helicopter. They were simply lying. I informed those consulates of the European countries and America based in Ankara that they had been lied to. That ship was deliberately scuttled and there weren't any drugs on board at all.

'They blamed me for everything; I was supposedly the cause of all the problems in the southeast. Whenever a secret service vehicle came under fire by Dev-Sol, my name was mentioned. If the PKK attacked a military vehicle, again my name. And it was me again when the police were attacked. Whoever got murdered in Istanbul, I'd done it. You could follow it daily in the newspaper headlines. But later, it was proved that I didn't murder the shipowner Ayanoĝlu. A certain Yavuz was arrested. He was apparently instructed to carry out the murder by Kürşat Yilmaz, a member of the ülkücü mafia and a former police officer. That girl is looking for her father's murderer. She can talk to me any time; I'll tell her anything she wants to know. If she keeps insisting that I did it, then I'm sorry for her.'

In 1992, in the middle of the sea between Pakistan and Turkey, a massive catch was made of 13,000 kilos of heroin and morphine base and twelve tonnes of hash on one ship, the *Lucky S*. It remained unclear who the owner was of this mega-shipment. Şeymus Daş, who according to Baybaşin worked with the Turkish secret service and who had a green passport, supposedly bought the consignment in Pakistan, but it was not possible to try him, as he was killed. The police put the ship under arrest on the open sea and brought it to the port of Marmaris.

In Baybaşin's view, all the fuss about the *Kismetim-1* was nothing other than a diversion created to allow the state's big shipment hidden in the *Lucky S.* to get through. Baybaşin declared to the press that a state gang, led by Mehmet Ağar, Necdet Menzir, Yahya Demirel and others, was responsible. 'The interception of this ship was pure show, intended to appease Europe and wipe out a couple of people. The ship was sailing under the Panamanian flag for a firm belonging to Tuğrul Türkeş [son of the founder of the Grey Wolves]. I tell you that all those drugs found their way onto the market! After all, with the confiscation of such a large shipment, you would expect the retail prices to rise, but that didn't happen. On the contrary, the heroin price dropped for a long time to twenty-five percent of the original price. Of course I'd been aware for a long time of what happened on ships like the *Lucky S.* The ship came as far as Marmaris and, from there, the stuff was taken to the port with small diesel oil tankers. After that, it went in police cars to the place of destination. Anyone with a yacht in the only marina in Istanbul, like me, could simply see what was going on. When it comes down to it, the fact that they intercepted the *Lucky S.* without seeing who was going to take delivery of the drugs inside the country proves it was the police themselves, doesn't it? They tried to give the world the impression that something was really being done about drugs, but not a single arrest was made in connection with the interception.'

All this was enough to make Baybaşin decide to leave the country. In the meantime, the Turkish authorities feared his continual revelations in the media, even abroad.

Honour

'In 1989, after I was released from prison, my family really wanted me to get married.' This man of the world, who was on an equal footing with the biggest gangsters, businessmen, politicians and civil servants in Turkey, the man who travelled around the capitals of Europe, got married, as his mother in Southeast Turkey had decided for him. 'I'd like to say that I primarily did it to have children. But there were other considerations, too. I'd caused my family a lot of distress in the past with my way of life and they'd had to put up with a lot. By marrying, I was doing what my family really wanted.

'I'd never seen or spoken to my fiancée before the wedding. My mother, my uncle and other blood relatives had spoken to the girl's family. The girl wanted to see me beforehand, but I refused, I was absolutely against it. After all, I might decide not to get married then. I knew myself well enough to realise there was a real chance I wouldn't want to get married if I saw her. A husband and wife have to really understand each other and I'd never come across anyone in my life who was like that. And on top of that, if things didn't work out, then I could say they'd got their way and it wasn't my fault. All the same, the most important thing was my mother. If she knew what I was getting up to, she'd strongly disapprove. She's still under the impression that I don't drink and that I honour my faith as highly as she does. She gives alms to the poor of Lice and Diyarbakir every month. She thinks I attach a lot of importance to my faith in Allah: leave it like that. She wanted me to get married according to the tradition. So I didn't go along with the girl's request; I only went to Diyarbakir a day before the wedding and we finished off all the preparations the same day. When it came to it, the mayor of Lice acted as witness and the chairman of Diyarbakirlilar, the active intermediary between me and the state; in 1989 they still had the impression that I would do everything expected of me. The evening before, a party was arranged without consulting me, to which five hundred people were invited. That was odd.

How can you have a party while people are being killed every day around you in the war? But the family insisted on celebrating.

'My wife turned out to be a very special person. She is extremely dedicated to her house and her work. She grew up in Diyarbakir, so someone always had to go with her to do the shopping in Istanbul. She is such an extraordinary person that I don't have to worry at all about what would happen to my children if I died. I'm sure that under her supervision they will have a good life and their honour will be protected.'

The overpowering significance of the *namus*, the family's honour, for which the man is fully responsible at all times whatever the consequences, is clear. And Baybaşin confirms that 'family' is really the family and not a metaphor for a criminal organisation.

'It's a shame that journalists ever felt they had to write about her. There was a piece in which it said I'd sent my wife to Arabia to organise my business. Unbelievable. Of course that journalist would have to answer for himself. But a journalist from the *Sabah*, Mehmet Kesim, had anticipated that and urged me not to take any measures. Oh, if what he had written had been true, then I wouldn't have minded. But this! That journalist would certainly have been killed if it hadn't been for Mehmet Kesim. I've forgiven him. Perhaps, in itself, it wasn't something to get angry about, but it's difficult to get justice in a legal, human fashion in Turkey. In this case it ended up with a court order for rectification. If I don't get that then, well, I'll have no choice. Like the police chief Karakaplan, who called me a bastard during the press conference. Then I had to take other measures. Of course he had every right to do his job, but not to call me a bastard. He suffered a fatal accident.

'Let me be honest about one thing. Anyone who harms me or my family will be punished. That's inevitable. It doesn't matter if I'm in prison or if I'm free. Luckily, my children are doing extremely well. My daughter is six years old.* I'm afraid she still hasn't been able to forget about what happened to me in Turkey. If she hears the word police she hides. Her teacher told me she starts crying when she hears a siren or an alarm. The police have raided our house several times recently, too. She finds that difficult to deal with. The others aren't bothered by things like that any more. Of course I want them to get the best education possible and at the weekends they get individual lessons in Kurdish. They have to

---

* This interview took place in 1997.

learn Kurdish regardless of their age. My daughter already speaks good English and French and she's now learning German, too. Turkish and Kurdish are on top of that, of course. My second child is eighteen months younger and the youngest is only a year old. I'm responsible for one of my sisters and one of my brothers, too. They're studying political science. I want their children to enjoy the best education, as well.'

Baybaşin developed into an industrialist and a Kurdish businessman. He sold the flour factory and the hotel he owned in Istanbul and instead played a central role in a trade community dealing in foodstuffs and electronics. 'We're also involved in textiles. I started building that up after I came out of prison in 1989. Of course I've got a criminal record, but it's never really caused me any problems, because I knew a lot of people in high places. During one of the conversations I had with Demirel at his home in Ankara he said, literally, "Whether it's opium or anything else, it doesn't matter. We're only interested in making sure your money goes in the right direction."' This corresponds with the impression top Turkish politicians have confirmed where the laundering of criminally obtained assets is concerned: it need not be an obstacle for gaining social esteem.

Hüseyin Baybaşin's story is a fascinating illustration of the typical career of a Turkish or Kurdish underworld boss. Coming from the tribal community in Southeast Turkey and living with the reality of vendetta, he later on managed to develop into a prominent drug *baba* in the big city and in Western Europe. When Baybaşin said all this, he was about to be released from prison. At the time, he was focusing primarily on stimulating economic growth in the area he comes from, Diyarbakir. He had also involved his family. He travelled to Paris, Germany and Belgium. 'I help open up Kurdish shops all over the place: clothes shops, shops selling foodstuffs like Kurdish wine, sugar, rice and macaroni. Everything has to be produced and sold under a Kurdish brand. We've even had talks in Taiwan about selling electronic equipment.'

On 29 March 1998, Baybaşin was arrested again on suspicion of involvement in large-scale drug trafficking and contracting murder. He was convicted and jailed for twenty years. In 2002, the court of appeal sentenced him to life, a sentence he was, at the time of writing, serving in the Dutch maximum security prison in Vught. His lawyers are convinced of his innocence and are attempting to prove that a conspiracy had been forged between senior civil servants and politicians in Turkey and the judicial authorities in the Netherlands, with the intention of silencing the outspoken Baybaşin. They plead that the technical evidence on which his conviction was primarily based consisted of doctored reports of his tapped telephone conversations. In January 2007, they obtained an abridged version of an extensive Turkish governmental report, of unclear origins, which describes the involvement of the government in drug trafficking in the 1990s (the 'Supplementary Report') and contains statements by witnesses alleging how Baybaşin was framed in various countries by 'parties with vested interests'. In April 2007, on the grounds of this material, the lawyers reported a number of extremely senior legal officials in the Netherlands to the Dutch Public Prosecution department for 'incitement and/or deliberate false imprisonment'.

We Know Us

8

An Unexpected Arrest

It is cold but busy at the Atatürk airport near Istanbul on Monday 23 December 1996. The passengers who have just arrived join the pre-sorted queues for customs, where their passports will be routinely stamped. Customs staff have to watch out at the end of the year: that's when high-ranking people come back from abroad to celebrate New Year's Eve at home. Perhaps a minister might arrive, an important politician, a senior civil servant, a prominent businessman or an eminent foreign guest, and they all expect to be treated with the necessary regard. A single mistake can mean the end of a career for the officer on duty.

Then customs receives a phone call. Someone wishing to remain anonymous has an important tip, 'There's a lady on the plane from Amsterdam with a suitcase full of money from heroin trafficking, destined for the PKK funds.' The chief of the airport police is alerted. The tip seems interesting enough, but they often get them and they usually end up leading to nothing. Often it's the personal action of someone wanting to take revenge. Still, the chief follows the steps. First, go through the passenger list. The name mentioned, Dilek Örnek, is indeed on the list for the flight arriving in half an hour. That doesn't necessarily mean anything, but still; supposing it's true? If an important money courier from the PKK, which he sees as a terrorist organisation, can be arrested under his supervision, that's a guarantee for furthering his career. Now, let's not count our chickens before they're hatched, but it can't do any harm to let the journalists know in advance. The regular army of reporters and photographers that hangs around the airport every day as long as there are planes taking off and landing, hoping to get a scoop, are informed of the possibility of something special happening today – in half an hour, to be precise.

After the plane lands, Dilek Örnek walks through customs with her luggage. She is a pretty twenty-two-year-old, born and bred in the Netherlands. She comes from a family of migrant workers in Hengelo, but is an example of second-generation social advancement. She's been trained as a secretary and that gives her plenty of opportunity to get a good job in the West. Now she walks towards the man standing waiting for her. They follow a regular routine. She can't remember how many times she's come with cases like this to hand over to him.* Once she's got rid of the cases, she'll go shopping in town. She wants to buy some shoes. Not that she doesn't have enough, because how many women have got two hundred and fifty pairs like her? Although she has to admit that Imelda Marcos has surpassed her. Then she'll fly south as quickly as possible. She's got her summer house in Antalya and her fiancé is waiting there.

'Passport?' asks the customs officer. She hands over her Dutch passport, hoping he'll hurry up. Something's wrong. Something is different from usual. But what? The officer flicks through her document, looks her straight in the eye and asks, 'Are you Dilek Örnek?' She confirms that she is. Why doesn't he hurry up? But the man takes a deep breath, changes his expression from nervous to pleased, and radiates pride as he orders her, 'Come this way with your cases, please.'

The Turkish journalists have understood that this is the lady it's all about. Photographers' flashes blind her. She has a brief moment of panic, but quickly recovers her composure, because nothing can go wrong. Of course she knows that importing criminal money is illegal, but the chance of getting arrested for it in Turkey is nil. She was assured beforehand that everything would be taken care of. After all, she has her contacts. When the cases are opened and do, indeed, turn out to be full of foreign money, the chief of the airport police invites the press in. Dilek can see the danger and hisses at the policeman that the cases are intended for Ayhan Akça. Even better, thinks the man, who doesn't know the name, we'll arrest the one who takes delivery of the money, too. The journalists, however, do know who Ayhan Akça is and dash out to find him. But he has already made a run for it.

---

* The Turkish papers did that for her later. The daily *Hürriyet* reported that this was the fifty-eighth time she had made the trip to Turkey with cases, though according to *Sabah* it was only the twenty-fifth time. The American State Department Bureau for International Narcotics and Law Enforcement Affairs stated in its *International Narcotics Control Strategy Report*, dated March 1997, that she had made the trip with drug money fifty times.

This is a man who has often been in the news over the past decade. He is a driver and guard employed by the chief of the Turkish police's special units and has become known as the suspected culprit of, among other things, the murder of the so-called king of the gambling joints in Turkey, Omer Topal. Has the head of the airport police realised at this point what kind of mistake he has made? The cases are destined for the police special department, not the PKK at all.

It also dawns on Dilek's fiancé, waiting in Antalya, that something has gone wrong. He immediately tries to flee abroad, but is arrested. Dilek is nothing but a courier, but her fiancé gives the impression of being less 'innocent'. He owns a restaurant in Spain and conducts business with Iranians based in various European countries. He knows the money comes from criminals whose work consists of liquidating people, extortion and other varieties of organised crime. On 5 May 1997, he nevertheless pleads before the court that he is only small fry. 'My share was no bigger than half a per cent,' he claims. But he understands now that the affair has been blown up out of proportion, that 'they've made my arrest into a second Susurluk'.

Dilek's personal drama was emphasised in an exclusive interview with the television presenter and journalist Savaş Ay, broadcast from the Bayrampaşa prison in Istanbul. This was a young woman talking who had become westernised through and through in her attitude to life and her aspirations. 'I like living in luxury, expensive clothes, dancing and travelling. I couldn't make ends meet on benefit in Holland. My aunt knew what I wanted and she said I could take foreign currency to Turkey and earn six thousand marks. That's what I did, although I haven't got as incredibly rich as the media is saying now.' It was worse for her and her fiancé to be arrested, as they were known in the Turkish community as belonging to the political left, where one would not expect any cooperation with secret elements of the state mechanism.

Dilek's story makes it clear that the organisation has no trouble recruiting new collaborators. A woman with a European passport who speaks foreign languages is perfect. The case received an extraordinary amount of attention in the Turkish media and it seriously upset the Turkish community in the Netherlands. The Dutch public at large failed to notice any of this, however, as the Dutch language media paid little attention to it.

Up to this point, we have seen the Turkish diaspora in Western Europe as an environment in which criminals from Turkey can operate invisibly from within. The example of Dilek Örnek, however, shows that the opposite also happens: people with a simple farming background in Turkey, who most likely never had any dealings at all with the underworld before, become involved when abroad. The Turkish mafia has a contagious effect.

A Neighbourhood Problem

In 1993, Amsterdam's Mercator district made national news in the Netherlands following a police operation with the intriguing name of 'Exodus'. The district police, the regional crime squad, the aliens department and the tax authorities had mobilised a team of no fewer than a hundred and sixty people to scour the neighbourhood on October 20. Two hundred and eighteen arrests were made, which were to lead to a hundred appearances before the public prosecutor and the referral of thirty-six people to the aliens department. The equivalent of roughly £300,000 was confiscated, plus three hundred and forty-five kilos of heroin, sixteen cars, a camper van and a truck. Six catering establishments were boarded up and one man, who was affiliated with ultra-right wing political circles and was seen by the authorities as the 'Mr Big' behind the scenes, was sentenced to twelve years in prison on appeal. His headquarters were in a room he had had built under his restaurant, accessible only via a secret door. In this den he received business contacts from all over Europe. The organisation he ran had already penetrated so far into the legitimate business world that money had been invested in Dutch catering companies, a sauna and a string of residential properties in the neighbourhood.

Arnhem's Spijker district hit the news at the end of 1995 when the case against the Metin family, known as the 'four Ms', who had established their headquarters there, came to court. According to the reports by the collaborating Turkish and Dutch police, between 1,200 and 2,000 people were allegedly involved. The police and the Arnhem council had already closed down twenty residential buildings and boarding houses and three companies due to drug nuisance between 1994 and 1996. The Turkish bars, snack bars and boarding houses above the Turkish companies were seen as the most bothersome. It was possible, with the police's identification registration system, to count the number of people in the region who had committed an offence, on whom a report had been made and whom the Public Prosecutions Department had not made a conditional decision not to prosecute. Nine hundred and fifty-eight offenders lived in Arnhem and 329 had meanwhile moved elsewhere. The vast majority of the offences were related to drug trafficking. An exceptionally high proportion of the offenders were Turks and Kurds. They proved to have developed their activities primarily within the Spijker district but lived largely outside the city.

Residents of the two districts in question had noticed more than ten years before the police operation that their neighbourhood was threatening to degenerate due to the growth of drug dealing. Dealing in Amsterdam's Mercator district had been on the increase since, fifteen years before, the police had cleaned out the Kop van de Zeedijk red light district to make that part of old Amsterdam liveable again. Mercator Square was one of the places to which the drug scene had gravitated. Foreign drug tourists quickly found out about the square. The police spotted cars with foreign number plates and arrested French, Germans and Belgians with notes in their pockets containing the instructions: 'Amsterdam, tram line 13, get out at Mercator Square.' There was a continual coming and going. The dealers in coffee shops and on the street worked in shifts: one for the morning, one for the afternoon and one for the evening. The consumers were primarily attracted by the constant supply of heroin and other drugs and the low prices.

Apart from the dealing itself, the local residents were bothered by the related trouble: cars arriving and leaving and often parked on the pavement, swearing, junkies in doorways, used syringes lying around, muggings, car and house break-ins, fights, stabbings and shootings.

In the course of the 1980s, the Arnhem area, close to the German border, had become an intersection for international drug trafficking. A Kurdish man who had already been living in the Arnhem area for twenty-four years and knew the criminal world well through his business, told us, 'It started in 1979 or 1980 with one man: Mahmut the Anarchist [this must be the same one as Huseyin Baybaşin's colleague, who had such excellent contacts in Europe – see page 233]. Together with a Turkish transport company, he smuggled heroin into Arnhem on a small scale. There were already some suspicions about who was involved in drug trafficking, but you didn't talk about it in public then.' In the 1980s, the number of people and groups involved in drug trafficking increased, reaching its high point, according to Turkish residents in the area, in the period between 1986 and 1994.

In the 1960s, boarding houses in the Spijker district had functioned as a kind of initial accommodation for migrant workers. In the 1970s and 1980s, one in five local residents was of foreign origin, with Turks the largest group. However, the eastern corner of the district developed into one of the biggest window prostitution zones in the Netherlands, reason for some Turks to move elsewhere. It was a time of dilapidation and impoverishment. The residents were annoyed by brothel owners, prostitutes and their clients rowdily settling their differences of opinion in public. 'The Spijker prison was full of junkies,' recalled a local beat cop. 'The Spijker district was a madhouse. When junkies wanted to buy gear, runners went to certain places to fetch it and run it back to the junkies. They were running around all day, from early in the morning to late at night. Then we started getting pushers, who first offered soft drugs free to school children and then, after a while, wanted paying for it. It was a bloody mess.'

*

Initially, the residents of Amsterdam's Mercator district had a lot of difficulty getting the issue of this crime on the political agenda because everyone could clearly see that drug dealing was affiliated with the immigrant groups in the district and the Turkish in particular. Even before 1990, a major police operation against Turkish coffee houses was cancelled due to a veto by Mayor Van Thijn himself, who was adamant that there would be no large-scale raid on the Turks. The problem took on even greater proportions. In addition to the influx of foreign customers, some three to five hundred junkies commuted to the district daily to buy their drugs. In 1992, no fewer than eight murders were committed in the police district around Suriname Square, under which the Mercator district also falls, as a result of the battle between criminal groups disputing the territory.

'The problems certainly didn't arrive overnight,' said a resident, who had been active in trying to keep the district liveable for more than twenty-five years. 'We could see it happening. The residents' committee walked through the district several times with the mayor and other councillors to show them the gravity of the situation, but we got no response whatsoever. Then suddenly, in 1990, there was a big panic. We'd already seen this coming fifteen years before and had been shouting it from the rooftops all that time, but we were met with nothing but indifference.' The big change was that the Mercator District Management Organisation had now begun to receive financial support and had even become 'Van Thijn's showpiece', as some residents expressed it. A separate community police team station was set up in Suriname Square with an annex in the middle of Mercator Square. Support was provided by the regional crime squad at headquarters. The first major operation was in 1992, under the name Marisol. A year later followed Operation Exodus, intended to clean up Mercator Square.

The operations were successful and the two areas saw a lot of improvement. The streets are now clean, a different use has been designated to the coffee shops and Arnhem now has a drop-in centre for drug users, to channel the problem. But has drug trafficking really disappeared? Action of the police and the judicial authorities in the drugs market is often accompanied by the dreaded displacement effect. This is also common in the neighbourhood-oriented approach to the drug problem. One criminologist has identified five forms of displacement when criminals are obstructed in their activities: The culprits change the time, their way of working, they seek another target, they concentrate on another type of offence or they change their operational area. The last form is the most commonly demonstrated; for example, one American study established that increasing police pressure on a certain place in the twentieth police precinct in New York led to the criminals relocating to another place. In fact, all municipal policy in the Netherlands aimed at fighting drug trafficking in a particular spot is doomed to have that same effect.

Someone who knows the Amsterdam Mercator district, having lived at various places in the area over a period of thirty-two years, concluded, 'Of course some things have changed cosmetically, the built-up area in particular is cleaner and tidier. But I've started seeing junkies and people doing deals with junkies in doorways again every day. Things are going on in certain cafés and coffee houses again and it's not just me saying it, it's the people who live around me, too. When you get big Mercedes parked on the pavement with the engine running and guys dashing in and out, you can easily work out what's going on. The shootings are still going on, too. It's shocking, there's congealed blood on every street corner. I knew half the victims, nice guys, each and every one of them, I would never have suspected a thing. When Mayor Van Thijn visited the neighbourhood, he had a cup of coffee at a Turkish coffee house, great. Two years later, the owner of the place was found dead there.'

Police people in the regional crime squad have also noticed that drug trafficking is threatening to come back or has perhaps simply been going on all this time. The price of heroin remains low, which means the supply is plentiful. An 'effect measurement' by the Amsterdam-Amstelland police in 1993 stated, 'The dealers and clients have anticipated the police's adapted approach. They have started dealing in a far more professional and cautious manner. The dealing has not disappeared from the district; it's simply spreading insidiously.' But where, exactly? First of all, private houses are still being used. A detective involved in all the operations said, 'I can name you ten addresses just like that where I can find heroin, in reasonably large quantities. After a while, the neighbours start getting bothered and then the business moves. We call it "house hopping".'

The Arnhem police were also forced to admit that their spectacular operations were followed by the initiative of the next group of dealers occupying the vacated positions. After the arrest of the Metin brothers, an important smuggling group at that time, detectives established that the drug traffickers were dealing with the setback by operating less visibly. After a few 'weeks of reflection' an old group, whose members had by that time served their prison sentence, took over the business and started all over again. Those 'old friends' have since been arrested again and the question is which organisation will now fill the gap in the market.

*

The entrepreneurial spirit of Turks in the Netherlands is demonstrated by a variety of companies unparalleled in minority groups. There are Turkish greengrocers, bakers, butchers, supermarkets, travel agencies, hairdressers, coffee houses, sandwich shops, bars, shoarma takeaways, garages, jewellers, translation agencies, driving schools, import and export companies, transport firms, removal firms, international telephone companies, boutiques, garment manufacturers, video libraries, furniture stores, snack bars, restaurants, solicitors' firms, banks, sports clubs, Turkish baths, mosques and so forth. Nothing unusual is going on in most of these companies, they are so many signs of economic vitality. But a number lend themselves to organised crime, some better than others.

Coffee houses traditionally play a major role as a place where Turkish and Kurdish men meet, but in the two neighbourhoods investigated, there were so many coffee houses, according to the residents, that everyone understood that they had to have a source of income other than serving coffee and tea. Drug trafficking was so integrated into the daily life of Turkish men in the neighbourhoods investigated in the 1990s that traffickers and those who were not involved simply sat next to and in the midst of one another. When a heroin shipment was expected, or when people decided to invest in an upcoming shipment, the hat was passed round fairly openly and everyone put in his few hundred or thousand. Import and export companies could serve as a place for unloading the drug shipments and loading money transports and the company itself could serve for laundering money. In view of the size of the Turkish and Kurdish communities, the number of this type of business is so large that it can hardly be possible for it to still be a healthy business sector.

On the corner of Hudsonstraat and Cabralstraat in Amsterdam's Mercator district are three virtually identical shops within a distance of less than a hundred metres; the crossroad is infamous for the number of scores settled there resulting in death or injury. Garages in both neighbourhoods are used for preparing hiding places for drugs in cars and for deploying cars brought in for repair for drug transports. The customer pays relatively little, but has to do without his car a day longer. This kind of car is used because the licence numbers are unknown to the police. Some Turkish travel agencies organise trips for the dealers and couriers. There is nothing illegal in that in itself, but someone working at such a travel agency in Amsterdam's Baarsjes district told us, 'We know who the traffickers are, you recognise people like that straight away. They come and book a return ticket just a day or two ahead for a few days in Turkey, Spain or Portugal, for example. A ticket like that is much more expensive than a ticket including the weekend, but that's no problem for them. The important thing with having a travel agency is to already have good professional contacts with Turkey. They can also serve as a cover for laundering money and sometimes they have contacts at air and sea ports in the goods transport and supervision sector.'

The police are well aware of the role of this commercial infrastructure and the municipality has closed several such companies in operations in Amsterdam's Mercator district. Just how many coffee shops were in Turkish hands at the time of the operations up to 1993 is not clear; estimations range from fifteen to forty. Of the two hundred and twenty catering establishments in the district, many have been closed since 1991. Ten of the seventeen premises have now reopened, under another name and with a new owner. They are inspected 'structurally', say the police; according to our spokesperson it is impossible to use them as a cover or employ illegal immigrants in subordinate positions. On average, more than a third of all these establishments change hands every year and some even six times within a year. The officials who issue the permits have noticed that naif starters in the catering business often accept conditions that make the agreements into strangulation contracts. It can't be easy to check all that.

Part of the income from drug trafficking is laundered in the Netherlands to pay for the lifestyle appropriate to the social status the traffickers have achieved, but most of the money earned goes to Turkey. That causes hardly any problems. The traffickers need only to transport the money and make sure it isn't intercepted. The slightness of the risk is reflected in the small amounts paid to transporters, typically five percent of the value or less. Turkish banks were also used for money laundering. That went without a hitch as long as money laundering was not prohibited in Turkey. The manager of a Turkish bank we interviewed at the beginning of 1996 said, 'Our bank accepts any amount of money transferred to an account holder's number. We don't ask about the origin of the money and we don't give any information on deposits to third parties. A customer can open a special account without having to prove his identity.' We can't name the bank where the man works, but he specifically stated that it was one of the most 'respectable' banking institutions in Turkey.

When the law came into force obliging banks to report unusual financial transactions things did change slightly. 'Actually, most Turkish banks in the Netherlands aren't real banks,' a financial detective told us. 'If they conduct financial business, they can't do otherwise than go through a real Dutch bank. That money traffic used to go on rather outside our control, but these days we are informed of anything over a certain amount.' The manager of a Turkish bank in the Netherlands confirmed that he was seriously cooperating with the checks, as 'we don't want to get bad name; we want to maintain a good relationship with our Dutch colleagues'.

These days, money couriers take cash to Turkey. Dilek Örnek was an example of a suitable person because, as a modern woman, she would not attract any suspicion. There are also men who travel disguised as migrant workers. Only the amounts they transport are sometimes rather high to pass for savings and it can't really be called normal for a migrant worker to take hundreds of thousands of pounds in savings to Turkey every couple of weeks.

*

A lot of older Turkish men who went to the Netherlands as migrant workers, were later reunited with their families and now have grown-up children, are terrified of the attraction drug trafficking has for their sons. All our interviews in the Turkish and Kurdish underworld have shown that the big change came in the course of the 1980s. While, before that, it was a select group of professional smugglers, increasing numbers of people are becoming involved in drug trafficking in varying functions and even to such a degree that parts of local Turkish and Kurdish communities have become dependent on this source of income for maintaining their social status, both at home and abroad.

The connection between high unemployment in the initial period of expansion and Turkish involvement in drug trafficking is clear. Amsterdam detectives told us that spectacular company closures, which hit Turkish workers, were followed after a few months by a sharp influx into the drug underworld. In coffee houses where the police tapped the phones in the event of concrete suspicion, they were suddenly hearing an increasing number of people unknown until then placing orders for drug shipments. This corresponds with what drug traffickers themselves have told us. One of the traffickers told a detective:

I'll give you an example from my own life. In the 1970s, going on holiday to Turkey was heaven for us and for my father, in particular. There, he was a king. But he lost his job and then things started getting awkward. Not only in Turkey, but in the Netherlands, too; we had to accept an enormous loss of face. Instead of once a year, now my father only went to Turkey once every three years and where, in the past, he had helped members of the family, now he was no longer able to. It was an enormous loss of power, our status was undermined. It wasn't just him it happened to, but a whole lot of that generation. They had worked at the NDSM ship-building factory and at Ford and right now I don't know anyone from that group who's still in work. My father earned twenty-three hundred guilders a month and now he had to make ends meet with eighteen hundred. After twenty years of hard work for a reasonable salary, now suddenly a minimum income. If you're prepared to be a *zulaci* [drug keeper], that brings in a thousand guilders a kilo and that's plenty to go on holiday with.

A member of the board of a Turkish association in Amsterdam recalled:

Drug trafficking used to be a subject hardly anybody dared talk about in public. It was a relatively closed world, characterised by the expression 'we know us'. But all that has changed now; now it's more like 'everyone knows us' or even 'everyone knows everyone'. It has become attractive, particularly to the young people. The young dealers wear expensive clothes and drive cars. When they go into a bar, they buy rounds. People without any future prospects easily step into that world. The parents are scared their children will see an example in those rich dealers. I, as father, smoke less and don't permit myself any luxuries, so that I can give my children more pocket money and buy nice clothes for them. But whatever you do, you can't compete with that luxury! You try everything to convince your children to live a respectable life. You can't do more than that. But I'm terribly worried, just like a lot of other parents.

And in Arnhem, a Turkish resident said, 'These days, you can talk about drug trafficking anywhere. Let me put it like this: In the past it was a taboo and now it's an everyday subject.' Police who know the community well can see how everyone is affected: 'When the dealers are quiet, walking round with tense expressions, then we know what's going on. They pace up and down in the street, go in and out of the coffee house. Then at some point they throw a party and we know there's another shipment in.'

*

Three or four ranks can generally be distinguished within a local community according to the degree of involvement in drug trafficking. First are the 'top dogs', who act as organisers. These are the people on whom police and the judicial authorities chiefly focus their attention, at least in the Netherlands. Second are the ones who carry out derived criminal activities, but who are nonetheless indispensable for the activity, such as couriers, stash keepers and money runners. They can be considered as suspects, but are not important enough to pursue actively. Third are those who fulfil supportive roles that are not always criminal in themselves, but without which the rest of the activities could not exist: restaurateurs and caterers, travel agents, car mechanics. Fourth are all those who benefit from the income and possessions of the first three categories without themselves being active, such as family members. Additionally, groups living in symbiosis with drug trafficking that exist by making traffickers the prey of their robbery activities deserve a separate mention. First are the 'collection agencies', consisting of groups of five or six men. They keep an eye on the financial settlement of the larger deals and their services are also used when business is conducted with the underworld outside the Turkish and Kurdish scene. According to one source, Nigerians in particular are terrified of these factions, who have a notorious reputation as enforcers. The second type is the gangs who blackmail or rob drug traffickers. They take advantage of the lack of legal protection for people doing illegal things or doing them inefficiently. This group also includes those who extort money from drug traffickers for political factions.

Altogether, the picture is of considerable Turkish/Kurdish involvement in drug trafficking. This does not mean, as we said earlier, that all those involved become filthy rich if they don't get caught, by any means. Contrary to the usual depiction of the millionaires that populate a mafia, most people involved in organised crime are not at all wealthy. But some are and they easily fulfil a sort of exemplary function for a lot of people.

The enormous expansion of the number of people engaged in this crime has to mean that the proportion of criminal amateurs is increasing. That is demonstrated by the clumsiness of those starting as couriers. The accuracy of this assumption is demonstrated by officer Akinbingöl's account of the figure of the *zulaci*, the one who hides a drug stash at home for payment. The drug traffickers approach people who have never had anything to do with trafficking in their life and distinguish themselves by their reliability and naiveté – after all, no-one will suspect them. The stash is delivered to these people in special packages, wrapped up and wound round with sticky tape. Every package is marked invisibly, so the boss can check if it's been tampered with. Stashing spreads the risk. The 'first' or basic *zulaci* stashes a large number of pounds or kilos and he is responsible for it all. No-one in the drugs world knows him and he stays home day and night. The first one gets a driver to take smaller packages to a few 'second' *zulacis*. The guarantee here is the same as in an espionage network: only three people, the first *zulaci*, the driver and the second zulaci, are informed. If the boss is really big, then the same system can include a third *zulaci*.

The amateurism of these stashers is apparent from the dangers threatening them and the errors they appear to make. First of all, they sometimes hide the gear inexpertly. Someone who had hidden half a kilo of heroin in the drawer of his gas oven had to throw it all away after his wife used the oven. He didn't know you can't heat heroin. The stasher can also become the victim of gangs of robbers who do nothing other than try to trace stupid drug stashers. Sometimes the temptation to try it themselves is too great and the stasher carefully sticks a screw in the package to remove a gram for himself. The punishment on discovery is merciless. People have also died of an overdose because they had no notion of the strength and purity of the stuff. Another thing that happens to amateurs out to make a quick profit is that they invest their money, receive their portion and only then start thinking about how to sell it. Without building up a market of your own network of customers, it doesn't work. The traffickers all know cases of idiots who, left with a shipment they have great difficulty in shifting, take great risks. These shipments are often ultimately stolen by a gang or confiscated by the police.

In the investigation into Turkish and Kurdish drug crime in Arnhem's Spijker district, the profile of the offenders was carefully examined. Drug trafficking was introduced there by professional smugglers and then, it seems, primarily marginalised young people without any future prospects yielded to the temptation of drug trafficking. But with the expansion of the crime, a lot of amateurs became involved. From 1990 to 1995, the Gelderland-Midden regional police recorded data on six hundred and seventy-nine people in their identification system. These include the data on a hundred and eight Turks convicted of drug offences. Over the same period, the Dutch Criminal Intelligence Service gathered data on seven hundred and four people, also recording the offences they were suspected of. Of the one hundred and sixty four Turkish suspects, the vast majority – a hundred and thirty-one – were dealing in hard drugs. This data was supplemented with data from the alien registration system and from the social services in Arnhem.

The analysis showed that the majority of the offenders were male and aged between twenty-one and fifty. The majority, fifty-nine percent of the offenders and sixty-eight percent of those registered by the CIS, were married. The majority turned out not to fit the stereotypical image of silly boys seeking adventure at all. In other aspects, they were simply family men. When the number of men on benefit was checked, fifty-eight of the hundred and eighty 'offenders' and twenty-six of the hundred and sixty-four CIS suspects turned out to be receiving benefit. That is a rather low percentage for a group of offenders consisting of 'underprivileged' people or people in hiding in the guise of a simple migrant worker. All the Turks and Kurds interviewed confirmed this impression: it was no longer the underprivileged Turks who were going into drug trafficking at all. A link to data from the aliens department showed that there were hardly any illegal immigrants among them. The drug trade has gradually come into the hands of developed and even prominent people; they are capable of organising the traffic internationally and they have a good command of languages. 'Some people think drug trafficking is easy,' said a Turkish businessman in the Spijker district. 'Nothing could be further from the truth. You have to be really smart and well educated to build a career in that world. Without any education, you won't get above the level of street dealing. I know drug traffickers here with university degrees. I also know someone with a university education who used to work in the central committee of a well-known illegal left-wing organisation and who is now active in drug trafficking.'

The results of this investigation are similar to a lot of study in the Netherlands into the social composition of people moonlighting. It is not the underprivileged, unemployed and uneducated who are doing it, but well-educated people, who moonlight in their spare time. It should be added, though, that this was a one-off measurement in one place, Arnhem; it is not clear whether these striking results would be the same in other local Turkish and Kurdish communities.

New Recruits

Drug trafficking has developed into an attractive career prospect in Turkish and Kurdish circles. In the usual descriptions of organised crime, the fervently longed-for admission into the exclusive, mysterious criminal organisation is the conclusion of a long apprenticeship, in which the aspirant has proved himself through courage and cleverness and which is graced with some degree of ritual. Here, there is no question of such a thing; the threshold for admission is low. The initiative lies with the aspirant himself and he should not wait until a vacancy presents itself in the organisation. The desire to participate is generated by continual confrontation with the wealth of successful traffickers and constant discussion of it. The most tempting example is set by the families who return to Turkey rolling in money after just a few years or sometimes after just one big deal, to lead a respectable existence, guaranteeing a steady future for the children. Whether this kind of thing actually happens is hard to say, but everyone in Turkish circles says he knows of a case. The chance of getting caught is slight and the earnings reputedly so high that even people with something to lose, such as regular work or the status of a good education, take the risk. And even if they were to be arrested, isn't that one big deal worth the prison sentence? The question is always: which is the one big deal? And when is the right time to stop?

An experienced drug trafficker told our fellow researcher Akinbingöl of his experiences. 'Recruitment is no problem at all,' he said. 'There are plenty of unemployed young men without any prospects in Dutch society. The coffee houses are full of that kind of guy. We don't have any special policy for approaching them; they come to us themselves. We have to keep our distance somewhat, because the second generation is sometimes childish and scared and they haven't got a clue what illegality is.' Another said, 'I can see in their eyes that they want to build up another way of life. They want to get rich quick and spend money like water on colourful nights out in Amsterdam. If you take these guys to a luxurious sauna, for example, and treat them to a massage by a woman, then they can't keep away from you, that becomes the dream of their life.'

From the traffickers' point of view, the recruitment of new personnel is effective and subtle. First, they gather information on people who are useable, usually people with financial problems and the capacity to keep their mouth shut. They have a cosy chat in the coffee house and after a couple of meetings, the traffickers help them out with a small amount of money, at most a couple of hundred pounds. Nothing is asked in return. In this way, they gain a reputation as a good person; they do it 'for Allah' or because the person involved is from the same area as they are. Every situation has its own line of reasoning. Then comes the moment when he says he would like to help more, but he's not made of money and the other will therefore have to get his hands dirty for once. Because he is a respectable young man who doesn't want to get involved in bad things, he mediates for an appointment with a legal Turkish company, in Italy or Spain, for example. Then, at some point, the person is asked to take care of a package or deliver cash somewhere. By then it has already become very difficult to resist a criminal career. Two experienced Amsterdam detectives confirmed this: 'They're terribly susceptible to earning money. Then they're put under pressure: "We'll look after you. We've paid for your ticket. Will you do this or that for us?" Young people are even approached in mosques: "Have you got a job?" "Come and have a chat with us about your future this evening." And it goes from bad to worse.'

A number of interviewed students told how they supplemented their income by drug trafficking. They said they had followed the example of the older generation: 'That family from the village where we come from started a couple of years ago. They think it's normal; they're not even ashamed of it. They talk openly about it and go round showing off. Like the way they furnish their house, the way they go on holiday, the way they go out. Fancy car. Just a certain air. They come round to our place and show off: "Yes, I've had an apartment built for each of my daughters."'

How is the contact made? 'At secondary school there are these eighteen-year-old guys who hang around in the snack bar across the road from school. They're trying to see if they can charm a girl. You want to belong and money is attractive at that age. So many girls are taken in by it that you think it's normal, too. It usually starts with those guys as friends and when you find out what he does, you approach the boy yourself: "I know what you're up to, haven't you got a little deal for me?"'

Wealth is the best advertisement and anyone who wants to can get in touch with the right people within the network of the local community just like that. During the investigation in Arnhem we got to know a group of young Turks, who agreed to an informal conversation. They were very friendly and told us freely that they had all been faced with the question, shall I do it or not? And that they had talked to their brothers and sisters about it, who usually advised against it. The girls, in particular, were dead set against it. One young man said, 'When I was still studying, my future didn't look very rosy. I wanted a nice car, a nice house, the good life. I thought, if you do it for a few years, then you'll have a lot of money.' His sister reacted rather disconcertedly on the spot. 'I never noticed,' she exclaimed. 'How did you dare do something like that? Didn't you think about us, our family and our name?' He replied, 'I didn't do it in the end, because I thought, How do I want to do through life? I'll always have to be on my guard. I wasn't scared of the police, because so what if you have to spend a couple of years inside? And if I'm careful and smart, I won't get caught anyway. But the most important thing was the damage to my good name.'

These conversations showed that there was a threshold, after all. In the rather more anonymous surroundings of Amsterdam, Turkish families where someone deals and families who are not involved get on more easily, but the community of Arnhem is like a little village and a strict separation is adhered to. 'If I bump into someone I know who's involved I avoid contact. If I can't avoid it I might say hello, but no more.' Drug traffickers told us the flip side of the coin, 'Once you're in it, you can't go back because they won't accept you any more,' and, 'Suppose I stop the drug trafficking today. Who can I go around with? The people from drug trafficking are my friends. They determine my social life. I go around with them day and night.'

Neutralisation

The ease with which people who commit crimes justify their activities is often astonishing. Of course the behaviour itself is bad and it is a good thing it's illegal, but the perpetrators hold special justifications for violating the prohibition. The simplest justification would be to reject the normative system, or at least part of it, in principle – 'your legal system is not mine' – but most offenders are not revolutionary or acting out of conviction and believe, like everyone else, in the standard itself. They don't think any differently about the values of faith, morals and justice than anyone else.

The academics Sykes and Matza distinguish five reasoning patterns in offenders to neutralise the culpability of their action in their individual case. They refer to such patterns as 'techniques of neutralisation'. The active form of the verb expresses very well what this is about. It is not rationalisation of behaviour afterwards, but devising grounds for justification in advance that make it possible to commit crime or continue to do so. In their own eyes, the offenders can't be blamed because they deny responsibility for this crime, they deny that any harm ensues from their actions, they are of the opinion that there are no victims anyway, they feel that those who condemn them for their behaviour are even more guilty than they, or their loyalties are of a higher order.

Which of these five neutralisation techniques do the perpetrators of drug offences use to justify their behaviour? It is not easy to find out. The police do have some idea when they question most indigenous drug traffickers, but their experience with Turkish and Kurdish suspects is that they always deny everything, so the question of how they got involved doesn't come into it. In empirical criminological investigation into problems such as these, it is usual to use the self-report survey method. The resesarcher asks a representative sample of people from a certain population category to tell them anonymously whether they have committed a particular offence in the past year or so many years. This research method is, however, quite suitable for finding out the incidence of misde-meanours. A lot of people will still honestly answer the question of whether they have stolen a bicycle in the past year. But Turkish and Kurdish residents of the Mercator district and the Spijker district inform-ing the researcher of whether they have dealt in heroin over the past year is out of the question. So we have to find another way to get the answer.

The following exposé of neutralisation techniques is based on three sources. First of all, a number of key figures within the Turkish and Kurdish communities in both Amsterdam's Mercator district and Arnhem's Spijker district were interviewed. Secondly, F. Akinbingöl interviewed twelve young Turkish drug traffickers informally. The most striking conclusion of his thesis is that there is no difference between the neutralisation techniques applied by the entire Turkish and Kurdish community to justify the behaviour of drug traffickers and the reasoning pattern of the young traffickers themselves.

As a third source, we used the 'broad social discussion' that started off in the Turkish community. In September 1995, once the problem had been brought right out into the open in the context of the hearings for the Parliamentary Enquiry Committee on Investigative Methods, that discus-sion got going. Mr E. Ateş, chairman of the Islamic Council for the Netherlands and, according to the Dutch daily paper *NRC Handelsblad*, a representative of the majority of Turkish mosque-goers, responded at the time with the remark, 'Now the whole country knows what we more or less knew ourselves.' The report prompted a lot of meetings, discussions in the media and the formulation of plans for tackling the problem. In April 1997, for example, the Association of Cooperating Turkish Organisations in the Province of Overijssel came up with a memorandum, *Traced and Incited*, which reflected on a round of discussions in the province. During those discussions it was continually stated that Turkish/Kurdish involvement in drug trafficking was a recent phenome-non. Before that, drug dealing was a taboo for those communities; it was only done by bad people without any morals. They kept saying that the current social problem was a sign of deteriorating values and standards in the Turkish community and that, now it has become such a general problem, everyone risks getting involved.

The initial reaction of a lot of people in the Turkish and Kurdish community was active denial. That is still often the case. Two Turkish councillors in Arnhem said they had plenty of contact with their community, but had actually heard and noticed nothing of Turks and Kurds having anything to do with drug trafficking. Others, on the other hand, had noticed something was going on, but knew little about it, as specific circumstances meant it did not happen in their immediate vicinity. A Turkish student said, 'If you study and have ideals, you don't do things like that. I'd stake my life on the fact that no Turkish student with any plans for the future will ever have anything to do with that business.' A young man active in a religious association said, 'Those who fear Allah will never do anything like that. The punishment the court imposes is nothing compared with the punishment Allah will deal out.' Some fathers do not do it because, as one of them put it, 'People who want to act as an example to their children after they die will never get involved in drug trafficking. I say to my children, "Listen, what you will inherit from me is an honest, respectable life and you should be proud of that. If you were to receive material goods from me that came from drug trafficking, you would ultimately be ashamed."' A Kurdish supporter of the PKK said, 'The entire Turkish state mechanism is after us. They're standing on every street corner waiting for us to make a mistake. If we suspect someone in our group is in contact with drug traffickers, then we tell him he had better leave.'

The mirror image of this exclusivity is the respondents' opinions of others. Members of religious associations were able to tell us that groups such as the PKK and Dev-Sol receive money from drug traffickers, willingly or otherwise. The PKK supporter was sure that all the drug trafficking in the Mercator district is in the hands of the Grey Wolves. Non-Islamic respondents questioned the origin of the millions they believe some mosque associations possess. The reasoning pattern is clear: the problem either doesn't exist or, if it does, there are particular reasons why it only involves other categories of Turks.

When it comes to the neutralisation techniques we heard from both traffickers and participants in the discussion who are not, themselves, involved in the business, we were struck by the similarities in the reasoning, although this is actually to be expected in a debate that troubles an entire community; not only do the traffickers themselves justify their behaviour, but the attacked Turkish minority responds as a whole. The neutralisation techniques here are of a collective character. We frequently observed the reasoning pattern implying that those who condemn the trafficking are even more guilty themselves.

Evidently nobody from the Van Traa Commission (see page 13) had wondered what impression the hearings and the entire investigation into the police and the judicial authorities' investigative methods had made on the public in ethnic minorities in the Netherlands. The revelations of the controlled supply of drugs has made a lot of Turks think the Dutch government consciously tolerates drug trafficking. The excessive investigative methods of the regional crime squad and, in particular, the financing by the police of a participating or 'growth' informer* and the setting up of a front store are, for them, the proof that the police – like in Turkey and other countries – are corrupt. A lot of people are convinced that the police know exactly which people are involved in trafficking, but deliberately refrain from taking measures, as this has become a major source of income for the Dutch economy. A drug trafficker used a corresponding argument when he said he was sure the police turned a blind eye to trafficking groups who sometimes provide the police with information. How can it be otherwise, he thought, 'because we've noticed that the police have quite a lot of informers amongst the Turks'. A Turkish woman from Arnhem said, 'I know a couple of drug traffickers from the past. I don't want to have anything to do with them, but a while ago I bumped into one at a party. He recognised me, but didn't dare speak to me. Then I said to him, "Whatever has happened, it's not your fault. It's the fault of the Netherlands and the Dutch police. They feed kilos and kilos into the market themselves. Listen, even the countries around us have problems with this country. How on earth can we just blame you?" I went away before he could react.' A drug trafficker told us himself, 'The Dutch government benefits from drug trafficking. Just suppose the drug tourism was to evaporate, that would be a blow for Amsterdam.' Another dealer, 'Everyone talks about the Netherlands and Amsterdam as the drug centre of the world these days. Slowly, it is shifting to Italy, France and Spain. In a few years' time, the Netherlands will simply be advertising job vacancies for Turkish traffickers. The Spanish authorities are investing in the Turkish mafia and the Netherlands will have to do the same, if they want to retain their economic interest.'

---

* This is a small-time criminal planted in the crime organization. His smuggling will be left alone and he is run by the police. After some time, he will rise in status in the criminal group and have access to the top. In this way, the police create a high-level informant.

This opinion is virtually always linked to the culpability of the Dutch drugs policy. And no wonder; isn't the government encouraging organised crime by tolerating the use of drugs and therefore indicating that there's not so much wrong with drugs? This is the first neutralisation technique: denying responsibility. If the government itself is guilty, a lot of people reason, then why shouldn't we take advantage of it? The Turkish expression is, 'The tap is running, so go and fill your bucket.' A drug dealer said to us, 'Why should I let someone else have this market if the Dutch government is turning a blind eye? Apart from which, the prison sentences in the Netherlands are ridiculously short. Surely that's a sign, too, that the government isn't taking the problem seriously?'

It is striking that actually nobody thinks about the fact that drug trafficking also produces victims. We continually heard the remark that 'our own children aren't addicted' and that they will do their utmost to spare them that fate. Anyway, didn't the drug consumers in Europe choose to become so themselves? We did not detect a scrap of compassion for people who are unable to control their use of drugs and become addicted. The theme of 'poisoning the unbelievers' was named by both drug traffickers and an imam in Amsterdam, who is incidentally keen to fight the crime. 'The dealer sells a bomb to Christians and not Muslims.' In Islamic circles there are serious discussions of whether drugs are *haram* (forbidden) according to the Koran. The use of alcohol is impermissible, but drugs are not mentioned often in the holy book. Some say that everything bad for the health should not be allowed. The Religious Affairs Department, a semi-autonomous body of the Turkish State Ministry with a large budget, recently decreed on the same grounds that smoking cigarettes is *haram*.

The fifth neutralisation technique was also brought into play by those who said that the poor in Turkey could be helped with the drug money and that the money benefits the Turkish economy in general and that of their own village in particular. Didn't President Özal himself indicate in the past that black money was more than welcome in Turkey? We also heard the claim to a higher loyalty from people who justify their actions on political grounds. A Kurdish man said, 'Why should I worry about a couple of junkies while my people are being slaughtered before the eyes of the whole world?' Another drug trafficker said, 'European countries take a hostile attitude to Turkey and to Turks in the Netherlands. I don't feel any responsibility for this society.'

In many discussions, we heard the argument that Dutch society takes poor care of ethnic minorities and that there is nothing wrong with grabbing an opportunity to profit when you can. This argument falls outside the scope of the neutralisation techniques, as it is more of a rationalisation. Without exception, what drug traffickers gave as the reason for their behaviour was that they weren't going to let themselves be exploited and belittled like their fathers: 'Even though he worked hard, my father achieved practically nothing'; 'I'm not going to live the same life as my father'; 'I don't want a life like my father, like an animal'; 'In this society they treat you like a dog. The people in the coffee houses, they're honest, brave and earn respect'; 'My parents haven't got a life, that's not going to happen to me'; 'In this society, Turks haven't got a chance, in all the time I worked in the cleaning business, I only saw one Turk in charge'; 'We're the Jews of World War Two.'

Respondents also feel the legal system discriminates: 'If a Turkish prisoner comes in and says what he's done, then we already know how many years he'll get, based on his nationality.' Here, we are typically faced with the reasoning of the second migrants' generation, which has adapted and wants to advance in the Dutch way, but those channels for social climbing are blocked as a result of discrimination. The degree to which their analysis is based on the truth doesn't matter; what matters is that this constitutes a rationalisation that offers a way to extenuate crime, especially for ethnic minorities.

The Future

In the late 1990s, the international heroin trade became a less important source of revenue for the Turkish underworld, as other drugs, in particular cocaine and ecstasy, became popular among European youth. One Turkish smuggler in Amsterdam even told us, 'Heroin is out of fashion for good. People don't use it any more. If you bring in a couple of kilos or so, your whole profit amounts to no more than a few thousand euros. And you are running the risk of ten years in prison.' Nowadays, sizeable amounts of ecstasy are being smuggled into Turkey from abroad and then supplied to consumers in countries in the Arab world.

The new business is human trafficking; Turkey is a major transit country for illegal migrants. A confidential report by the Illegal Migration and Refugee Affairs Agency in Ankara in 2001 gives an impression of the scope of this flow. A total of 29,426 illegal migrants were apprehended in Turkey in 1998; in 1999 this rose to 47,529, in 2000 to 94,514 and, in the first nine months of 2001, the number of arrested migrants without documents was 100,053. The largest numbers of migrants currently originate from Iran, Iraq, Afghanistan and various African countries. The average price for transportation to Europe is £3,500. It is less dangerous for smugglers than drugs, the prison sentences are shorter and they can more easily neutralise the criminality of their acts by claiming that they are helping people in need. And there is some truth to that.

There is enormous pressure to leave the country. In 2001, A & G Research Bureau organised a survey among no fewer than 100,000 people in Turkey. When asked whether they would like to live abroad, twenty-three percent said yes, as did 43.5 percent in the poverty-stricken region of eastern Turkey where most Kurds live. Faruk Akinbingöl describes the system in detail in his book *Knooppunt Istanbul* and notes that smugglers actively recruit their clients in Turkey's poorer villages. There is plenty of demand in Western Europe for cheap, illegal workers and the demand is now linked to the supply by a new underworld of Turks and Kurds setting up temporary job agencies. Even more than drug traffickers, human traffickers work in a chain structure of independent cells. If one cell is taken out of the chain, the police and judicial authorities are not likely to get any further. Things went dramatically wrong in 1999, when a lorry that had been chartered by a Turkish entrepreneur to transport a load of illegal Chinese immigrants arrived in Dover with the corpses of fifty-eight people who had died from suffocation.

Before concluding, it is important to consider the extent to which the Turkish state has still been involved in organised crime since the parliamentary investigations of 1997. According to Fikri Saglar, a member of the commission and of the Republican People's Party, not much has changed since then; we have not been able to establish the whole truth, due to political and bureaucratic repression and the fact that witnesses have failed to appear or given incomplete evidence. The report simply cannot be complete. The question remains too whether or not the state is involved in human trafficking.

It has become more difficult to neutralise state intervention. As long as a campaign was being waged against the Kurdish PKK, the state could afford to take plenty of chances. Funding was needed and the state was in danger. The people who played an active role did not feel guilty because they were serving sacred state aims. Following the arrest of its leader Öcalan, however, when the PKK stopped its armed struggle, the matter was no longer as simple. Devlet Bahceli, the new leader of the Grey Wolves, made every effort to improve their image. His efforts were partially successful. People in the party who were involved with the underworld were removed from their positions – in any event there is now no evidence of any such ties.

We would like to conclude, though, with a little food for thought: if Bülent Ecevit was ignorant of the existence of the state gangs in 1974, then Recep Erdogan, the prime minister at the time of writing, is well aware of its details. But Erdogan of course is pro-Islamic, and Kemalist circles are far too distrusting of religious circles to reveal their secret pacts with the underworld.

So if the Deep State is continuing, how are *we* expected to know?

Acknowledgements

To enable us to gather the material, we appealed to a long list of people and institutions. First Fazilet Okuducu and later Gülay Öntaş assisted us, and Ankie Lempens also participated in the research. Faruk Akinbingöl gathered material amongst drug dealers in the Netherlands, from which we also benefited, and in March 1998, he graduated from the Free University of Amsterdam in cultural anthropology with a thesis entitled *Temptation and justification; 'Neutralising techniques' for Turkish delinquents in the Netherlands*. Numerous police and legal officials throughout Europe, including Turkey, also assisted. We would like to thank, in particular, Messrs Kazim Yeşilgöz and Sinan Yerlikaya of Ankara for contributing their efforts and all those affiliated with the Dutch embassy and consulate in Turkey who did likewise. Anne Brambergen acted as our interpreter in Italy.

Several of these research results were published. Appendices VIII and XI of the final report by the Parliamentary Enquiry Committee on Investigative Methods (the 'Traa Committee') include the initial findings on the Turkish underworld in the Netherlands, which caused quite a stir on publication. The Northern and Eastern Netherlands Interregional Investigation Team then enabled Yücel Yeşilgöz to conduct research, following which, together with Ankie Lempens, he published *A Study of Turkish Drug-Related Crime in the Mercator District of Amsterdam*. Together with Frank Bovenkerk, they published an abridged version of this piece in the literary journal *De Gids*, 'Organised Crime as a Neighbourhood Problem' (volume 199, number 7/8). In 1997, they examined Arnhem. The report again attracted a great deal of attention, as the overwhelming majority of the culprits turned out to be family men and not, as everyone had thought, a marginalised second generation of migrants. *A Study of Turkish and Kurdish Drug-related Crime in the Spijker District of Arnhem* was a joint publication by the Northern and Eastern Netherlands Interregional Investigation Team and the Willem

ACKNOWLEDGEMENTS

Pompe Institute for Criminal Law and Criminology and was written by Yeşilgöz, H. Regterschot, M. Maas, B. Lentfert and G. Beering. We feel privileged to have the scientific cooperation between this Interregional Investigation Team and the Pompe Institute: the researchers are always given the freedom to publish their findings.

A lot of people have been nice enough to provide the manuscript of this book with critical comments and suggestions: Sjoukje Botman, Bernice Bovenkerk, Martin van Bruinessen, Eeuwke Faber and also Messrs. R.B. Eigenman, D.J. Korf, A. Smaling, M. Neefe, J. Regterschot, K. Valk, J. Huuskes, D. Shekary and A. Ram. It goes without saying, however, that we take full responsibility for the content. As always, we have been able to rely on the secretarial support of Wieneke Matthijsse, Annie Milzink, Kathelijn Korver and Maartje Visser. We would like to thank the Willem Pompe Institute and the Besouw fund for their financial contribution to the research and Gerda Blok and Frank van Galen for all their efforts in that respect.

In 1998, the first edition of this book was published in Dutch under the title *De maffia van Turkije* (Meulenhoff Publishers, Amsterdam). A translation in Greek subsequently appeared with Kastaniotis Publishers in Athens. Turkey followed with *Türkiye'nin mayfyasi* for Illetisim in Istanbul. In 2004, two updated chapters appeared in the extensive survey of *Organized Crime in Europe* edited by Cyrille Fijnaut and Letizia Paoli published by the Springer series *Studies of Organized Crime* in New York. We have tried to update our description of the Turkish mafia in this English edition on the most important points.

The major source for all those delving into the history of modern organised crime in Turkey is the work of Uğur Mumcu. The tragedy is that this writer himself became part of this history in a grisly manner. Mumcu started his career as an assistant to the Law Faculty of Ankara University. After the military coup of March 1971, he was first arrested and then placed in service as a 'soldier of unreliable category', even though, on the basis of his status within the Turkish system, he should have been entitled to an officer's rank. Once back in society, Mumcu wrote about this episode in a book that gained him national fame. He then embarked on a career as a columnist for the left-wing Kemalist daily newspaper *Cumhuriyet* and became an investigative journalist. Mumcu was the first in Turkey to conduct serious research into the criminal organisations in his country and their international branches abroad.

One of his most important books, *Arms Dealing and Terror*, published in 1982, exposes the relationships between international arms dealing and the problem of terrorism. It turned out that criminal organisations were smuggling in arms in collaboration with both right-wing and left-wing organisations, under the protection of governmental officers. Mumcu showed that religious and extreme-right parties were involved in drug trafficking. He then conducted research into the attack on Pope John Paul II in Rome in 1981. In that research he again demonstrated connections between the criminal organisations in Turkey and figures in the extreme right. His 1984 book on the subject posed new questions on the attack: was the CIA involved? And the Turkish secret service? What was the role of the Bulgarians? What was the motive? These questions are still left partially unanswered.

He was asked to appear before the court of Rome as an expert. On 24 January 1993, Uğur Mumcu was blown up in Ankara by a car bomb. The perpetrators are, to date, unknown. The Turkish secret service and a specially formed parliamentary investigation commission looked into the murder but, so far, without result. Mumcu's family say the culprits should be sought in the vicinity of the Susurluk accident. To this day, the press still speculates about the truth.

Turkish media offer a wealth of material on organised crime. We gathered documents over a period of approximately ten years, some of which came from the original editions of these newspapers in Istanbul and some from special editions for the European market. The Turkish media are organised in conglomerates. The largest groups are the Doğan group, including the biggest daily newspapers in Turkey, *Hürriyet* and *Milliyet,* and the Sabah group, which has also been publishing European editions for the past decade or so. Other newspapers available in Europe and which we have also occasionally used as sources are *Özgür Gündem, Politika* and *Özgür Politika, Zaman* and *Türkiye.* Left-wing critical papers in Turkey, such as *Yeni Yüzyil* (of the Sabah group) and *Radikal* (of the Doğan group), are not yet available in Europe. Our colleague Gülten in Turkey has closely followed *Yeni Yüzyil*, in particular. In addition to the newspapers, there are also some Turkish weeklies such as *Nokta* and *Aktüel*. There is also an excellent English-language paper, *Turkish Daily News,* which allows non-Turkish-speaking readers to follow the daily news and is now available online. We have made sure that we cast our net as widely as possible. The political tint of most daily newspapers in

Turkey is right-wing, but there are also papers of a social-democratic tone and those that are left-wing or even ultra-left.

The television stations are grouped under the same economic conglomerates. Channel D belongs to the Doğan group; Channel ATV belongs to the Sabah group; TGRT is affiliated with the *Türkiye* newspaper; TRT INT is the official government channel; HBB is an independent station broadcasting primarily right-wing propaganda and Kanaal 7 is religious and demonstrates its democratic leanings by inviting both left-wing and right-wing speakers to participate in discussion programmes. Organised crime is dealt with by all channels in the form of reports, discussions, interviews and spoken commentaries. For our purposes, the media needs to be handled with discernment. There is a lot of speculation and comment in the press, which often makes such contributions biased. For this book we have only used them where facts are concerned and then only if they are mentioned in several newspapers.

We also interviewed a number of police officers who were involved in investigations into the Turkish underworld, as well as civil servants from the National Security Service. It appears that the police forces in every European country have had and still have specialists in this field. We interviewed them in Rome, Wiesbaden and Brussels. Several European countries and the United States have police liaison officers stationed in Istanbul and Ankara for bilateral or multilateral police cooperation. Enquiries were conducted amongst the assembled community of liaison officers in Istanbul and with some individually.

A trip to Ankara and Istanbul in 1997 during the aftermath of the Susurluk scandal also produced a wealth of interview material with such diverse persons as the ambassador for the Netherlands, the chairman of the Parliamentary Enquiry Commission investigating the Susurluk case, several Turkish politicians and a former police reporter who currently writes books on the old underworld of Istanbul.

We examined Interpol files on certain figureheads in the Turkish underworld. This information is not used directly as such, but serves to verify the material we have gathered on the life stories of prominent figures. We also interviewed people who, themselves, worked in drug trafficking. Three times, we held extensive discussions in prison with godfathers of various standing. Striking is the detail in which, and how easily, they recount their experiences. On the other hand, we are well aware that they only talked about those things they were prepared to reveal and that all they said was coloured by their own, biased view. We considered comparing the accounts from such interviews with what is known to the police and the judicial authorities about those involved, but rejected the idea, as it would have caused us a hopeless conflict of roles.

And then there is ethnography. Since 1996, the Northern and Eastern Netherlands Interregional Investigation Team has given the Willem Pompe Institute the opportunity to investigate the everyday aspects of Turkish and Kurdish organised crime in the Netherlands. We used what the police refer to as 'open sources': chiefly interviews with local residents, local politicians and prominent members of Turkish and Kurdish organisations, but also newspaper reports and data from administration systems. We combined these with information detectives had obtained from 'closed' sources, which they, in turn, anonymise and aggregate and then combine with their own information.

Notes

Introduction

13   Four criminology professors … the Netherlands: Cyrille Fijnaut et al. (1998): *Organized Crime in the Netherlands*, Kluwer Law International, The Hague, 1998.

18   'Organised crime … be illegal': G. W. Potter, *Criminal Organizations; Vice, Racketeering, and Politics in an American City*, Waveland, Prospects Heights, 1994..

19   According to … the local rulers: Eric J. Hobsbawm, *Bandits*, Pelican, Harmondsworth, 1969; A. Blok, *The Mafia of a Sicilian Village*, Basil Blackwell, Oxford, 1974.

20   The criminological counterpart … military lines: Donald R. Cressey, 'The Functions of Criminal Syndicates' in Patrick J. Ryan and George E. Rush, eds., *Understanding Organized Crime in Global Perspective. A Reader*, Sage, Thousand Oaks, 1997

20   Since 1971 … baba or father: Engin Bilginer, *Babalar Senfonisi*, Cep Kitaplari, Istanbul, 1990.

21   Well-organised crime … poorly organised: Butz Peters, *Die Absahner; Organisierte Kriminalität in der Bundesrepublik*, Rowolt, Reinbeck bei Hamburg, 1990.

21   The British criminologist … way around: Mary McIntosh, *The Organisation of Crime*, MacMillan, London, 1975.

22   Certainly, these gentlemen … organised crime: H. Abadinsky, *Organized Crime*, Nelson Hall, 1991.

23   It is clear … department in question: Aykol C., *Kontr-Gerilla*. Ankara, Ani-arastirma, 1990.

23   The renowned American … World War II: See the reference by Margaret E. Beare, 'Corruption and Organized Crime: Lessons From History' in *Crime, Law and Social Change*, 1997, 28 (2).

24   There is also … and Italy: Frank Bovenkerk, 'De misdaadbiografie' in *Biografie Bulletin*, 1996, 6 (1).

24   Criminologists have … organised crime: James M. O. Kane, *The Crooked Ladder: Gangsters, Ethnicity, and the American Dream,* Transaction Publishers, New Brunswick and London, 1993; Margaret E. Beare, *Criminal Conspiracies: Organized Crime in Canada*, Nelson Canada, Toronto etc., 1996; Robert J. Kelly (ed.), *Organized Crime: A Global Perspective*, Rowmam & Littlefield, Totowa, 1986.

25   Indeed, some … business community: Abadinsky, op. cit.

25   The 'favourable' … goods and services: Robert K. Merton, 'Social Structure and Anomie' in *Social Structure and Social Theory,* The Free Press, New York, 1957, (originally pub. 1938); Daniel Bell, 'Crime as an American Way of Life' in *The End of Ideology,* The Free Press, New York, 1960 (originally pub. 1953).

25   This latter option … Latino ghettos: William J. Wilson, ed., *The Ghetto Underclass, Social Science Perspectives*, Sage Publ., Newbury Park etc., 1993; Christopher Jencks and Paul E. Peterson, eds., *The Urban Underclass*, The Brookings Institution, Washington D.C., 1991.

25   This book aims … it appears': R. J. Kelly, op. cit.

Chapter 1

28   'The country's legal … Turkish Mafia': *Euromoney*, November 1994.

29   The inheritance mafia … nuclear substances: Sources for this section are the newspapers and periodicals *Hürriyet, Milliyet, Sabah, Politika, Turkish Daily News, NRC Handelsblad, Aktüel* and *Nokta*.

33   One lady … and the media: Frank Anechiarico, 'Beyond Bribery: The Political Influence of Organized Crime in New York City' in C. Fijnaut & J. Jacobs (eds.), *Organized Crime and its Containment: A Transatlantic Initiative,* Deventer, Kluwer, 1991.

34   Organised crime … a criminal role: J.J.M.Van Dijk, *Criminaliteit als keerzijde.* Arnhem, Gouda Quint bv, 1991; Lawrence E. Cohen and Marcus Felson, 'Social Change and Crime Rate Trends: A Routine Activity Approach' in *American Sociological Review*, number 44, 1979.

34   He once said … economic system: Halil Nebiler, *Ben Devletim Vururum*, Istanbul, BDS Yayinlar, 1994.

35   More in keeping … a pension: The story on the Çiller family is taken from the *New York Times* of April 1997.

35   'Together, the Turkish … as clever': *Nokta*, 30 July to 5 August 1995. See Mustafa Tören Yücel, *Türk Ceza Siyaseti & Kriminolojisi*, Ankara, Hakim, Genel Müdür, 1996.

36   'Unlike conventional … market forces': Alfred McCoy, *The Politics of Heroin: CIA Complicity in the Global Drug Trade*, New York, Lawrence Hill Books, 1991, p. 2.

37   The American and … of opium: See Marcel de Kort, *Tussen patiënt and delinquent,* History of Dutch drugs policy, Hilversum, Verloren, 1995; and also McCoy, op. cit.

38   Consulting these documents … black market: Alan A. Block, *European Drug Trafficking and Traffickers Between The Wars,* Hamburg, Paper, International Society of Criminology, 1988.

38   The farmers … paid cash: C. Lamour and M. R. Lamberti, *Les grandes manoeuvres de l'opium*. Paris, Seuil, 1972.

39   But in other countries … be found: At least according to the organised crime historian Alan Block, on whose findings we base our work. See Alan A. Block, op cit.

39   The same observation … in Paris. Observatoire Géopolitique des Drogues, *Atlas Mondial Des Drogues*, op. cit.

39   Their networks … trading partners: The same argument can explain the relative over-representation of ethnic minorities and immigrants in American organised crime. See Frederic D. Homer, *Guns and Garlic*, West LaFayette Indiana, Purdue University Press, 1974.

41   In describing … products illegal: See Peter Reuter, *Disorganized Crime: Illegal Markets and The Mafia,* Cambridge, Massachusetts, 1986, MIT Press.

41   Historical research … before the war: See for example P. Jenkins, 'Narcotics Trafficking and the American Mafia: The Myth of Internal Prohibition' in *Crime, Law and Social Change*, vol. 18, number 3, 1992.

41   Historical research … and Chicago: Observatoire Géopolitique des Drogues, *Atlas mondial des drogues,* Presses Universitaires de France, Paris, 1996.

42   One estimate … New York: Lamour and Lamberti, op. cit.

43   He claimed … daughter's wedding: See *The Heroin Trail*, op. cit.

44   The Sicilian Badalamenti … Avni Musullulu: Shana Alexander, *The Pizza Connection; Lawyers, Drugs and The Mafia*, London, W. H. Allen, 1989.

45   The end of … against drugs: D. W. Rasmussen and B. L. Benson, *The Economic Anatomy of a Drug War*, London and Boston, Rowman & Littlefield Publishers, 1994.

46   The market … to heroin: De Kort, op. cit.

50   Research was … some time: *Milliyet*, 13 January 1996.

50   The heroin and … in demand: Graham Farrell et al., 'Cocaine and Heroin 1983-93, A Cross-National Comparison of Trafficking and Prices' in *British Journal of Criminology*, vol. 36, number 2, 1996.

52   To date … little effect: For a recent good overview, see Transnational Institute, *Losing Ground. Drug Control and War in Afghanistan*, TNI Briefing Series, Amsterdam, 2006.

55   On the contrary… foreign currency: See *De Volkskrant*, 4 May 1997, which quotes the *Far Eastern Economic Review*.

57   The theory … by this route: Werner Wegner, 'Die Balkanroute' in *Der Kriminalist* numbers 1-3, 1992, and by the same author, 'Balkan-Route contra Seidenstrasse, Die tödlichen Rauschgiftstrassen von Asien nach Westeuropa' in *Organisierte Kriminalität in Deutschland*, Schmidt Römhild, Essen; Northern and Eastern Netherlands Interregional Investigation Team and IPIT, *Turkse heroïnesmokkel over de weg*, Nijverdal, 1996; General Directorate of Security, Department of Anti-Smuggling and Organized Crime, *An Overall Assessment of Illicit Traffic in Drugs*. Ankara, 1996.

60   The bag … is big: F. Bovenkerk and A. Lempens, 'De branche van het wegtransport' in Appendix IX of *Inzake Opsporing*, Parlementaire Enquêtecommissie Opsporingsmethoden, The Hague, Sdu Uitgeverij, 1995.

61   A lot of … the timetable: For this overview, see the publication by the Interregional Investigation Team and IPIT, op. cit.

61   The following passage … at this point: Henk de Jong et al., *Turkije Handboek*, Northern and North-eastern Netherlands Core Team and Rotterdam-Rijnmond Regional Crime Squad, Sdu Uitgevers, The Hague.

63   The police … other's psychology: Also see Dick Hobbs, 'Professional and Organized Crime in Britain' in M. Maguire et al.

(eds.), *The Oxford Handbook of Criminology*, Oxford, Clarendon Press, 1994.

63 The racket ... the 1970s: See *The Geopolitical Drug Dispatch* of 22 August 1993.

64 A banker ... your activities': *Financial Times*, 2 October 1996.

65 That, too, was rejected: Nebiler, op. cit.

66 In the meantime ... was discussed: See www.fatf-gafi.org.

Chapter 2

67 Highwaymen live ... no followers: Y. Kemal (1984), *Memed, My Hawk*. London, Fontana.

68 'Once upon a ... said went': Bilginer, op. cit.

68 For more about the *kabadayi* we recommend *Sayili Firtinalar, Eski Istanbul Kabadayilari* by Refi Cevad Ulunay (born 1890), who spoke to several old *kabadayi*. Another Turkish journalist who wrote about the underworld of yesterday's Istanbul is Ergun Hiçyilmaz, see his book *Yosmalar, Kabadayilar*, 1996.

69 'viewed as neutral ... personal interest': Feroz Ahmad, *The Making of Modern Turkey*, London, Routledge, 1993.

70 'small traditions': Erdogan, 1999.

70 The theory of ... for Turkey: Ergil, 1997.

70 Despite the lengthy ... ethnic groups: P.A. Andrews, *Ethnic Groups in the Republic of Turkey,* Wiesbaden, Dr Dudwig Reichert, 1989.

70 The administration ... actual power: Erik J. Zürcher, *Een geschiedenis van het moderne Turkije,* Nijmegen, Sun, 1995.

70 In his book ... the rebellions: R. Zelyut, *Osmanli da Arşi Düşünce ve Idam Edilenler*, Istanbul, Alan Yayincilik, 1986.

70 'It offered them ... wrote Zelyut: Zelyut, op. cit.

71 'Bloodthirsty Turks ... they run': Çetin Yetkin based this comment in *Etnik ve Toplumsal Yönleriyle Türk Halk Hareketleri ve Devrimleri* (1974) on the words of the Seljuq author Kerimeddin Mahmud.

71 'In the Ottoman ... other minorities': Yetkin, op. cit.

71 Particularly in the ... good roads: Hobsbawm, op. cit.

72 He, however ... the peasants: A. Blok, op. cit.

72 They always have ... prophetic movements: W.F. Wertheim, *East West Parallels: Sociological Approaches to Modern Asia,* The Hague, W. van Hoeve Ltd, 1974.

73   According to one ... numerous followers: *Sosyalizm ve Toplumsal Mücadeleler Ansiklopedisi,* 1730-1.

73   The Babai ... second-class citizens: C. Şener, *Alevilik Olayi,* Istanbul, Topumsal Bir Başkaldirinin Tarihçesi, Yön Yayinlari, 1989.

74   Bedreddin lived ... wise man: Yetkin, op. cit.

74   Pir Sultan ... in 1590: Mehmet Bayrak wrote an excellent study on the Alevite leader under the title *Pir Sultan Abdal* in 1986.

75   The Ottoman Empire ... Celali's followers: M. Akdağ, *Celali Isyanlari,* Ankara, Dil Tarih Coğrafya Fakültesi Yayinlari, 1963.

77   Cevat Ulunay ... soccer today: Ulunay, op. cit.

77   One important pillar ... the empire: Zürcher, op. cit.

79   His friends ... a weapon: Ulunay, op. cit.

79   It is based ... of violence: Compare Jane and Peter Schneider, *Cultural and Political Economy in Western Sicily,* New York, Academic Press, 1976.

80   In the event ... council of elders. Ulunay, op. cit

81   Some of them ... or ministers. Bilginer, op. cit.

82   There are innumerable ... Arnold Rothstein: Paul Gregory Kooistra, *American Robin Hoods: The Criminal as a Social Hero,* thesis, University of Virginia Sociology Dept., 1982

83   Nevertheless, his life ... his memoirs: S. N. Tansu, *2 Devrin Perde Arkasi,* Istanbul, Pinar Yayinevi, 1964.

84   The Ottoman police ... later recounted: Ibid.

84   Chrisantos was ... the police': Ibid.

85   He felt it ... his memoirs: Ibid.

85   Abdullah did ... with Iraq: Bilginer (1990) and Hiçyilmaz (1996) both include passages about this *kabadayi* and Ulunay (1994) has written a long story about him and interviewed him.

86   He went to ... with her': Bilginer, op. cit.

87   This was the ... his honour: For the codes of honour, see Yeşilgöz's thesis, *Allah, Satan en het recht,* Arnhem, Gouda Quint, 1995.

89   Murad Sertoğlu ... about his life: Including M. Sertoğlu, *Çakircali Mehmet Efe,* Istanbul, Güven Basimevi, 1955.

89   This is precisely ... the Ottomans': Sertoğlu, 1955.

89   His departure for the plain now left some room for the rise of new *efe:* Ibid.

90   One of the ... 'social rebels': *Sosyalizm ve Toplumsal Mücadeleler Ansiklopedisi,* Istanbul, Iletişim Yayinlari, 1988.

91　'If every eşkiya … nine hundred eşkiya': *Yön*, 2 September 1966.

Chapter 3

94　According to the … his *abi*, or 'big brother': Bilginer, op. cit.

94　It was less … departed's soul: See *The Heroin Trail*, op. cit.

95　The founding of … dictatorship: Zürcher, op. cit.

95　Mussolini had seen … and branch: Christopher Duggan, *Fascism and the Mafia,* New Haven and London, Yale University Press, 1989.

96　Unlike other farming … for support: Ahmad, op. cit.

98　'Thirteen guns! … the Netherlands': Bilginer, op. cit.

98　'Just like in American … Kabadayi Heybetli': *Hürriyet*, 3 March 1995.

101　In 1956 … the affair: Beşikçi Ismail, *Orgeneral Muğlah Olayi, Otuzüç Kurşun*, Istanbul, Bilim Dizisi, 1991.

101　Uğur Mumcu … 1960s and 1970s: Mumcu, op cit.

102　The same primitive … today: A.K. Cohen, 'The Concept of Criminal Organization' in *The British Journal of Criminology,* vol.17, number 2 (1977).

102　'the role of … as heroes': Yücel, op. cit.

102　Hüseyin Uğurlu … arms dealing': Mumcu, op. cit.

103　The lawyer declared … in Pötürge': Uğur Mumcu, *Silah Kaçakçilĝi ve Terör,* Istanbul, Tekin Yayinevi, 1995; Mumcu, op. cit.

103　According to … Sporting Affairs: Nebiler, op. cit.

103　Apart from … immigrant community: *Hürriyet*, 28 November 1997.

103　'We are the … the separatists': *Hürriyet*, 11 December 1997.

105　The definitive anecdote … explain his actions: This story is featured in the book by the well-known *Milliyet* journalist Halit Çapin: *Bir kabadayinin Anatomisi, Ejderhayi Kovalayan Kiz,* Istanbul, Parentez, 1995.

106　One minute … for help: *Hürriyet*, 27 September 1994.

106　It was only … the *kabadayi*: Çapin, op. cit.

107　Dündar Kiliç swore … in Diyarbakir: Çapin, op. cit. Also see *Nokta*, 9 October 1988.

107　As Kiliç recounted … of glasses': Çapin, op. cit; *Hürriyet*, 8 October 1994.

107　'You can … make him famous': Çapin, op. cit.

108 So when someone … ten minutes: Ibid.

108 The next day … all its details: See the Turkish dailies of 22 May 1969.

108 'I learned … an interviewer: *Nokta*, 9 October 1988.

108 'I've always been … thy neighbour': Bilginer, op. cit.

109 'Who does something … on me': *Hürriyet*, 10 October 1994.

109 'You can see … be innocent': Ibid.

109 'Their aim was … their ambition': *Hürriyet*, 10 October 1994 and Bilginer, op. cit.

110 'I haven't been … in 1988: Bilginer, op. cit.

110 'I can't speak … years now': *Nokta*, 9 September 1988.

110 When, during … my honour': Halil Nebiler, op. cit. This anecdote is reminiscent of the telephone conversation the American gangster Meyer Lansky had with the film actor who had played him in the *The Godfather Two*. Lansky first asked the actor how his two small children were and then, 'Couldn't you have portrayed me a little more sympathetically in the film? After all, I am a grandfather already!' This story can be found in Robert Lacey's *Little Man: Meyer Lansky and The Gangster Life,* Boston etc., Little, Brown and Company, 1991.

111 The country … so forth: Soner Yalçin, *Behçet Cantürk'ün Anilari,* Ankara, Öteki Yayinevi, 1996, p. 198, 199.

112 Were they not … illegal business: See Bilginer, op. cit., and Yalçin, op. cit.

113 At each meeting … Bulgaria, incidentally': For an overview of such organisational structures, see a publication from the German police, by Konrad Freiberg and Berndt Georg Thamm, *Das Mafia-Syndrom. Organisierte Kriminalität: Geschichte, Verbrechen, Bekämpfung,* Hilden, Verlag Deutsche Polizeiliteratur GMBH, 1992.

114 The form and codes … criminal networks: Joseph L. Albini, *The American Mafia: Genesis of a Legend,* New York, Appleton-Century-Crofts, 1971; Mark H. Haller, 'Organized Crime in Urban Society: Chicago in the Twentieth Century' in *Journal of Social History*, number 5, 1971-2; Dwight C. Smith Jr., *The Mafia Mystique,* New York, Basic Books, 1975; Alan A. Block, 'History and the Study of Organized Crime' in *Urban Life*, number 6, 1978.

115 Yet others feel … commercial reasons: Frederico Varese, 'How Mafias Migrate: the Case of the 'Ndrangheta in Northern Italy',

discussion papers in *Economic and Social History*, University of Oxford, 2005.

115 Painstaking historical research ... legal authorities: Henner Hess, *Mafia: Zentrale Herrschaft und local Gegenmacht,* Tübingen, J.C.B. Mohr, 1970. Also see Anton Blok, op. cit.

116 Various authors ... patronage systems: Pino Arlacchi, *Mafia Business: The Mafia Ethic and The Spirit of Capitalism,* Oxford, Oxford University Press, 1988.

116 In 1983 ... commercial crime structure: Pino Arlacchi, *Leven in de Mafia: Het verhaal van Antonino Calderone,* Amsterdam, Nijgh and Van Ditmar, 1993; Pino Arlacchi, *Addio Cosa Nostra: La Vita di Tommaso Buscetta,* Milan, Rizzoli, 1994.

116 On this basis ... let him examine: Tullio Bandini et al., *La criminatità organisata, Moderne metodologie di ricerca e nuove ipotesi esplicative,* Milan, Dott. A.Giuffrè, 1993. Also see Eeuwke Faber, 'Pino Arlacchi onder vuur: van Mafia Business naar Addio Cosa Nostra' in *Magazine voor Criminologie*, vol. 37, number 2, 1995.

122 The operation ... Gambino family': Howard Abadinsky, op. cit.

124 In a study ... operating units: Yesilgöz et al. (1997), op. cit.

129 The following day ... like women"': *Milliyet*, 15 February 1995.

130 Her father ... Alaattin Çakici': *Hürriyet*, 12 December 1996.

130 Later investigation ... mafia activities: The report on the hearing for the inquiry commission, *Susurluk Komisyonu Tutanaklari 1*, Istanbul, Kaynak Yayinlari, 1997.

131 At the end ... these people!': Turkish papers, 5 November 1993; Yalçin, 1996, op. cit.

131 'As the PKK ... Kocakaya families': *Nokta*, 29 January 1994.

131 'There will be ... happens to me': Yalçin, op. cit.

133 He was dressed ... and Davidoff: *Hürriyet*, 17 January 1994.

133 Cantürk's own newspaper ... state responsible: All Turkish dailies, 23 January 1998; *NRC Handelsblad*, 24 January 1998.

Chapter 4

136 The commercial infrastructure ... a refuge: Mumcu, op. cit.

136 The number of ... with 10,000: 1995 Yili Raporu, *Çalima ve Sosyal Güvenlik Bakanliği*, report, Ankara, 1996.

137 The people from ... the Netherlands: J. den Exter, 'Regionale herkomst van Turken in Nederland' and J. den Exter and E. Kutlu, 'Emirdağ: over de effecten van migratie op een Turks district', both in *Migrantenstudies*, number 9 (1993).

137 They place themselves ... other Turks: M. Alkan and R. Kabdan, 'Droom of werkelijkheid? Succes onder Turken in Nederland' in R. Gowricharn (ed.), *Binnen de Grenzen,* Utrecht, de Tijdstroom, 1993.

138 Added to this ... seeking work: Roger Zegers de Beijl, *Documenting discrimination against migrant workers in the labour market. A comparative study of four European countries,* International Labour Office, Geneva, 2000.

139 It is therefore startling ... general crime rates: Michael Tonry, ed., *Ethnicity, Crime, and Immigration: Comparative and Cross-national Perspectives,* Chicago and London, University of Chicago Press, 1997; A. P. Schmid, *Migration and Crime: A Framework for discussion*, Proceedings of the Ancillary Meeting held on 3 May 1995 in Cairo, Egypt. Milan, ISPAC, 1996; Ineke Haen-Marshall, ed., *Minorities, Migration and Crime*. Beverly Hills and London, Sage, 1997.

140 The French system is quite different: Tim Boekhout van Solinge, *Drugs and decision-making in the European Union,* Mets en Schilt Pubishers, Amsterdam, 2002.

146 No attempt was ... Turkish press: See for example *Il Tempo*, 3 April 1996.

147 The northern Italian ... through violence: P. Arlacchi and R. Lewis, *Imprenditorialità illecita e droga. Il mercatot di droga a Verona,* Bologna, Il Mulino, 1990.

150 R.Weijenburg ... a Chinese concern: R. Weijenburg, *Drugs en drugs-bestrijding in Nederland,* The Hague, VUGA, 1996.

151 As the headquarters ... Spielfeld investigation: Weijenburg, op. cit.

153 This involves ... are Turkish: D. Siegel and Y. Yesilgöz, *Natachas and Turkish men: new trends in women trafficking and prostitution*, in D. Siegel et al., *Global Organized Crime: Trends and Developments*, Kluwer Academic Publishers, Dordrecht etc., 2003.

153 Investigative journalists ... Grey Wolves: Stella Braam and Mehmet Ülger, *Grijze Wolven, Een zoektocht naar extreem rechts*. Amsterdam, Nijgh & Van Ditmar, 1997.

153 In 2001 ... in the Netherlands: Special theme bulletin from the

Amsterdam/Amstelland regional police, *Grijze wolven in Nederland*, 2001.

155 Back in 1979 ... political connections: Paolo Serri, '"Türkische Ameisen" – der Weisheit letzter Schluss' in Stephanie Pauls (ed.), *Krieg dem Rauschgift! Für eine internationale Anti-Drogen-Koalition*, Wiesbaden, Campaigner Publ. Deutschland GmbH, 1979.

155 In the same ... heroin traffickers: Interpol files, for example.

157 The Kurdish community ... convinced nobody: See the reports in *Het Belang van Limburg* from 22 November 1996.

161 On the other ... drug trafficking: *Turkish Daily News*, 5 May 1997.

162 After clan boss ... twenty-two years in prison: See a well-informed article in *The Guardian*, 28 March 2006.

164 The policy of ... the department: Detective Akibingöl interviewed Messrs Yilmaz and Gümüş and Bovenkerk and Öntaş spoke to Mr Çalişkan. It is typical of the rapid turnover at the top of Turkish political circles that a new head of department was appointed only weeks after our last interview.

168 Istanbul has become ... drug trafficking: Ö.F. Akinbingöl, *Knooppunt Istanbul. Mensensmokkel via Turkije*, Meulenhoff, Amsterdam, 2003.

169 Anthropologists call this form of contact 'friends of friends': Jeremy Boissevain, *Friends of Friends: Networks, Manipulators and Coalitions*, Oxford, Basil Blackwell, 1974.

Chapter 5

176 Çatli had played ... ex-president Elçibey: For Çatli's life, see S. Yalçin and D.Yurdakul, *Reis, Gladio'nun Türk Tetikçisi*, Ankara, Öteki Yayinevi, 1997.

176 The major ... group are: The report was referred to as the 'second MIT report', after a first MIT report was written in 1987. An attempt was initially made to bring the second report out in the major media, but they did not dare publish. Both the second and the first were, however, leaked via the same media.

177 The underworld figure... suspected murdered: Tarik Ümit was kidnapped in early March 1995 by still unknown culprits. A couple of days later, his luxury Chevrolet Camaro was found in the same area where two Iranian Kurds had been shot dead. The Turkish

media described Ümit as both a spy for MIT and the police and a crony of Dündar Kiliç. *Milliyet* wrote that Ümit maintained relations like an octopus. One of his arms worked for Dündar Kiliç, another for MIT. He was co-owner of Yahya Demirel's (the president's cousin) bank in Cyprus. He maintained relations with both the Kurdish underworld boss Behçet Cantürk and with the *ülkücü* Alaattin Çakici. His daughter offered a reward of 500 million Turkish lira to the one who could trace her father. *Milliyet* wondered, 'If Ümit was a spy for MIT, why didn't the government do anything?' Dündar Kiliç denied being partners with Ümit, but did say, 'He worked for me and, at that time, he was a good guy. He wanted to get rich and he did. But how he managed all that in such a short time is something you'll have to investigate.' The fugitive Çakici called *Hürriyet* to say he had had nothing to do with Ümit's kidnapping. Nothing more was heard of him. His last contacts were with the people in the group the report speaks of. The report also contained the names of various people who have been shot or stabbed to death by unknown culprits, such as Behçet Cantürk and Savaş Buldan. The report does not make it clear whether these people were killed by the group, too, but the reader gets that impression.

178 Çatli's coffin ... Allah is great': Turkish newspapers, 6 November 1996.

178 He was taken ... perfectly well: *Milliyet*, 16 November 1996; *Hürriyet*, 11 November 1996.

179 'This chance occurrence ... was insignificant: *Milliyet*, 6 and 7 November 1996.

179 Çatli had obtained ... chief of police: *Sabah*, 4 and 5 December 1996.

179 But he let ... lose face': *Milliyet*, 7 and 8 November 1996.

180 'Don't worry ... for Susurluk': *Hürriyet*, 15 November 1996.

180 But she ... thanks to him: *Milliyet* and *Hürriyet*, 9 November 1996.

180 'Anyone who fires ... honourable people': *Yeni Yüzyil*, 23 November 1996.

180 As there were ... thirty-six hours: *Sabah*, 30 August 1966.

181 'After the payment... to me"': *Ifade Tutanaklari, Susurluk Belgeleri*, compiled by Veli Özdemir Istanbul, Scala, 1997.

181 Based on the fingerprints ... of the state: *Hürriyet*, 7 December 1996; *Sabah*, 12 April 1996.

182 Some of the … Topal (murdered)': *Milliyet*, 24 December 1996.

182 'I first discovered … dirty business': *Yeni Yüzyil*, 5 December 1996.

183 'one minute without … good': *NRC-Handelsblad*, 3 February 1997.

183 A sociological study … be punished: *Hürriyet*, 11 June 1997.

184 'I have not committed … else matters': *Hürriyet*, 28 November 1997.

184 'I chose … his comment: *Milliyet*, 5 December 1997.

184 'If we come … wipe it out': *Hürriyet*, 3 December 1996.

184 'Yes, it's possible … house,' said Bucak: Özdemir, op. cit.

184 The next day …. for drug smuggling': *Milliyet*, 22 January 1997; *Hürriyet*, 23 January 1997.

185 Another drawback … before it: *Hürriyet*, 3 January 1997.

185 The files… could be released: *Radikal*, 17 March 1997.

186 'Ultimately, it … president everything': *Sabah*, 13 December 1996.

186 Yilmaz voiced … had been named?': *Susurluk Komisyonu Tutanaklari 1, Doğu Perinçek ve Mesut Yilmaz'in Açiklamalari*, Istanbul, Kaynak Yayinlari, 1997.

188 The report simply cannot be complete: Saglar and Ozgonul, 1998.

188 According to the … been severed: Ibid.

189 The Minister … bottom of it: See http://web.amnesty.org/library/Index/ENGEUR440332005

190 'We will do … General Ozkok: See the Turkish newspapers of 21 February 2006.

Chapter 6

193 Internal enemies … are other Turks': Yeşilgöz, 'A Double Standard: The Turkish State and Racist Violence' in Tore Djörgo & Rob Witte, *Racist Violence in Europe,* London, Routledge, 1995.

195 Prominent Turkey expert … new coup: Ahmad, op. cit.

195 Throughout this … Uğur Mumcu: Mumcu, U., *Silah Kacakciligi ve Teror,* Istanbul, Tekin Yayinlari, 1995.

196 To give an … one mortar: Ali Birand, *12 Eylül, Saat: O4.00*, Istanbul, Karacan, 1984.

198 A total of 62,000 … billion U.S. dollars: *Turkish Daily News*, 11 August 1997 and 15 September 1997.

199 Various famous … quietly eliminated: Alain Labrousse and Laurent Laniel, 'The World Geopolitics of Drugs 1998/1999', *Special Issue of Crime*, 2001, *Law and Social Change* 36 (1-2).

200 The Kurdish issue … northern Iraq: Christopher de Bellaigue, 'The Uncontainable Kurds' in *The New York Review of Books*, March 1, 2007.

203 But smuggling is … sufficient investigation: Mehmet Eymür, *Analiz, Bir MIT Mensubunun Anilari,* Istanbul, Milliyet Yayinlari, 1991.

203 According to … Grey Wolves: Ali Yurtaslan's confessions were published in 1980 by the Aydinlik publishing house.

204 This was a … NATO organisation: Zürcher, op. cit.

204 In Turkey … was set up: Serdar Çelik, *Türk Kontr-Gerillasi,* Berlin, Ülkem Presse, 1995; Müller, op. cit.; Parlar, op. cit. Zürcher, op. cit., however, gives a different date. We quote from his book: 'Another organisation that appears to have played a role in the supression of the left wing is the mysterious "counterguerrilla", an underground organisation of right-wing civilians paid and equipped by the army. The counterguerilla was set up in 1959 with American support to organise the resistance in the event of a communist take-over. Its existence was acknowledged only twenty years later (in the 1980s, this type of organisation, such as Gladio in Italy, reveived a lot of publicity in other NATO countries).' Zürcher's source is unknown. But if we compile all the information, it cannot be ruled out that 1952 was the year in which it was established and 1959 the year when the organisaion was given its new internal function.

204 Various sources indicate … possible sabotage: Akyol, op. cit.; *Milliyet,* 5 and 6 September 1992; *Yeni Yüzyil,* 23 December 1996.

204 An accident, was the court judgement: Yavuz Donat, *Yavuz Donat'in Vitrininden,* Ankara, Bilgi Yayinevi, 1987.

205 Gladio is … both cases: C. Dündar and C. Kazdaĝi, *Ergenekon, Devlet lçinde Devlet,* Istanbul, Imge 4th edn. 1997.

205 'There is such … associated organs': Inci Hekimoĝlu, *Vatan Yahut Susurluk, Siyasi Cinayetler,* Istanbul, Papirus, 1997.

205 A second suspect … Oflu Ismail: Mumcu, 1994, op. cit.

208 When questioned by … same time: Mumcu, 1994, op. cit.; *Sabah,* 25 November 1996.

209 They did, indeed … twenty Armenians: Nezih Tavlaş, 'Türk-Israil Güvenlik ve Istihbarat Ilişkileri' in *Avrasya Dosyasi,* number 3, 1994.

209 The costs of … special funds: Eymür, Analiz, *Bir MIT Mensubunun Anilai,* Istanbul, Milliyet Yayilari, 1991.

211 The weekly magazine *Nokta* also declined: Sinan Doğan, MIT *Raporu Olayi*, Istanbul, Kaynak Yayinlari, 1988.

212 In his function … accident in Susurluk]: Ağar's career has since been dealt with extensively in several publications, such as C.Dündar and C. Kazdağli, *Ergenekon, Devlet içinde devlet*, Ankara, Imge Kitabevi, 1997.

213 The relationship between the nephew of President Demirel and Enis Karaduman has some rather colourful sides. Yahya Demirel and Karaduman met in Sweden in the early 1980s. Later, they did business together. In July 1985, Karaduman asked for his money back; this was $1,300,000. Yahya had paid half, but didn't come up with the rest (Nebiler, op. cit.). Karaduman then kidnapped Yahya. He was stripped, tortured and photographed. Yahya's father then announced that he would pay his son's debt of $780,000. He did call it extortion, however, and informed the Swiss police who freed Demirel.

213 The time from December 1992 to the beginning of 1994 was a black period for the underworld. A total of fifteen important men were killed. These included the drug smuggler Şehmus Daş on 25 December 1991; the drug trafficker and owner of *Kismetim 1* on 31 December 1992; the famous boss of Ankara, Inci Baba, on 5 December 1993; and the drug trafficker Behçet Cantürk on 15 January 1994. Then followed the death of Enis Karaduman. The latter was referred to by the Turkish media as 'the most dangerous man in the world'. He was the son of a factory owner. First he went to a mililtary school, but then he exchanged that life for the underworld. He was arrested many times for drug trafficking and other crimes, such as attempted murder. His name has also been linked with arms dealing. He was known for his prison escapes. As he kept adopting new identities, he was also referred to as the 'man with a thousand and one faces'. He had relationships in the film and music scene, the best known with the film star Ahu Tuğba. On the night of 24 January 1994, he went to a restaurant in Hendek, a small town in the province of Adapazari. He was with five men. Due to the poor service, he got into a row with the restaurant owner. At that point he became so angry he said to the owner: 'I've written your death warrant.' Then he drew his gun. But the gun misfired and that was the end of Karaduman.

213 A spokesman ... draft form: Turkish newspapers, 24 February 1988.

213 It was later ... early stage: Doğan, op. cit.

214 'Almost every ... remains unsolved': The unofficial report by the Turkish parliament, *TBMM Faili Meçhul Cinayetler Komisyonu, Sonuç Raporu*, part 7, 1995.

214 Legally, the department ... JITEM: Soner Yalçin, *Binbaşi Cem Ersever'in Itiraflari,* Istanbul, Kaynak Yayinlari, 1994.

214 According to these ... Southeastern Turkey: The Turkish parliamentary report, op. cit.

215 According to Baykal ... special units: *Milliyet*, 22 September 1995.

215 According to Karakaş ... Kurdish civilians': *NRC-Handelsblad*, 2 December 1996.

215 A gang from ... in Yuksekova. *Milliyet*, 7 September 1996; *Sabah*, 27 September 1996.

216 The gang was also ... a full picture. *Hürriyet*, 27 February 1997 and 8 July 1997.

217 Among his less-known ... and the army: S. Parlar, *Osmanli'dan Günümüze Gizli Devlet.* Bibliotek Yayinlari, Istanbul, 1996. Both Parlar and Özkan state that the first Turkish secret service was set up on the advice of the English ambassador Stratford Canning and that its first head was a foreigner, Civinis Efendi, who had earlier been employed by the Russian Tsarina. He stole her diamonds and then fled to the Ottoman Empire. First, he pretended to have various functions in different places, such as an imam. He travelled through Anatolia as a rich Italian tourist. According to these sources, Civinis also worked for employers other than the Ottoman Empire.

217 According to an American ... doubt their loyalty': P.H. Stoddard, *The Ottoman Government and the Arabs, 1911 to 1918,* Ann Arbor, Michigan, Princeton University, 1963.

217 Erturk, one of ... the organisation: S.N. Tansu, *2 Devrin Perde Arkasi, Teşkilat-i Mahsusa M. M. Grup Başkani Hüsamettin Ertürk'ün hatiralari*, Istanbul, Pinar Yayinevi, 1964.

218 The fact that ... Celal Bayar: Stoddard, op. cit.

218 As both had ... Black Arm: See T. Özkan, *Bir Gizli Servisin Tarihi*, Istanbul, Milliyet Yayilari, 1996. A police station is still called a *karakol* in Turkish.

218 Mustafa Kemal ... the military: Stoddard, op. cit.

218 'Until then ... Ecevit said later: *Milliyet*, 28 November 1990.

219 The costs … the Americans: Çelik, op. cit.

219 The former … national heroes: For Mrs Çiller's 'special agency' also see Dündar and Kazdağli, op. cit.

Chapter 7

223 It is difficult … chronological order: David Henige, *The Chronology of Oral Tradition,* Oxford, Clarendon Press, 1974.

229 In 1995 … recounted exactly: Turhan Temuçin, *Azrailin Öbür Adi,* Ankara, Ümit Yayincilik, 1995.

240 He received … broken ribs: *Aktüel*, 14-20 July 1994.

245 According to … heroin cargo: *The Geopolitical Drugs Dispatch*, 22 August 1993.

247 Şeymus Daş … was killed: *Ekonomi Politika*, 24-31 January 1993.

248 Baybaşin declared … was responsible: *Özgür Politika*, 14 April 1996.

Chapter 8

256 This is a man … Omer Topal: *Hürriyet*, 14 January 1997, *Milliyet*, 2 July 1997.

256 'My share … a second Susurluk': *Hürriyet*, 6 May 1997.

261 One criminologist … operational area: René Hesseling, 'Verplaatsing: een pleidooi voor het rationele keuze perspectief' in *Magazine voor Criminologie,* vol. 35, number 22, 1993.

261 The last form … another place: J.C. Press, *Some Effects of An Increase in Police Manpower in the 20th Precinct of New York City,* New York, Rand Institute, 1971.

263 Coffee houses … and tea: Yeşilgöz, op. cit.

267 Contrary to … all wealthy: A.G. Anderson, *The Business of Organized Crime,* Stanford, Hoover Institution Press, 1979.

271 'That family … my daughters'': Maya Gersons, *Turken en schurken,* Report on post-graduate sociology study, University of Amsterdam, 1996.

273 They refer … of neutralisation': G.H. Sykes and D. Matza, 'Techniques of Neutralization: A Theory of Delinquency' in *American Sociological Review*, number 17, 1957.

274 First of all … were interviewed: In Amsterdam, the interviews included a municipal officer, a politician, an expert in drug traffick-

ing who was not personally involved, two representatives of the Islamic movement Milli Görüş, two members of the Turkish Social Democratic Association, a worker at a Turkish travel agency and a number of drug traffickers themselves. In Arnhem: all the Turkish councillors and ex-councillors of Turkish origin, members of the board of Turkish youth clubs, members of the Arnhem mosque association and a number of Turkish and Kurdish drug traffickers.

279 Faruk Akinbingöl ... in his book: Akinbingöl, F., *Knooppunt Istanbul. Mensensmokkel via Turkije,* Meulenhoff, Amsterdam, 2003.

280 The report ... be complete: Saglar and Ozgonul, 1998.

283 The largest groups ... even ultra-left: *Hürriyet* means 'freedom'. It is a right-wing nationalist paper, for which left-wing critical columnists also sometimes work. *Milliyet* means 'nationality'. This daily sails the course of the political centre in Turkey and has a social-democratic character. *Sabah* means 'morning'. It is a paper for which both right-wing and left-wing columnists write. Columnists are far more important to the news and its interpretation in Turkey than in the Netherlands. The paper's policy can be described as right-wing/liberal. *Yeni Yüzyil* means 'new century'. This paper has a left-wing view. *Türkiye* means 'Turkey'. It is an extreme-right, nationalist paper. All these daily newspapers admit to toeing the Kemalist line editorially. *Zaman* is a religious paper and *Özgür Gündem, Politika* and *Özgür Politika* represents various variations of a pro-Kurdish left-wing paper, which are therefore non-Kemalist. *Nokta* and *Tempo* are serious, liberal weeklies. That also applies to *Aktüel*, but this magazine also covers sensual subjects.